The Metaphysical Mode
from
Donne to Cowley

The Metaphysical Mode from Donne to Cowley

BY EARL MINER

PRINCETON UNIVERSITY PRESS

PRINCETON, NEW JERSEY

1969

L. C. Card: 75-83686

SBN: 691-06170-X

Publication of this book has been
aided by the Whitney Darrow Publication Reserve Fund
of Princeton University Press

Printed in the United States of America
by The Maple Press Company,
York, Pennsylvania

In Memoriam

BRADFORD A. BOOTH

as having wrought

In the same Mines of Knowledge; and thence brought
Humanitie enough to be a friend,
And strength to be a Champion, and defend.

PREFACE

"Will it *do*," asked James Russell Lowell, "to say anything more about Chaucer? Can anyone hope to say anything, not new, but even fresh, on a topic so well worn?" The same questions may well be asked about the Metaphysical poets (and about other writers that might be named). Each reader of this book can best judge for himself whether it says anything new or "even fresh." I can say for myself that like Lowell I have found a stimulus in my subject that has led me, as it has led others, to commit their ideas into writing. From Dr. Johnson's writings, one would not have expected him to occupy himself, as he does in his *Life* of Cowley, with what he calls "the Metaphysical race." But he did, and I have been similarly moved. More particularly, I have felt the need for a book on these poets that would simplify the approach to them in some respects and discriminate more finely in others. I have not aimed to describe the Metaphysical sensibility or to narrate the historical development of Metaphysical poetry; nor have I aimed to give a purely analytical examination of the poems. What I have sought to do is to discriminate Metaphysical poems from poems in other styles (by the same or by different poets) and to differentiate between the kinds of Metaphysical poetry written by the various major writers of that race. It goes without saying that I follow the *consensus lectorum* in the belief that there was such a "race" and that it included certain poets but not others.

It is true of course that seventeenth-century poets of all persuasions shared more with each other than they do with us. But I do not think that it follows from this basic historical premise that it is necessary for us to drop labels of convenience such as "Metaphysical," provided of course that we remember that they are designations for styles and views of life which may merge or which may characterize different works in a total canon. Some recent critics would have us drop these labels, but I believe that they have overreacted to inadvisable uses of such terms. The differences in ways of understanding life in the seventeenth century were as numerous as in most other times. For example, we can acknowledge that what is called the rise of capitalism or the Civil Wars were experiences shared by men and women of the time. But what was common experience was reacted to very differently by people who felt their interests and beliefs clear, or who felt themselves divided in allegiance. Similarly, in speaking of poetry we may use as it were party names for convenience sake to designate kinds of perceptions and the styles employed to convey the perceptions. I well appreciate that level of generalization that regards seventeenth-century poetry as a whole, and that which regards each seventeenth-century poem as a distinct entity. The level I have sought, however, lies between, my purpose being to discriminate one complex of seventeenth-century perception, and one range of styles, from others. I should feel no hesitation in writing about certain poems by Marvell in a book on Cavalier poetry, or in one on Restoration poetry, and sometimes the poems might be some of those discussed here. But Marvell is a complex case, and the elements discussed would be different. "Metaphysical" or "Cavalier" are to me convenient ways of speaking, on a middle level of generalization, about numerous poems that I respond to differently from other poems because they have differing perceptions of life. From this level we may move easily to the lower level to consider uniquely discrete poems or to the higher level with a better conception of what may be thought to be the seventeenth-century sensibility.

Our modern equivalent of Macaulay's schoolboy would no doubt offer several principal characteristics distinguishing

Metaphysical poets from those writing in other styles. One is the union of thought and feeling, an undissociated sensibility, if that is the positive complement to T. S. Eliot's "dissociation of sensibility," which he said was wrought by the "two most powerful" poets of the seventeenth century, Milton and Dryden, who, in spite of doing certain things surpassingly well, showed a "dazzling disregard for the soul." It is a pity that such nonsense became the cant of a generation, because it is demonstrably false historically, false in certain premises, and false in application. Although much might be said about the notion (it can be traced in other guises to the later eighteenth century), it is enough to indicate one's consent with the last chapter of Frank Kermode's valuable book, *Romantic Image*.

Other criteria our schoolboy might offer are "strong lines," wit, and conceits. The first was attributed to Donne by his contemporaries, the second by his contemporaries and everyone since, and the last was judged a particular version of the second by Dr. Johnson. I think each is very significant, but also that each requires discrimination and that even taken together they are insufficient as criteria. Donne uses conceits. So do Wyatt and Surrey, the Elizabethan sonneteers, Jonson, and Dryden. Donne is among our wittiest poets. The wit of Jonson, Dryden, and Pope is also remarkable. Donne often uses strong lines. So do Hall, Marston, Jonson, and Chapman. Quite apart from the need for such discrimination, it is also necessary to say that Donne himself wrote some poems that do not qualify under such heads: "Sweetest love, I do not goe," for example. After Donne the tendency to drop strong lines accelerates, and wit often disappears along with the conceit.

I had originally thought to try to clarify such matters with an initial chapter discussing the formation of Metaphysical poetry out of the alternatives of the 1590's and a final chapter describing the absorption or redefinition of the style in the Restoration and the eighteenth century. After writing them, however, I judged that their purely historical emphasis distracted from my main purpose, and I accordingly discarded them. The chapters retained include four of discrimination and one of demonstration, through analysis and commentary, of my views of the way in which certain Metaphysical poems work.

My first chapter posits the private mode as the chief "radical" of Metaphysical poetry, that feature differentiating it from the social and public modes of other poetry written in modern English before the late eighteenth century and the Romantic poets. The second chapter treats the forms, modes, and structures of Metaphysical poems in terms of their versions of time and place. My conclusion is that Donne's "dramatic" use of time and place—with well-defined characters and situations creating a momentary, intense experience—gradually accommodates and then yields to other treatments. At this point, I must enter a plea for taking my terms like "dramatic" in an adapted sense. We often use them very loosely, and to do so is perhaps inevitable, as is also the lack of discrimination that results. I have just described what I mean by "dramatic" and I sometimes quote the term to remind the reader that its use is adapted. The same is true of "narrative," "meditative," and "argumentative" along with their variants as nouns. Dramatic treatment of time and place yields, then, to "narrative" with its emphasis upon relation and sequence; drama may yield to "meditation," in which time and place are less part of a situation or sequence than a point of musing; and the drama may yield to "argument," in which something of the air of dramatic address is employed without other significant development of time and place. In the third chapter I seek to define major features of

Metaphysical wit in terms reflecting the poets' use of an older logic and rhetoric. The problem in doing so for readers today is that to us the old terminology and procedures are unknown or unwelcome. Another problem has bedevilled attempts to get at Metaphysical poetry in such terms: the fact that poets in other styles were taught the same rhetoric, the same logic. Since discrimination requires differences as well as some degree of similarity, I have chosen two rather simple logical or rhetorical features that, I believe, distinguish Metaphysical wit from wit of other kinds: definition and dialectic. In the fourth chapter, I discuss the thematic range of Metaphysical poetry in terms of complementary elements that I designate (again in adapted senses) as "song" and "satire," the former a tendency to affirmation, the latter a tendency to denial, both being capable of expression in lyricism or in satire, or in mixtures. In the fifth chapter, I examine Donne's wonderful elegy, *The Perfume;* my favorite poem by Herbert, *The Flower;* and a particularly baffling poem by Marvell, *The Nymph complaining for the death of her Faun.* The approach to each combines the historical and critical exercises.

The major effort of the book is, then, to discriminate poetic features that are particularly important to the Metaphysical style and differences possible within the style: in other words, what is lasting and what changes, what is general to the style and what is peculiar to individual writers. To reduce such effort to a crude paraphrase, I argue that Metaphysical poetry is private in mode, that it treats time and place in ways describable in terms of the "dramatic," the "narrative," the transcendent, the "meditative," and the "argumentative"—and that these terms provide in their sequence something of a history of the development of Metaphysical poetry. I argue further that the wit of Metaphysical poetry can be characterized as definition that is, as those

logical or rhetorical processes bringing together or separating
(whether in metaphor or idea) matters of similar or opposed
classes; and as that dialectic, or those processes, that extend
such matters by their relation in logical and rhetorical procedures. Finally, I argue that the thematic range of Metaphysical poetry can best be represented in terms of satiric denial
and lyric affirmation. My lack of concern in this book with
continental poetry is a major omission. I have left out such
consideration for the same reason that I dropped two historical chapters after writing them: the belief that it would be a
distraction from my main purpose.

I have preferred to aim for a simple scheme within which
discriminations might be made. I believe that Simplicity and
Discrimination are among the Muses of criticism, although
I may have invoked them to no avail. I have also simplified,
no doubt more culpably, by not mentioning systematically
the very numerous scholars and critics to whom I am indebted or to whom I am, in some sense, responding. In particular, I have avoided taking issue with those who have gone
before me, at least by name, unless they are writers whom
I particularly respect. Otherwise I mention only those whose
comments seem to me to bear immediately on a given, limited point, where the reader may well wish to have amplifica-
tion or an alternative view. I have numerous debts from two
decades of reading these poets, and I hope that it is clear
that editors, scholars, and critics have been of continual use
to me. Editions apart, there are three studies that I should
like to distinguish for their meaningfulness to me. I find the
tone and approach of J. B. Leishman particularly appealing,
especially in *The Monarch of Wit* (London, 1951). I value
the wedding of scholarly truth and critical interpretation by
Joseph H. Summers in *George Herbert: His Religion and Art*
(London, 1954). And to my mind the most useful study of
the whole group of Metaphysical poets is the very valuable

and stimulating study by Robert Ellrodt, *L'Inspiration Personnelle et L'Esprit du Temps chez Les Poètes Métaphysique Anglais,* 2 parts in three volumes (Paris, 1960). The bibliography in the second volume is useful for its comprehensiveness and its inclusion of a number of works by continental scholars. To adapt a line from a ninth-century Japanese poem, "The knowing ones will know" when I have taken from such books or differed from them. If I have not, in a bibliographical sense, set out with the Hobbesian aim of "instructing the ignorant," I trust that in other respects I have at least succeeded in "soothing the learned in their knowledge."

Although I have tried especially to avoid arguing with real or imagined opponents, I have not hidden my feelings about the poets or their poems. Donne, Herbert, and Marvell seem to me of a different order from the other poets I deal with. Donne's Satyres and Elegies seem to me much more powerful than they have been given credit for being, and much more important to an understanding of his other poems than has often been thought. I think Donne's *Anniversaries* more closely concerned with Elizabeth Drury and John Donne than does any recent critic I know of. I think the eighth stanza of Marvell's poem, *The Garden,* an anticlimax, an unfortunate flaw in a great poem. I think Cowley far more important as a Metaphysical poet, indeed as any kind of poet, than Traherne. These and other judgments will be found explicit and implicit in the book, but they will be found set forth in terms of the poems rather than in terms of my responses to Scholar *a* and Critic *b.*

Metaphysical poetry is among our most valuable English literary inheritances. It is, to paraphrase Jonson, the first poetry in the world for some things. Donne's characteristic immediacy engages every reader at once, and in the classroom I have found that he comes, as it were, closer to teaching himself than any other English poet but Chaucer. What is in some ways the most extraordinary thing of all is that the Metaphysical poets are but one constellation in that amazing galaxy of the seventeenth century: Shakespeare and the drama, early and late; Milton; Dryden, lately the subject of a revival; Jonson, apparently next to be revived. The variety and the scale of the achievement are remarkable throughout the century, and if the Metaphysical poets are not as various as others they are more intense. Reading one of these poets for perhaps the hundredth time, one is teased into asking, will it do *not* to try to say something more about them, if only to confirm their achievement?

Los Angeles   E. M.
June, 1968

ACKNOWLEDGMENTS

SOME OF my many debts to earlier students of Metaphysical poetry are suggested by references in the Preface, text, notes, and the concluding bibliographical note on the editions I have chiefly consulted. Others will be quickly recognized by knowing readers, and the book itself is meant to repay in some measure what I have taken from those who have preceded me. I am also grateful to the unstinting favors of the staff of the Clark Library, where this book was begun and completed, and to the numerous courtesies given me at the Bodleian Library, where a major portion of these pages was written. A Fulbright lectureship at Oxford University entailed other occupations but also provided some time for work on this book. I am deeply grateful for that lectureship and for the courtesies extended me by Oxford University and, in particular, the Warden and fellows of St. Antony's College. The continuing support of the Committee on Research of the University of California, Los Angeles, has greatly assisted me.

Among the individuals immediately important to this book, Professor John McManmon deserves my warm thanks for his assistance with what are to me the considerable difficulties of patristic Latin. Mr. Ronald Baar has checked my quotations; he and Mr. Robert Mundhenk have also earned my thanks for helping with proof on an emergent occasion. Miss Miriam Brokaw, Associate Director and Editor of Princeton University Press, has shown an enthusiasm for my work that would gratify the heart of any self-centered author. I also greatly appreciate the celerity and accuracy of the staff of the UCLA Central Stenographic Bureau and the courtesy of its head, Miss Ellen Cole.

Students of seventeenth-century English poetry are perhaps uniquely blessed in having readily to hand excellent editions with well-printed pages and valuable commentary. What Dr. Johnson termed with some justice the dull duty of an editor makes possible what I believe can equally accurately be described as the assured excitement of readers using such excellent editions. The best editors are not invisible in their work, and if I single out the editions of my friend Dame Helen Gardner, it is only because her editions of Donne have stimulated me most frequently to thought and even, on occasion, to disagreement.

I owe most grateful thanks to the publishers who have so promptly given me their permission to quote from the excellent texts published by them. I gratefully acknowledge the following permissions: The Clarendon Press to quote from: William Alabaster, *The Sonnets*, eds. G. M. Story and Helen Gardner (1959); Richard Crashaw, *The Poems*, ed. L. C. Martin (1957); John Donne, *The Divine Poems*, ed. Helen Gardner (1952); John Dryden, *The Poems*, ed. James Kinsley (1958); Lord Herbert of Cherbury, *The Poems*, ed. G. C. Moore Smith (1923); George Herbert, *The Works*, ed. F. E. Hutchinson (1941); Henry King, *The Poems*, ed. Margaret Crum (1965); Richard Lovelace, *The Poems*, ed. C. H. Wilkinson (1930); Andrew Marvell, *The Poems and Letters*, ed. H. M. Margoliouth (1927); Thomas Traherne, *Poems, Centuries and Three Thanksgivings*, ed. Anne Ridler (1966); and Henry Vaughan, *The Works*, ed. L. C. Martin, 2nd ed. (1957). Messrs. Routledge and Kegan Paul Ltd. to quote from *The Poems of Andrew Marvell*, ed. Hugh Macdonald, 2nd ed. (1956). Doubleday and Company, Inc. to quote from *The Complete Poetry of John Donne*, ed. John T. Shawcross (1967). The Macmillan Company to quote from *The Collected Poems of W. B. Yeats* the last stanza of "Sailing to Byzantium." The editors of *Modern Philology* have graciously permitted me to reprint, in altered form, an article on *Marvell's Nymph complaining for the death of her Faun* which first appeared in their pages.

THIS book is dedicated to the memory of Bradford A. Booth, rather than to my son and daughter, as originally planned. They knew of my original intention but have willingly foregone whatever pleasure they might have taken in a dedication in favor of my giving what honor I can to the memory of my sometime teacher, loyal friend, and colleague, whose death on December 1st, 1968, brought irresistibly to mind my many debts to his goodness. Although he published my first printed essay in the journal of his foundation, *Nineteenth-Century Fiction*, I am neither a Victorianist nor a critic of the English novel. It does not belong to me, therefore, to set forth details as in a Festschrift. But I trust that the reader of this book on the Metaphysical poets will not take it amiss that the page of dedication should quote lines from a poem addressed by Ben Jonson to a learned teacher and friend.

TABLE OF CONTENTS

The Metaphysical Mode
from
Donne to Cowley

THE PRIVATE MODE

this dialogue of one.
— Donne

THE MOST distinctive, and distinguishing, feature of Metaphysical poetry is its private mode. Strong lines barely survive Donne. As for wit, although considerable differences in use may be discriminated, it may be found in poetry from Wyatt to Pope. The same may be said of conceits. But it cannot be said of Elizabethan poetry, of Cavalier poetry, or of Restoration poetry as it must be said of Metaphysical that it is at root private. The private mode is simply the most crucial feature of Metaphysical poetry, distinguishing it not only from other styles but also from poems in other styles by the same poet, whether King or Cowley, Marvell or Vaughan. Moreover, the exploitation of the private mode distinguishes Metaphysical poetry from all other modern English poetry before the Romantics. An outline of some of the salient features of the two great periods of private poetry may serve to stress the importance of the mode to each.

To start with a brief characterization, then, Metaphysical poetry developed at a time when poetry was being given increased intellectual dignity; it developed out of earlier lyric and satiric poetry; it protested with satire against social myth and ritual; it rejected eloquence in favor of natural language; and it grew up in the shadows, not in the lights, of the court. Romantic poetry developed at a time when poetry was being given increased emotional weight; it developed out of earlier descriptive and reflective forms; it protested with lyricism and narrative against social claims; it rejected poetic diction

3

in favor of a more natural language; and it completed a gradual shift from court to urban scene to country estate to natural setting. Conceived of in terms of such origins, the private mode of Metaphysical poetry was a humanist poetry that proved anti-humanist in some major respects, a court poetry that brought fully into question the hegemony of the court, and a poetry of nature (in then current senses) that put an old rhetoric and ornament to uses other than adornment. The private mode did not bring all this about. Rather, it is poetically symptomatic of a number of forces—religious, political, and intellectual; and it is the vital principle of such forces as they operated in Metaphysical poetry.

The private mode is usually distinguished by a polarity with its opposite, the public mode, as practiced normatively from Dryden to Dr. Johnson. The primary bases of distinction involve esthetic distance and assumptions about the poet's (or his speaker's) relation to other men and women. In terms of esthetic distance, so this explanation runs, the private mode takes its stance between the three chief esthetic points—the world of the reader, the world of the poet/ speaker, and the world of the poem in its subject and characters. The stance involves considerable detachment from the world of the reader, or rather, from the reader in the world. The poet/speaker moves close to the world observed and portrayed in the poem, to the other characters in the poem, to the situation, and to the subject. The second stanza of *The Extasie* shows Donne's choice of esthetic distance in its description of the two lovers:

> Our hands were firmely cimented
> > With a fast balme, which thence did spring,
> Our eye-beames twisted, and did thred
> > Our eyes, upon one double string.

The male speaker communes as closely with the unnamed woman of the poem as might easily be conceived. The first four lines of *The Vanity of Human Wishes* show at an equal extreme how Dr. Johnson has taken the public stance:

> Let observation with extensive view,
> Survey mankind, from China to Peru;
> Remark each anxious toil, each eager strife,
> And watch the busy scenes of crouded life.

Here the speaker is at one with his audience and removed, by thousands of miles as it were, from a situation observed so generally that it contains only "scenes" with no specific individuals. Dr. Johnson's proper norms are bonds between the speaker and his creator in his world and the reader in his world. Their worlds are the same and are immediately shared by others. The convenient symptoms of the private mode are speech approaching dialogue or monologue, with use of the singular first and second person pronouns; the symptoms of the public mode are allusion and public detail, with use of the plural first, second, and third person pronouns.

Such an explanation of the differing points of esthetic distance in the two modes implies what might be termed their sociological bases. The public mode is concerned to affirm that which distinguishes men in their own persons, needs, and sense of integral being, while at the same time joining them in what all men meaningfully share. When the bonds between men seem to have broken or to have become inimical to the integrity of private personality, a private response is the most valuable. We shall see that just such an impulse underlies Donne's early poetry and indeed continues to define Metaphysical poetry. We can readily appreciate how natural it was that the immediate experience of an individual, especially the transactions of his private heart, should have come to be the major concern of poetry for several crucial decades. This is sufficiently clear, even obvious, to any reader of Donne. What requires greater stress is the fact that when public poetry is successful, it is personal—it bears upon our persons

5

as well as what may be called our publicity;[1] and equally
that when private poetry is successful it bears upon recurrent
individual human experience in a way that must be called
universal. It is as though Donne's lovers with their twisted
eye-beams exclude us as readers entirely from the scene but
welcome us back as human beings witnessing a drama in our
own lives. Just as it is necessary in any discussion of public
poetry to discuss its personality as well as publicity, so is it
necessary in a dicussion of private poetry to emphasize its
universality as well as privacy. I stress this reciprocal feature
the more because it confirms our impressions of drama and
immediacy in reading private poetry (as the next chapter will
discuss in other terms), and because the rest of this chapter
will be chiefly concerned with the privacy rather than with
the universality of the private mode.

Before going on to such a discussion, however, I must im-
pose upon the reader's patience with a few more general
remarks. There is a considerable artistic space between the
extremes of private and public poetry; numerous gradations
are in fact possible. Poetry prior to, and contemporary with,
Metaphysical poetry is for the greater part neither public nor
private but something between. It is social in the sense that
it defines its manners, its decorum, and its relation between
the speaker/poet and the reading audience by implicit, accepted conventions, or in the sense that an extreme fiction
like that of *The Faerie Queene* has as its general aim the
fashioning of a gentleman and as its particular significance
ethical and historical truth. But poetry of a middle esthetic
distance may use the first person singular in such varied ways
as the autobiographical of Spenser's *Epithalamion* or the fictional of much of *The Shepheardes Calendar*. Such varieties
of middle esthetic distance constitute the norm in English

---

[1] I have treated this aspect of the public mode in *Dryden's Poetry*
(Bloomington and London, 1967), ch. i.

6

before Metaphysical poetry. From that norm diverged to the one side the public poetry of the Renaissance, often in learned tongues and usually on the affairs of the great, as to the other side such private poetry as may be found occasionally in passages of Sidney and frequently in the sonnets of Shakespeare. Of the two divergent Renaissance modes, the public is by far the more fully developed (which is not to say *ipso facto* the more interesting) before the last decade of the sixteenth century. Insofar as Metaphysical poetry represents a shift or rebellion from an orthodoxy of esthetic mode, it involves therefore a change from a dominant middle esthetic distance and a subordinate public mode which was thought to possess the dignity of social gravity and ceremony.

Donne did not proceed from this earlier norm to those twisted eye-beams in one sudden change. The way in which he effected the shift can be observed in the forms he chose to write much of his earliest poetry—elegy and satire—and in his handling of them. The love elegy involved a departure from the dominant conventions usually and rather loosely labelled Petrarchan to the classical model of the Roman elegists and, in Donne's case, especially Ovid, as Grierson and others have observed.[2] The urban, household scene of *The Perfume*, in which the lovers attempt their assignations in spite of family precautions, is especially Ovidian. (See ch. v below.) It also introduces into poetry the new conception of love in opposition to the society in which the lovers find themselves. The animosity to the family reaches such heights

[2] See for example Dame Helen Gardner's Commentary on the *Elegies*, pp. 122, 124, 126, 128, and 131. Donne's use of the Roman love elegy is treated at length in ch. v. This is a convenient place to refer to the Bibliographical Note on the texts chosen for quotation in this book, and to point to implications of the choice: e.g., the *numbers* for the Holy Sonnets are those of Helen Gardner, not of Grierson. (See "Major Editions Used and Consulted.) As subsequent notes show, I am indebted to both editions, as well as others, for commentary.

7

as the wish that the girl's "immortall mother" and stupid father will die. Such impatience grows to the conclusion: "What? will hee die?" Another elegy, *Jealosie*, is equally Ovidian or Roman in its general situation of adulterous love. The Ovidian debts are important to consider for those who wish to treat the elegies biographically. But they are equally significant for what they show of a rejection of the courtly society presumed by almost all Elizabethan love poetry. They permitted Donne to introduce passionate young men as speakers in very specific amatory situations. The sarcastic opening clause of *The Anagram* hits off the Roman and heterodox note perfectly: "Marry, and love thy *Flavia*. . . ." The highly unorthodox speaker addresses a man with a "Roman" mistress of surpassing ugliness. Such other openings in the elegies as "Natures lay Ideot, I taught thee to love," "By our first strange or fatall interview," "Here take my Picture, though I bid farewell," or "Come, Madame, come, all rest my powers defie" show how successful Donne was in creating the air of actual speech, that is to say, of conversation between a clearly defined male speaker and a largely implicit woman listener in situations that owe little to the characters and situations of contemporary love poetry.

If the rejection of existing social conventions is largely implicit in the elegies—although to an age sensitive to decorums it must have been shockingly obvious—it is basic to the satires. Three of the numbered satires (I, IV, and V) are directed against the court and its courtiers, the second against "all this towne," as best represented in the lawyer of the poem. The third, on religion, is far less satiric in any usual sense, although it does reject facile reasons for adhering to any given position and concludes with a rejection of the national claims of any state religion. In all five, the integrity of the individual provides the authority for satire of society, as the opening of *Satyre IV* shows:

8

Well; I may now receive, and die; My sinne
Indeed is great, but I have beene in
A Purgatorie, such as fear'd hell is
A recreation and scant map of this.
My minde, neither with prides itch, nor yet hath been
Poyson'd with love to see, or to bee seene,
I had no suit there, nor new suite to shew,
Yet went to Court.   (1–8)

In *Satyre III*, the general biblical injunction, "Hold fast that which is good," becomes far more personal: "Keepe the'truth which thou hast found" (l. 89). The individual is assumed to be right (if he can find his way through wise doubting to truth), and social notions are thought utterly wrong. Repeatedly, the bitter observation of the court shifts to the private response of the speaker. He is revolted to the verge of nausea by what he sees.[3] He repeatedly struggles to be alone, to scurry back to his private lodging, or to find his spiritual home.

Satire of the court is by no means original with Donne. Its corruption had been shown by Skelton and Wyatt early in the Renaissance and still earlier in the middle ages by the complaints of the Plowman and even by the handsome indirections of Chaucer's *Nun's Priest's Tale*. Closer to hand were Spenser's embittered attacks upon a court that could not be trusted. *Mother Hubberds Tale* (1591) almost certainly antedates Donne's first satires, as *Colin Clouts Come Home Againe* (1595) perhaps postdates them. Yet Spenser's protests are from one within the system who obliquely uses the beast fable or pastoral and who, in any event, dedicates

---

[3] To my mind, no one has better caught this feeling of the time than Robert Ellrodt in *L'Inspiration Personnelle et L'Esprit du Temps chez Les Poètes Métaphysiques Anglais* (Paris, 1960); see particularly Pt. II, ch. ii, "La Nausée." Hereafter cited as Ellrodt, *Les Poètes Métaphysiques Anglais*.

his poems to such exalted and puissant patrons as Sir Walter Raleigh. Donne's satires are more immediate, for if they usually do not name names they are not fables or pastorals. Like Spenser's poems they judge the court (as we shall see) by what it should be in the light of what it seems really to be to someone who is disaffected; they also show what the court is when judged by a speaker who feels his personal integrity under threat.

For such reasons, although the satires are themselves in a form in which it is difficult to avoid writing public poetry, Donne succeeds in making them private. As a result, they offer little hope of change, of the satirist's voice being heard. He speaks but to himself and is the more embittered because no one will hear him. That quality has led to some disagreement as to Donne's classical model. The crabbed strong lines have led many in his day and ours to associate him and the other late Elizabethan satirists with Persius, while the embittered, personal invective employed by Donne is thought to display kinship with Juvenal. Yet the closest specific resemblance of any of the satires is to one by Horace,[4] as Dryden had suggested more generally on the basis of prosody and the plain style.[5] Donne goes farther, however, than any of the three Roman satirists in creating a speaker who is not only incoherently bitter like that of Persius, indignant like that of Juvenal, and detached like that of Horace, but quite simply private. The Donne of the satires constitutes himself as a personal, unloyal opposition to the Establishment, angry with the world for its indiffer-

[4] See H. J. C. Grierson, *Donne's Poetical Works*, 2 vols. (Oxford, 1912), II, 117, who points to Horace, *Satire I*, ix as the model for *Satyre IV*. For general discussion of Roman influence, see Ellrodt, *Les Poètes Métaphysiques Anglais*, Pt. II, ch. vi.

[5] See *Of Dramatic Poesy and Other Critical Essays*, ed. George Watson, 2 vols. (London, 1962), II, 144.

ence to him, and angry with himself for his partial involvement with it. When we come to consider the motives for
such private response, we must not forget such partial involvement or the seemingly first-hand experience the satires
record. Donne does not strike out, as do the Romantics so
often, from their private sensibility at an abstract Society, nor
at an indifferent modern world such as that in some of the
writings of recent decades. He attacks what he purports to
have seen, even to have been dragged into willy-nilly. "Well,"
he writes, "I may now receive, and die"—*after* having been
at court.

Both in his satires and elegies, then, Donne reacted against
the conventions of the social world and against that world
itself. The reactions have in common, in two such different
spheres as those of satire and the love elegy, retreat to the
integrity of the private self. To transform that retreat into
poetry, Donne chose to present the experiences of the private
speaker in his encounters with the public world or with love,
the latter a subject long hedged by conventions that he
overthrew with a remarkably easy hand. This is not to say
that, writing when he did, he could escape composing some
poems that were genuinely public or others set in the middle
esthetic distance of earlier writers. His verse letters, epicedes,
and epithalamia show as much. Yet even in them the private
voice seeks to speak out. The "Elegie on Mris Boulstred"
begins, "Death I recant, and say, unsaid by mee . . ." with
two first person singular pronouns in the first line of a public
poem. *The Elegie on the untimely Death of the incomparable Prince Henry* (an event which probably provoked more
public poetry than any before it in England) both begins
and ends with attention to the speaker himself. The Som-
merset epithalamion is preceded by an elaborate personal
apology for not being on hand for the marriage. What is

perhaps most revealing of all is the verse letter, *The Calme*, which moves as the satires do from the observed outer world to the private reaction:

> What are wee then? How little more alas
> Is man now, then before he was? he was
> Nothing; for us, wee are nothing fit;
> Chance, or our selves still disproportion it.
> Wee have no power, no will, no sense; I lye,
> I should not then thus feele this miserie. (51–56)

The suffering of the men aboard a becalmed ship becomes finally his own. In other words, even those acknowledged exceptions—those poems written in forms favoring the public or the social mode—show signs of his private impulse breaking forth.

What is after all of greatest importance is that Donne's finest poetry is in the private mode, that whatever he may have felt called upon to do in those public poems holding least interest today, he struggled in them with his private self, and he found full expression for that self in private poems. It is remarkably unnecessary for us to sift Donne's works. Popular response over the centuries has already done this, showing that whatever is of truly first importance comes from a private response to himself and his world. Upon consideration, it may be said that Donne's public poems prove the same truth negatively. They are not true to life. But when he became a public figure, when he assumed a sure place in his society, then he could speak out in his sermons for the "world" in terms that showed how deeply his remarkable personality was involved.

Donne's crucial redirection of poetry into the private mode was followed by the rest of the poets we call Metaphysical. The "Metaphysical race" begins to die out when the private response no longer most matters, or matters only as convention, in the more trifling poems of Godolphin, Cleveland, and even Cowley. To put it otherwise, when Cowley and Cleveland are most successful they are often least private, most anticipatory of later styles. In order for Metaphysical poetry to be, then, it was necessary that the intimate, the significant because different, the personal, in a word the private, be taken as that which is most essential. Given the course of events in the century, the surprising thing is not that Metaphysical poetry was steadily eroded or compromised by other kinds, or that it lasted so short a time, but that it lasted as long as it did. Most of the poets writing in the first half of the century became more and more drawn into public and social concerns by the Civil Wars, as was shown by their poetry; sometimes, as in Milton's case, by their prose rather than their poetry; or sometimes by their silence. Yet more remarkable still is the career of Vaughan, beginning with strong Royalist commitment in the wars and ending as a private poet dead but five years before Dryden. Strong as were the forces that opposed it, and many as were the poetic alternatives to it, the private impulse clearly accounts for much that is central to seventeenth-century experience.

The crucial element in establishing the character of private poetry is the means by which the poet expressed such private necessities of experience in his poetry: the speaker of the poem, the man or woman separated from the world and speaking of his experience apart from it. Although there is no question but that we can describe the important features of the private mode if only we can describe the conditions of the speaker of the poem, the problem is enormously complex. Apart from the biographical connection, which in Donne, if not always in the others, is very slippery, there are three important aspects of the speaker's function which may usefully be considered: the development of his attitudes in the poem, his relation to the situation of the poem, and the identity of his audience. The first of these—the development of attitude—has usually been discussed in terms of the "drama" or structure of the poetry, with attention given to such twists in direction as those which frequently mark Metaphysical poems. In "Womans constancy" Donne gives a familiar example:

> Vaine lunatique, against these scapes I could
> Dispute, and conquer, if I would,
> Which I abstaine to doe,
> For by to morrow, I may thinke so too.   (14–17)

In "The Collar," Herbert probably gives the best-loved example of all such change in the speaker's attitude:

> But as I rav'd and grew more fierce and wilde
> At every word,
> Me thoughts I heard one calling, *Child!*
> And I reply'd, *My Lord.*   (33–36)

Since such developing attitudes or changing tones have so often been analyzed, there seems little need to expatiate upon a known and indeed immediately felt truth. The second feature of the function of the speaker—his reaction to a situation—is one that the next chapter will be concerned with, if from a slightly different point of view. Such elimination leaves us with the third feature: the identity and use of the speaker's audience.

It may seem so obvious as to make statement vain that the audience of the love poems is commonly a single woman, and that of the religious poems God. There may seem to be no problem to consider. But the truth is that both the audience and the speaker of Metaphysical poetry are far more complicated than the obviousness of these statements implies. In Herbert's poem "The Collar," there is at the end something approaching conversation between the speaker and God, but,

14

until that point, to whom has the speaker been relating all his rebellion? "I struck the board, and cry'd, No more. / I will abroad." There is something here suspiciously like a narrative past tense: "A Gentle Knight was pricking on the plaine." What needs to be admitted at once is that a Metaphysical poem (like many other kinds) does not have a single audience but, potentially at least, three distinct kinds: the speaker himself as audience; the "dramatic" audience of another person in the poem; and the vicarious audience of the reader, to whom the poem is in some sense related. All three can be illustrated by one of Donne's most familiar poems, "The Indifferent," which begins:

I can love both faire and browne,
Her whom abundance melts, and her whom want betraies,
Her who loves lonenesse best, and her who maskes and plaies,
Her whom the country form'd, and whom the town,
Her who beleeves, and her who tries,
Her who still weepes with spungie eyes,
And her who is dry corke, and never cries;
I can love her, and her, and you and you,
I can love any, so she be not true.

The pronouns of all but the last part of the eighth line leave us with three possibilities for the identity of the audience. Either the "her's" suggest that he is musing to himself, that he is addressing some as yet unspecified friend in the poem, or that he is speaking as it were into the air, that is, to the reader. The last part of the eighth line and all the second stanza introduce what seems a completely different audience: the specified women addressed in the second person:

Will no other vice content you?
Wil it not serve your turn to do, as did your mothers?
Or have you all old vices spent, and now would finde out
    others?

Or doth a feare, that men are true, torment you?
Oh we are not, be not you so,
Let mee, and doe you, twenty know.
Rob mee, but binde me not, and let me goe.
Must I, who came to travaile thorow you,
Grow your fixt subject, because you are true? (10–18)

This stanza requires us to revise our impression of the three possible audiences for the first stanza. The direct address suggests that the audience is one of women: "Wil it not serve your turn to do, as did your mothers?" Without this plural, or without the end of the eighth line ("you and you"), we would surely suppose that the second stanza addresses but one woman, as the tone suggests: "Let mee, and doe you, twenty know. / Rob mee, but binde me not." What the second stanza also does is eliminate the friend as a possible audience for the first stanza and make it most difficult to believe that the speaker is addressing himself or—except over a great gulf of private poetry—us.

Yet in this strangely shifting (but not in that unusual) poem of Donne's, the third stanza sets us right by denying a second-person audience altogether:

Venus heard me sigh this song,
And by Loves sweetest Part, Variety, she swore,
She heard not this till now; and that it should be so no more.
She went, examin'd, and return'd ere long,
And said, alas, Some two or three
Poore Heretiques in love there bee,
Which thinke to stablish dangerous constancie.
But I have told them, since you will be true,
You shall be true to them, who'are false to you. (19–27)

"Venus heard me sigh this song." The first two stanzas have been a love complaint, not of the usual Petrarchan sort, to be sure, but still modelled on it and a complaint all the same. The pretense that the speaker was addressing women was bravado; he was addressing himself and us. He was soliloquizing. The remainder of the third stanza gives us the proper "dramatic" audience, the audience within the situation, Venus, who goes out for heretics like a pursuivant, comes back, and tells the speaker what she has done.

We have, then, three audiences: Venus within the situation, the reader exterior to it as to the whole world of the poem, and the speaker himself. Now which of these is most important to the speaker, to the poet, and to the poem? The presence of Venus defines the situation of the poem; we certainly should never have guessed it without her. But, more fundamentally, the reader is also addressed: "*Venus* heard me sigh this song." Someone is being told. The verb is the verb of relation, in a quasi-narrative past tense. The reader as audience is of great significance for what it tells us of the tone of the poems: it reminds us how fictional they are, how far the speakers of other poems, with other audiences and other situations, are free art. After all, Venus is not to be met with every day. The inclusion of the reader as audience establishes the fact that we are being given a poem, a fiction. The interior audience, or the dramatic audience within the situation, Venus, emphasizes this the more. The most active or "dramatic" character in the poem, she is the most patently fictional. Both of these audiences in "The Indifferent" should serve to remind us how seldom Donne's poems are autobiographical, even when most personal in addressing some "you," when most exclamatory in mood, or when most active with motion. By calling a character Venus in this poem, he has given away a game well concealed in many other poems; obviously there are many Venuses in his poems, even those in which the speaker talks with the accent of direct address. We shall return to the interior or dramatic audience after considering the other two further.

"*Venus* heard me sigh this song"—the sigh tells us that the speaker has been addressing himself, uttering a complaint, soliloquizing. If Donne had not shown us as much, we should not have believed it. But who is that "me" in soliloquy? He is a person apparently in his chamber, sighing over the fact that some women have insisted, of all things, on fidelity in love. In other words, the private speaker is as fictional as is Venus and is not to be identified precisely with the private poet. Outside the poem, as a general supposition, that is to be sure our bond with Donne himself—he and we may meet in pure poetic faith over what is known to both as a fiction. The extent of the fictionalizing process must be the same for the speaker as for the person he addresses, Venus, and the extent to which they are fictional renders the poem more wholly free, "dramatic." The extent to which they are fictional divides the poet from his speaker and the dramatic audience, Venus, from the reader. On the other hand, as other poems show, to the degree that the speaker and the poet move closer together (as in "Batter my heart, three person'd God"), the reader as audience is set at greater distance. And to the degree that the reader is addressed, the dramatic audience grows distant, as is shown (to take a different poet) by Traherne in his poem, "The Author to the Critical Peruser":

> The naked Truth in many faces shewn,
> Whose inward Beauties very few hav known,
> A Simple Light, transparent Words, a Strain
> That lowly creeps, yet maketh Mountains plain,
> Brings down the highest Mysteries to sense
> And keeps them there; that is Our Excellence:
> At that we aim; to th' end thy Soul might see
> With open Eys thy Great *Felicity*,
> Its Objects view, and trace the glorious Way
> Wherby thou may'st thy Highest Bliss enjoy. (1–10)

The address to us critical perusers excludes address to God, at least in theory.

The proviso about theory is necessary. Donne obviously can shift his audience, or more accurately make us revise our impressions about who is being addressed. To take for illustration one of his somewhat lesser known poems, the eighth of the 1633 Holy Sonnets, he may begin with address to the reader and go on to address a dramatic audience:

Why are wee by all creatures waited on?
Why doe the prodigall elements supply
Life and food to mee, being more pure then I,
Simple, and further from corruption?
Why brook'st thou, ignorant horse, subjection?
Why dost thou bull, and bore so seelily
Dissemble weaknesse, and by'one mans stroke die,
Whose whole kinde, you might swallow'and feed upon?
Weaker I am, woe'is mee, and worse then you,
You have not sinn'd, nor need be timorous,
But wonder at a greater wonder, for to us
Created nature doth these things subdue,
But their Creator, whom sin, nor nature tyed,
For us, his Creatures, and his foes, hath dyed.

The audience shifts from that of the reader (and speaker, who is included in that "wee") to animals in lines 5–10 and back to the reader and speaker ("us") thereafter. While the reader is addressed, the possibility of a dramatic audience seems remote, and as the dramatic audience of horse, bull, and "bore" is addressed the reader grows remote. What this poem and such a familiar one as "The Indifferent" show is the fluidity, or kinesis, of the audience in Donne's poems. Quite simply, the audience may change very nearly at will and may be as patently fictional as Venus or a horse, while the poet and the reader stand at either end, bound to each other by a varying fiction.

The two crucial terms of the poetic relationship are, then, the poet and the reader, in Metaphysical as in all other poetry. What Donne's two poems show him doing is achieving private poetry by establishing the terms upon which poet and reader are to meet. They may be joined by the "wee" of the Holy Sonnet, though kept apart by its dramatic audience —the animals whose very fictional character sets the reader at a distance—insuring the privacy of the poet. The dramatic audience is a means of assuring privacy not just because it distances the reader, but even more because it brings the poet closer—sometimes to the point of identity—to his speaker and even the dramatic situation, which in Donne's lyrics at least is seldom anything but private.

The remarkable thing about Donne's poetry is that in it he shifts the audience addressed, or its distance from him and from the reader, with such astonishing ease. *Goodfriday, 1613. Riding Westward* is a fine example of his varying or manipulating the audience. The title and the religious devotion create two presumptions: that the poet and the speaker are very nearly congruent, and that the situation is one of private musing on a to him private occasion. The opening lines implicitly address the reader, however: "Let mans Soule be a Spheare." The address is made explicit a few lines later: "so, *our* Soules admit [Pleasure or businesse] / For their first mover" (11. 7–8; my stress). The private occasion and the address to the reader come together as the poet-speaker informs us of the situation:

Hence is't, that I am carryed towards the West
This day, when my Soules forme bends toward the East.
(9–10)

With these lines the grammatical subject shifts to a dominant "I," which in this poem is capable either of inclusion with the common human estate of the reader or of restriction to a situation. The former possibility is realized early in the poem, the latter at its end, when suddenly a dramatic audience is introduced by the address to Christ:

and thou look'st towards mee,
O Saviour, as thou hang'st upon the tree . . .
Restore thine Image, so much, by thy grace,
That thou may'st know mee, and I'll turne my face.

(35–36, 41–42)

By the end, the reader is set at a very great distance; however deeply moved, we fall silent and wish ourselves unobtrusive when a man is at prayer.

Such distancing of the reader raises other problems. It places great stress upon the speaker of the poem, whose relation to the poet is less easily decided than any other of the esthetic relationships that come about because poetry is a complex species of address. In reading the religious poems we usually assume a congruency, even an identification, of poet and speaker. In other poems, like "The Apparition," we assume a complete separation:

When by thy scorne, O murdresse, I am dead,
And that thou thinkst thee free
From all solicitation from mee,
Then shall my ghost come to thy bed,
And thee, fain'd vestall, in worse armes shall see;
Then thy sicke taper will begin to winke,
And he, whose thou art then, being tyr'd before,
Will, if thou stirre, or pinch to wake him, thinke
Thou call'st for more,
And in false sleepe will from thee shrinke,
And then poore Aspen wretch, neglected thou
Bath'd in a cold quicksilver sweat wilt lye
A veryer ghost then I;
What I will say, I will not tell thee now,
Lest that preserve thee; 'and since my love is spent,
I'had rather thou shouldst painfully repent,
Than by my threatnings rest still innocent.

21

No one would seriously argue that Donne identifies himself with the speaker here. The speaker and his audience are entirely "dramatic," in the sense that I have been using the term, even to the point of the creation of a second drama in the future, when the dead speaker will come as a ghost to where the "murdresse" lies with some man unable to satisfy her unbounded sexual desires. Donne has many such poems and very few that are private which do not have an element of drama. As we have seen, when they are wholly dramatic (again in the sense used here), the reader is greatly distanced. The poet may also be distanced, however; all depends upon the kind of fiction that acts as the bond between the poet and reader.

Yet even in those poems in which the identification of poet and speaker seems certain or probable, there is distance between them. The valedictory poems provide a convenient example. In "A Valediction of my name in the window," "A Valediction of the booke," and "A Valediction of weeping" the hyperbole and the address in highly complicated syntax and imagery stamp the poems with a strong degree of fiction —and fiction, precisely, of the "dramatic" kind. If one has any doubts on this score, one need only compare the poems with Donne's letters to see the difference between address by a real person and address by a fictional speaker. The same is true, although less obviously and less wholly, of "A Valediction forbidding mourning" and even of the song, "Sweetest love, I do not goe, / For wearinesse of thee." But what these poems as a group show is that the greater the pressure of a dramatic audience (as in the first three named), the greater may be the distance between poet and speaker.

I have discussed the relations of poet, speaker, audiences, and reader chiefly in reference to Donne, because he is most various and most masterful in handling them. More than that, after him there is a gradual change in practice which, as it goes far enough in this or that direction, renders poems by

those we consider Metaphysical indistinguishable from Cavalier, Elizabethan, or Restoration poems in respect to their
address and, indeed, their degree of privateness. What happens is that the dramatic audience either disappears or loses
that incomparable liveliness it has for Donne. After him,
Herbert is most consistently successful in maintaining the
conviction of a dramatic audience, a conviction that depends
not only upon a poem's being addressed to someone, which
in itself hardly makes it "dramatic," but upon the fictional
reality in the poem of the person addressed. This reality is
most truly dramatic when the audience itself is given speech,
as in Herbert's poem, "The Quip":

> The merrie world did on a day
> With his train-bands and mates agree
> To meet together, where I lay,
> And all in sport to geere at me.
>
> First, Beautie crept into a rose,
> Which when I pluckt not, Sir, said she,
> Tell me, I pray, Whose hands are those?
> *But thou shalt answer, Lord, for me.*
>
> Then Money came, and chinking still,
> What tune is this, poor man? said he:
> I heard in Musick you had skill.
> *But thou shalt answer, Lord, for me. . . .*
>
> Yet when the houre of thy designe
> To answer these fine things shall come:
> Speak not at large; say, I am thine:
> And then they have their answer home.
>
> (1–12, 21–24)

The situation is specific; the speaker is addressed; and even
God is given words to speak. Yet on occasion Herbert loses
the vivacity of the dramatic audience, as in "Life":

23

I Made a posie, while the day ran by:
Here will I smell my remnant out, and tie
          My life within this band.
But time did becken to the flowers, and they
By noon most cunningly did steal away,
          And wither'd in my hand. . . .
Farewell deare flowers, sweetly your time ye spent,
Fit, while ye liv'd, for smell or ornament,
          And after death for cures.
I follow straight without complaints or grief,
Since if my [scent] be good, I care not if
          It be as short as yours.
                    (1–6, 13–18)

There is address, to the flowers, but they are only flowers, and the poem is too shot through with the *sic vita* treatment of nature to be wholly dramatic.

With Crashaw, there is little life in the dramatic audience, for although there is usually address, it is the passion of the speaker rather than any response of a dramatic audience that determines the poem ("Vexilla Regis"):

Look up, languishing Soul! Lo where the fair
Badg of thy faith calls back thy care,
     And biddes thee ne're forget
     Thy life is one long Debt
Of love to Him, who on this painfull TREE
Paid back the flesh he took for thee.   (1–6)

The later Metaphysical poets more or less lose the functioning dramatic audience. In "The Garden" Marvell does indeed use address to "quiet," "Innocence," and "Trees," but his speaker, like Bacon's Pilate, does not stay for an answer. "The Definition of Love" is wholly undramatic, as is most of his Metaphysical poetry. His dialogues, "Between the Resolved Soul and Created Pleasure" and "Between the Soul and Body," are excellent poems, but surprisingly undramatic. To adapt Donne's phrase, they are monologues of two, parallel remarks often with little relation to each other. *The Nymph complaining for the death of her Faun* and *Upon Appleton House* achieve more fully felt situations, not by drama but by "narrative," by events in a sequence related or spoken to the reader as audience. The one poem that is dramatic after the fashion of Donne's situations is "To his Coy Mistress," but its address is as Cavalier as Herrick's in "Corinna's going a Maying." The poem is more properly not so much a Metaphysical poem as one of the numerous poems in F. R. Leavis' "line of wit" that has accessions of Metaphysical wit and imagery. It is significant that dramatic address was possible to Marvell only on price of his turning Cavalier or searching out such other ambiguous forms as the dialogue or narrative.

With Vaughan and Traherne, the dramatic *audience* is all but completely lost. Vaughan's typical method is that of "The Retreate":

> Happy those early dayes! when I
> Shin'd yet in my Angell-infancy.
> Before I understood this place
> Appointed for my second race,
> Or taught my soul to fancy ought
> But a white, Celestiall thought. (1–6)

"The World" (the famous one of that title) is a seeming exception, since the "doting Lover," the "darksome Statesman," and others described in the poem do act or speak. But the point is that they do not interact with the speaker or address him. The governing feature of the poem is the speaker's words.

> I Saw Eternity the other night
> Like a great *Ring* of pure and endless light,
> All calm, as it was bright,

> And round beneath it, Time in hours, days, years
> > Driv'n by the spheres
> Like a vast shadow mov'd . . .   (1–6)

Traherne sounds the same note in "On Leaping over the Moon":

> I saw new Worlds beneath the Water ly,
> > New Peeple; and another Sky,
> > > And Sun, which seen by Day
> > > Might things more clear display.   (1–4)

What happens in all these poems is that there is a great simplification of speaker and audiences. With the diminution and gradual disappearance of dramatic situations the poems change in their kind of privateness. The absence of drama makes the speaker more closely identified with the poet, and the reader more distant. When Traherne writes, "I saw new Worlds," he uses a verb of lyrical relation, but because of the strong meditative strain from Herbert on, the lyric relation is rather to the speaker himself than to any but a distant reader. Although the dramatic situation in Donne's poems often separates us from the speaker, the meditative musing and self-address of the later writers (or of some of Donne's religious poems, out of which the later strain appears to have developed) keeps us equally distant. It will be clear, therefore, that the privacy of the poetry is maintained, even though the drama gradually disappears.

Yet the loss of the dramatic audience is a real one, both poetically in its diminution of poetic range and historically in its signalling the decline of Metaphysical poetry. Cleveland and Cowley, who were to Dryden and Dr. Johnson among the last of the Metaphysical race, show best how the new modes we associate with the Restoration were being first practiced in the admission of social decorums and public subjects, and even more radically in the growing lack of faith

26

in the integrity of the dramatic or narrative speaker. He is beginning not to matter much. And with Vaughan and Traherne we have the meditational speaker who in addressing himself is often almost indistinguishable from the speakers of Elizabethan moral poems with their somewhere audiences. But the private mode does continue so long as there is a private speaker, or rather so long as the poet has faith in him cut off—as in Vaughan's poem, "The World" —precisely from the world and its inadequacies.

The process of change is partly one of yielding to new or older modes unlike Donne's and partly one of simplification. With Donne, the private speaker is often immured in his privateness by the intervention of the dramatic audience between the poet to the one side and the reader to the other. The later poets could assure the privateness of the poet and the poem best by identifying the speaker with the poet in a way simplifying Donne's technique or merely by claiming experience for oneself ("*My* love is of a birth. . . ," "*I* Saw Eternity the other night") and speaking to oneself about the matter. Insofar as the reader is involved, it is presumed that he will not so much hear as read. Moreover, later Metaphysical poets were writing at a time when new convictions about the relation of the speaker to other men were challenging the older view of his separation, when new situations were being devised in a public arena specifying time and place with what was often historical accuracy. *Paradise Lost* and *Absalom and Achitophel* show that the change had irrevocably come. The last Metaphysical poems are flowers out of season.

What is common to all the Metaphysical poets is a private speaker conscious of, often explicit about, his alienation from what is repeatedly termed the "world." Donne's anti-court satires, his attack upon such social units as the family (or more often his simply ignoring them—how many children had John Donne?), and his repeated attribution to lovers of

27

the role of saints or priests opposed to "the layetie" show how marked was his insistence that his poems turn their backs upon the world. "The Canonization" is the most explicit:

> For Godsake hold your tongue, and let me love,
>   Or chide my palsie, or my gout,
> My five gray haires, or ruin'd fortune flout,
>   With wealth your state, your minde with Arts improve,
>   Take you a course, get you a place,
>   Observe his honour, or his grace,
> Or the Kings reall, or his stamped face
>   Contemplate, what you will, approve,
>   So you will let me love.   (1-9)

Others may conduct the business of a worthless world. He, with his marvelously and characteristically observed "five gray haires," will love. The opening of "The Sunne Rising" is similar:

> Busie old foole, unruly Sunne,
>   Why dost thou thus,
> Through windowes, and through curtaines call on us?
> Must to thy motions lovers seasons run?
>   Sawcy pedantique wretch, goe chide
>   Late schoole boyes, and sowre prentices.
> Goe tell Court-huntsmen, that the King will ride,
> Call countrey ants to harvest offices.   (1-8)

"A Valediction forbidding mourning" is equally certain of the superiority of shared private love to anything else that the rest of the world might know:

> So let us melt, and make no noise,
>   No teare-floods, nor sigh-tempests move,
>   'Twere prophanation of our joyes
>   To tell the layetie our love.   (5-8)

In these poems, or in *The Extasie*, where the motif of the unity of the lovers is yet more marked, the dramatic situation is sometimes rather attenuated in comparison with other poems by Donne. They are dramatic monologues premonitory of Browning's. Each is, as Donne says in another context in *The Extasie*, a "dialogue of one." The woman (sometimes the man) addressed, or God, is seldom given anything to say. But the audience is felt as a presence in Donne's poetry, a fact distinguishing it (and most of Herbert's poems) from the increasingly narrative or other address in later Metaphysical poems. What is retained in them from Donne is the speaker, cut off from the world and superior to it in his integrity or in the worth of his experience. The private speaker is the norm of consciousness, of integrity in a world lacking in clear-sightedness, a world corrupt.

If there is any explanation current as to why the Metaphysical poets should have required such speakers, it is probably that they modelled their poems upon the formal religious meditation or that, more generally, the experience they treat is meditational.[6] There is no question but that meditational forms do underlie some of the poetry, although, as I have argued, the replacement of drama by meditation is a symptom of the decline of Metaphysical poetry rather than a *sine qua non* of its origin, which was in satire, elegy, and love lyric, which thus far no one has argued to be meditational. In any event, to offer a form of religious devotion as an explanation as to why poets sought the private mode is only to remove the problem one step. Why should the Metaphysicals have used song, dialogue, or meditation in the first place?

The traditional explanation, which exists still in spite of its obvious historical unpersuasiveness, is Jacobean melancholy. Dark clouds are said to have blackened England after

[6] See Louis L. Martz, *The Poetry of Meditation*, Yale Studies in English 125 (New Haven, 1954). About the same time Dame Helen Gardner and the late Helen White were making similar discoveries, much to the benefit of our understanding, as my earlier remarks about the meditational nature of later Metaphysical poetry will have suggested.

1603. Since Donne set the terms of private poetry in the last ten or twelve years of Elizabeth, however, and since it was those years that produced (along with a good deal else) satire by writers as various as Donne, Hall, Marston, and Spenser, the notion of bright Elizabethan and dark Jacobean England is of course absurd. Recently it has become increasingly common for scholars to speak of a late-Elizabethan depression and a Jacobean recovery. Such a generalization fits the historical facts somewhat better but still puts the problem at one remove. Why did the pessimism or optimism arise in any case, at whatever date? Was Donne affected by either? The best historical answer to date, at least that most carefully set forth, is that economic and therefore social dislocations at the end of the sixteenth and early in the seventeenth century produced certain literary responses, or at least that these alterations were reflected in literature.[7] Donne has a very few, and brief, passages glancing at economic matters. In *Satyre IV*, ll. 103–107, he criticizes the licenses or monopolies granted "to some Courtier"—thereby referring to the economic abuse most commented upon by his contemporaries. A single line (105) in *Satyre II* refers to the conservative ideal of feudal country order, with "th'old landlords" generosity to his household and his alms to the poor. In juxtaposition the two passages suggest a view of these matters very like that of Jonson, or indeed like that of most of the writers from Wyatt to Dryden, who neither understood nor liked "the rise of capitalism" and the attendant breakdown of an old order whose ways of life they romanticized. But a half dozen or so lines in Donne cannot be used to base a very substantial edifice of interpretation, especially in view of their resemblance to views of writers altogether different

---

[7] See L. C. Knights, *Drama and Society in the Age of Jonson* (London, 1937; Penguin Books, 1962). Ellrodt is more pertinent to poetry, however; see *Les Poètes Métaphysiques Anglais*, Pt. II, chs. i and ii.

from him. We must search elsewhere for the springs of that response of Donne's to the world that led him to retreat to private integrity.

The best initial guides are the prosaic dates, which may be set forth most simply *seriatim*. (Those still uncertain are marked "ca.")

1591 At Thavies' Inn; 6 May 1592 admitted to Lincoln's Inn.

ca. 1591–1598 *Satyres*.

1593 Only brother, Henry, died in prison, having been committed for harboring a priest.

ca. 1593–1596 *Elegies*.
ca. 1593–1602 Earlier poems of *Songs and Sonnets*.

1596 With Essex on Cadiz Expedition.

1597 On Azores Expedition.

1598–1602 Secretary to Egerton, Lord Keeper.

1600–1601 Incomplete satire, *The Progress of the Soule*.

1601 Execution of Essex; married Ann More.[8]

The persistent feature of the decade is satire, both in openly practiced forms and in infusions into such other genres as

---

[8] The dates given for the Satyres, ca. 1591–98, are conventional, although John T. Shawcross, *The Complete Poetry of John Donne* (Garden City, N.Y., 1967), presents strong evidence indicating 1597–1598; he believes the Elegies date from ca. 1592 to 1598. W. Milgate, *Donne: The Satires, Epigrams and Verse Letters* (Oxford, 1967), accepts the conventional dates for the Satyres, though he thinks the five major Satyres may have been copied out as a "book of satires" (and—my sheer speculation—revised somewhat with then current allusions?) in 1598, when Donne was serving Egerton. The dates for the Elegies are those of Dame Helen Gardner and, details apart, are conventional: *Donne: The Elegies and The Songs and Sonnets* (Oxford, 1965). Shawcross finds "most inconvincing" her dating of the *Songs and Sonnets* into two groups, prior to 1598, and 1607–1614; his only positive amendment is a return to a sense of pre- and post-Anne More. These discrepancies between accounts by eminent scholars should excite in us a hesitation like that shown by Robert Ellrodt on *The Songs and Sonnets*. See "Chronologie des Poèmes de Donne," *Etudes Anglaises*, XIII (1960), 457–62.

epigrams, love elegies, and songs. The element distinguishing Donne's satire from that of Dryden and Pope is not that theirs was "neoclassical" and his not: he follows classical models more closely than does Dryden. It is rather that they were at one with, "in" with society or the "establishment," whereas he was at variance with it, "out." A closer comparison to Donne is that suggested earlier in this chapter: with the Spenser of *Mother Hubberds Tale* and *Colin Clouts Come Home Againe*, the former published in 1591, the latter in 1595, and both written in response to the court. With the exception of *Satyre III*, which concerns religion and which is only very partially satiric, Donne's satires are also directed against the court or "all this towne." Grierson's words will serve to describe the unfulfilled aim of *Metempsychosis. The Progresse of the Soule:* "A satirical history of the great heretic in lineal descent from the wife of Cain to Elizabeth." As he says, "Women and courtiers are the chief subject of Donne's sardonic satire in this poem," [9] and when one of the women happens to be Elizabeth I, one can see that to Donne something has gone wrong enough to elicit a decade of reaction whose direction is more or less described by the word satire.

It is not my purpose in this chapter to describe the nature of Donne's satire (see ch. iv) but to attempt to discover its motives. In brief, the parallel with Spenser runs close. Both had hopes of preferment, indeed both obtained enough preferment to satisfy many people, Spenser by virtue of his poetry and service, Donne for his parts and his attendance upon the great. Both felt that they had slid on the slopes of patronage, and both reacted in very human fashion. Donne had tried to get on and felt that he was failing. On the record of his satires, he thought the reasons for his failure to be that the court was corrupt and that he was not a courtier

[9] *Donne's Poetical Works*, II, 219.

content to flatter, wheedle, intrigue, and bribe. *Satyre V* is the more remarkable for its address to Egerton, Lord Keeper, and for the scorn it heaps not so much upon the great, who exploit suitors, as upon the suitors themselves, who do not realize the vanity of efforts which only undo them. It is yet more remarkable for its implications, which spare not even the "Greatest and fairest Empresse," Elizabeth (1. 28). *Satyre V* stands apart from, or perhaps rather caps, the other satires by virtue of its reference to specific people in ways that are unmistakable. The fact that, just as he was himself getting on, Donne chose to criticize the suitor rather than the powerful does not do him a great deal of credit, but along with the general sense in the satire of malaise and of criticism directed as well at the powerful, the fact is less important. Quite plainly, the court was something Donne had experienced and which in spite of its attractions threw him back on his own resources of integrity. Here is one reason why he became a private poet.

There is another constantly recurring emphasis in the satires, whose terms suggest that it was to Donne both an explanation and a source of fear: religion. As Grierson put it succinctly, "Throughout the *Satyres* Donne's veiled Catholic prejudices have to be constantly borne in mind." [10] Donne's Catholic background and continuing susceptibility to his family's religion provided an explanation to him in the sense that they revealed a religious integrity unsullied by the court corruption of informers and pursuivants.[11] But they also gave him, at a greater depth, his self-questioning hesitation over his search for preferment—an agony that was to recur more evidently before him when he was urged by James I and by his friends to enter Anglican orders. Even more (and this I find deeply moving), his satires reveal the suffering of fear,

[10] *Donne's Poetical Works*, II, 121.
[11] See *Satyre II*, 92–96; *III*, 89–92; *IV*, 137–40, 215–17; *V*, 65–68.

almost of terrors, both of the anti-Catholic court and of himself. In *Satyre IV*, his imagination creates of the guards at Court great giants, Askaparts, to whom his reaction is physical: "I shooke like a spyed Spie" (IV, 237). The attitude runs throughout *Satyre IV* and touches *Satyres I, II,* and V. Even "At home in wholesome solitarinesse"—which is, incidentally, a proof of the degree to which private poetry came in his case from a desire to retreat to private integrity— even there (IV, 155), like Dante he "dreamt he saw hell," the hell of court and of such dangers as the Askaparts. Significantly, although the first part of *Satyre IV* purports to recount what was seen on a visit to court (ll. 1–154), it is the remainder, which is a vision seen "in wholesome solitarinesse," that is the more fearsome. Even more than *The First Anniversary, Satyre IV* gives a sense that the outer world has oppressed or threatened Donne's private inner world almost to the point of destruction.

Such nightmares argue a deep, obsessive fear which is no great wonder, considering the methods of pursuivants and the fact that in these years his brother died in prison for harboring a priest. What my explanation implies is that Donne had real attachment to Catholicism. Grierson and others have thought so and the evidence, not that he was a communicating Catholic, but that he suspected he should be, is provided by *Satyre III*.[12] The problem of religious truth and certitude after the Reformation is that, to all sides,

[12] I have some fears that this discussion will be taken as an indictment of Donne's religious integrity when it is rather an attempt to show how the motions of his integrity influenced his poetry. It is essential to an understanding of the seventeenth century that one feel why it was that most of the greatest writers changed their religion at least once: Donne, Jonson, Milton, Marvell, Dryden, Rochester, and Wycherley. The pressures upon people in those days are treated in the sentences immediately following in the text, and it seems a sound principle to give all these men the benefit of any doubt over a conflict between interest and religion.

there was just one true religion by which a man might save his immortal soul. One had therefore above all else to "Seeke true religion," as Donne put it, asking immediately, "O where?" (*Satyre III*, 43). Donne gave himself an oblique answer, one he found difficult to hold to:

> but unmoved thou
> Of force must one, and forc'd but one allow;
> And the right; aske thy father which is shee,
> Let him aske his.   (*Satyre III*, 69–72)

The significant element is the biblical echo: "Remember the days of old, consider the years of many generations: ask thy father, and he will shew thee; thy elders, and they will tell thee" (Deuteronomy 32:7). To Donne personally, with *his* father, the injunction surely meant an acknowledgment of Catholicism as "the right" religion. Again, in a reference to Elizabeth's use of pursuivants, those unscrupulous and cruel ferrets of Catholics, he urges:

> Keepe the'truth which thou hast found; men do not stand
> In so ill case, that God hath with his hand
> Sign'd Kings blanck-charters to kill whom they hate,
> Nor are they Vicars, but hangmen to Fate.   (III, 89–92)

And again there is a biblical allusion: "hold fast that which is good" (I Thessalonians 5:21). Such steadfastness could only argue holding to Catholic "truth"—if Donne could convince himself that he had found it. (The first half of the verse charges that one "Prove all things"; Donne seems to have found some conflict between the two halves.) Significantly, the rest of the poem addresses the "Foole and wretch" whose soul is "tyed / To mans lawes"—to the Church by Law Established in acts of the civil authorities. There were of course numerous ecclesiastical establishments throughout Europe, but the English situation of the poem shows again that Donne has Catholic truth in mind.

The revulsion from the court and the self-assessment that he was, or should be, a Catholic are ample reasons, I believe, for Donne's turning away from the "world," for his turning with satirical scorn and wit, whether playful or mordant, upon the court. In brief, there are reasons more powerful than Jacobean melancholy or economic changes for Donne's turning to private subjects, private attitudes, and private poetry to recapture an integrity threatened by the court from without and from religious uncertainty within. As Dame Helen Gardner says of poems in *Songs and Sonnets*, "The values of love are set over against the values of the court and the world." [13] Often this contrast of public falsity and private integrity is wholly implicit. Often, in the early poems, it involves a contrast between the private integrity of the speaker and the worldliness of the person addressed. "Breake of day," spoken by a woman, makes this point clear:

> Must businesse thee from hence remove?
> Oh that's the worst disease of love,
> The poore, the foule, the false, love can
> Admit, but not the busied man.
> He which hath businesse, and makes love, doth doe
> Such wrong, as when a maryed man does wooe.
>
> (13–18)

At other times the world is treated as a standard of corruption and pain, as in "The Curse" upon "Who ever guesses, thinks, or dreames he knowes / Who is my mistris."

> May he dreame Treason, and beleeve, that hee
> Meant to performe it, and confesse, and die,
>   And no record tell why:
>   His sonnes, which none of his may bee,

[13] *The Elegies and The Songs and Sonnets*, p. ix.

36

Inherite nothing but his infamie:
   Or may he so long Parasites have fed,
   That he would faine be theirs, whom he hath bred,
   And at the last be circumcis'd for bread.   (17–24)

The public world is not only rejected; it is made a curse upon itself. The most consistent and explicit of the earlier lyrics in such rejection of the world is "The Will," a legacy of all the speaker's good or striking attributes to those in the world who should, but do not, possess them, or who possess them but should not:

   My constancie I to the planets give,
   My truth to them, who at the Court doe live;
   Mine ingenuity and opennesse,
   To Jesuites; to 'Buffones my pensivenesse;
   My silence to'any, who abroad hath beene;
      My mony to a Capuchin.   (10–15)

Such approaches sometimes become yet more explicit, as in "The Canonization":

With wealth your state, your minde with Arts improve,
   Take you a course, get you a place,
   Observe his honour, or his grace,
Or the Kings reall, or his stamped face
   Contemplate, what you will, approve,
   So you will let me love.   (4–9)

The lovers become saints or priests practicing mysteries far above the laity. Love, the most typical subject of private poetry, is in itself a retreat from the world, but in Donne's formulation it is also a defense and a challenge to even the existence of the "world." Next to love, "Nothing else is."

Before continuing briefly with other poets who continued the private mode as a revulsion from the world, I must seek to show that what Donne rebelled from also fascinated and attracted him. In this respect his private poetry is probably less completely private than that of the Romantic poets. The evidence to show the attraction held for Donne by the public world is both biographical and poetic. His reading law no doubt took him into the society of other witty young men of some fortune and ambition, but his solicitation of patronage and his work for Egerton exemplify the hopes he felt for rising in the very court he criticized. His feelings appear to have been genuinely ambivalent. Such is, at least, the natural interpretation to put upon actions literary and social which are in sum ambivalent. The mixed feelings affect the poetry generally by providing us with some understanding of the force of emotion invested in his satires, elegies, and other poems. The verse letters, dating from about 1597, and the even more occasional poems—the epithalamia, epicedes, and *The Anniversaries*—reveal in the seventeenth century tendencies present in his outlook from the sixteenth. More than this, his earliest poems themselves show an absorption with the public world. For all their private standpoint, the satires are poems in one of the most public of genres and concern a public world. Although based in tone upon Persius or Juvenal and in substance and style upon Horace, his satires grow to a considerable extent from the native medieval complaint. Spenser's substitution of the pastoral shepherd or of beasts for the medieval Plowman had taken the important step of moving forward, allegorically as it were, toward experience with the court. The experience occasioned revulsion, but revulsion after contact. Donne goes a step further in his satires (as well as in his elegies and most other poems) of urbanizing his poetry, a fact which itself gives his poetry a new social context.

The best evidence of the poetic importance of these strains in confluence is provided by the identity of his satiric narrator. Of course he is the plain man and his is a private voice. More than that, if but negatively, he is not a simple Plowman or a Colin Clout. But most importantly, as we have seen in *Satyre IV*, when he is "At home in wholesome solitarinesse," he cannot forbear imagining the nightmare world of the court, whose guards affright his memory, and whose informers or pursuivants make him shake in public like a spied spy, whose activities would cause his private life to be haled into public view. In the end, he could not hope to lead a private life in London or at the court. Like Colin Clout, he would need spiritually to go home again in the country, but, unlike Spenser's *alter ego*, he could not or would not go. With few exceptions, and those often agonized, Donne's poems are set in the city or at court, if anywhere. Yet more than this, in the very first satire, the private life envisioned as the alternative to the public is a life of contemplation—but of the very public world from which he recoils:

> A way thou fondling motley humorist,
> Leave mee, and in this standing woodden chest,
> Consorted with these few bookes, let me lye
> In prison,' and here be coffin'd, when I dye;
> Here are Gods conduits, grave Divines; and here
> Natures Secretary, the Philosopher;
> And jolly Statesmen, which teach how to tie
> The senewes of a cities mistique bodie;
> Here gathering Chroniclers, and by them stand
> Giddie fantastique Poëts of each land.
> Shall I leave all this constant company,
> And follow headlong, wild uncertaine thee?   (1–12)

His sources of comfort are divines, scientists, statesmen, historians, and poets. In contemporary terms, the scientific natural philosopher was a student of the retired, contemplative life, and a couple of the other comforters are ambiguous

as to their public or private status. But the statesmen, even
if read in books, exemplify the very world his satires attack.
Like Spenser, then, Donne's reaction against the court is a
reaction against a public society not so much because it was
public as because it was corrupted from the ideal in his mind.
Nothing could be more significant than the imagery he uses
to describe the private world to which he retreats. The
imagery is dominantly restrictive, suggestive of painful con-
finement and death. His chamber is a "standing woodden
chest" in which he is "coffin'd"; and, while private, he is "In
prison."

More than that, there is another major strand of imagery
that, with a seeming paradox, describes private experience in
terms of the very world revolted from. Donne's astronomical
and cartographic imagery is well known, and we find it, if less
frequently, in subsequent Metaphysical poets. "The Sunne
Rising" shows an intimate knowledge of the sun's habits in
going around the static earth; in "A Valediction of weeping,"
the lover finds globes in his beloved's tears; and in Marvell's
poem, *The Garden*, the Mind creates world and sea after
world and sea. There are of course numerous other examples,
many of which, especially in Donne, rest on the conception
of the human microcosm of the universal macrocosm. As
Donne begins Holy Sonnet 2 (1635), "I am a little world
made cunningly." The effect of such correspondences is very
often to transcend the ordinary, customary, faulty world by
finding that the private world of the lovers or of the wor-
shiper contains the larger universe.[14] This transcendence of
the restricted, immediate world to the total universe is often
very sudden, but what is of equal importance to the thrill we
often feel is the naturalness, the assurance we so often find.
"I Saw Eternity the other night"—the tone is perfect, like

[14] In "Donne and the Rhetorical Tradition," *Kenyon Review*, xi
(1949), 571–87, William Empson lays great stress on what he calls
Donne's "repeated metaphor of the separate world" of lovers.

nothing else that one can think of in English poetry. We are convinced that the lovers *can* make "one little roome an every where." And we admire their ability to find in the woman with the speaker in the curtained bed all states, in the man all princes, and then, most extraordinary of all, to find that "Nothing else is." Such transcendence will be found in somewhat different terms in Herbert's poem so significantly entitled "The World" and in both of Vaughan's of that title. Usually one of two movements is involved after the rejection of the world (best exemplified in *The First Anniversary*). Either there is a soaring to an eternal, distant world (as in Crashaw, Vaughan, Traherne, and sometimes Marvell and even Donne), or the eternal, larger world is made to represent the values of the little world of the lovers or worshipper. A somewhat similar but nonetheless different tendency may be found in the lesser terms of diction and verse texture. Imagery is often taken from the very public or customary world that the poet rejects. This is a very happy tendency in that it allows the poets to fill out their private worlds with terms of experience rendering them widely available, shareable and, in a word, "universal." The best Metaphysical poetry very well knows the world it rejects, and it often comes near to retrieving what it so ostentatiously throws away. This great counter-pull is of the utmost significance to us readers, enabling us to participate in the private world and to affirm what seems at times to deny us entrance. The counter-pull is to be distinguished, however, from that transcendence of the customary world made possible by seeing a greater, ideal world in the private. The counter-pull draws the poet back into the customary world, but the transcendence enables him to fly clean out of it. Both factors assist in the universalizing of private poetry; but it is that privateness, however qualified, that remains the radical feature of Metaphysical poetry.

It should afford no surprise that the counter-pull of the

world and even its transcendence testify to a tension in Donne's poetry that reflects the ambivalence of his life. On balance, he was led to be a private poet by the tension, but the vector of public ambition and concern with larger worlds was not to be resisted. The books to which he wishes to return (but from which he is haled forth) in *Satyre I* are, moreover, representative of the sources from which he draws much of his imagery for the poems in *Songs and Sonnets*— "grave Divines," "the Philosopher" or scientist, "jolly Statesmen," "gathering Chroniclers" (they least), and "Giddie fantastique Poëts." In no special order, some of his images are those of "Mermaids," "the Sunne," "Nature," "Law," "a murderer," "Marriage rings," "officer," "Tyrans, and their subjects," "Venus," "oathes," the "God of Love," "natures law," "warres lawe"—and so on through the full range of images and conceits for love poems that have made him for all readers the essential witty and Metaphysical poet. Whole poems, like "The Legacie" and "The Will," are founded upon social conceptions. Poems like "The Canonization" draw their imagery from the full range of authors specified in the opening lines of *Satyre I*. His divine poems show the same assimilation of the public and learned into the private world.[15] A few sonnets may be given as ready examples, those beginning, "This is my playes last scene" (3), "At the round earths imagin'd corners" (4), "Death be not proud" (6), "Batter my heart, three person'd God" (10), and yet others. In the last, for example, the imagery of siege and vassalage is clearly public, and the chastity or ravishing implies the social bond of marriage. Donne's is commonly a private poetry written in public diction and imagery, a fact well reflecting the ambivalence of his own experience, just as

---

[15] I should say again that the numbers are those of the 1633 sonnets given by Dame Helen Gardner in *The Divine Poems*, not the numbers given by Grierson.

the private references in his later, public sermons retain something of the same tension.

There is nothing in the appeal of the public world to Donne or in his use of it for imagery to unmake the private mode of his poetry. But it is true that in his poetry, and much to its complex betterment, the tension between the two worlds is far greater, far more a part of the poetic scene and process, than in subsequent Metaphysical poetry. As in so many other respects, Donne's followers in this respect simplify his complex Metaphysical weaving, either by untangling it into the separate public and private poems of King, Cowley, Cleveland, Marvell, and Vaughan, or by accommodating Cavalier and other traditional elements, as in Carew or Godolphin, as again in Cowley and Marvell. Such simplifications often resulted in poetry complex enough and to spare in other ways, as Marvell preeminently shows; but the breadth of human life behind the poetry and in the poetry, as well as much of its intensity, has been refined into different components. In "To his Coy Mistress," Marvell is Metaphysical only by admitting a Cavalier concern with time and ritual; Traherne and Vaughan hold the public world of the Protectorate or Restoration at bay with neo-Platonism and "Hermeticism." More significantly, in the first stanza of "The Garden," Marvell glances at the public life only to reject it; in *An Horatian Ode* on Cromwell, he glances at the retired private life only to reject it. Although similar rejections are found aplenty in Donne, they do not entail a glance and then a veering away, but a use of public experience to convey a superior private world. If a poet with a mind so very complex and in some ways so divided as Marvell's can be said to simplify Donne's complexities, it is not likely that any of the other poets we count Donne's followers approach him, in their poetry, for complexity.

Given what I have called the simplifications of Meta-

43

physical poetry after Donne, we must look not to single poems but to the larger canons and the lives of the later poets for evidence of the tensions and ambivalence to be found throughout Donne's poetry. As is well known, Herbert's ambivalence is to be found in the contrast between his early secular ambitions and his later saintly life at retired Bemerton. Some poems—for example, "The Quip," "Vanitie," "The Pearl," "The Collar," and *The Flower*—show in their glances back upon the secular world or in their moments of rebellion that Herbert had some sighs left for the world of fame and public service that he had given up. But he returns to his vocation with wholehearted acceptance after such deflections, and the general tenor of his poetry is certainly that private quiet of a person who has turned his back on "the merrie world." It is difficult to imagine the late Herbert (or Crashaw, Vaughan, and Traherne, for that matter) a bishop, but Henry King, author of one lovely Metaphysical poem, "The Exequy," proved his right to the mitre not only by his living longer than Herbert but also by a dedication to public issues reflected in most of his verse. Herbert's life nearly breaks into two divisions; King's is a public life apart from one or two exceptional poems.

Cowley and Cleveland managed to separate the public and private poetry they wrote into different periods or aspects of their lives and into different poems. After Donne, Marvell is obviously the most complex of the Metaphysical race and, in respect to its fusion of public with private concerns, *Upon Appleton House, to my Lord Fairfax,* is the most complex of his poems. It is a poem on the retired life but addressed to a public figure, the great Puritan general and a lord, yet a man himself ambiguously active and retired:

> From that blest Bed the *Heroe* came,
> Whom *France* and *Poland* yet does fame:

> Who, when retired here to Peace,
> His warlike Studies could not cease;
> But laid these Gardens out in sport
> In the just Figure of a Fort.   (281–86)

The first four lines sound, it must be confessed, rather like some unfamiliar reach of *Hudibras*; in this passage, the public world is not in itself very well conceived. But it *is* conceived, and Marvell's imagination fires when the paradox of a warring garden occurs to him. For the full effect of the conception, we would need to set *The Garden* side by side with *An Horatian Ode*. In addition, *Upon Appleton House* shows that affection for the small and quaint which can be found in most of Marvell's poems before the Restoration. And yet he pictures such details in the guise of war:

> When in the *East* the Morning Ray
> Hangs out the Colours of the Day,
> The Bee through these known Allies hums,
> Beating the *Dian* with its *Drumms*.
> Then Flow'rs their drowsie Eylids raise,
> Their Silken Ensigns each displayes,
> And dries its Pan yet dank with Dew,
> And fills its Flask with Odours new.   (289–96)

After beating his flowers to the colors, Marvell is off on an allegory of the Civil Wars read through Fairfax's career. In *Upon Appleton House* Marvell adjusts the genre of poems like Jonson's "To Penshurst" by adapting the political ruminations of Denham's *Cooper's Hill*. But a civil war of flowers is purely Marvellian and closer in its balance of active and retired, if not of public and private, than anything since Donne. Apart from this poem, however, Marvell's complexities are of other kinds—of ideas and apprehensions, of expressive glances and deflections, rather than of modes—and if "The Definition of Love" stands at one pole of his work as a Metaphysical poem, the satires he wrote after the Restoration stand at the opposite as public poetry.

To a considerable extent, therefore, the ambivalence of the private poetry of Donne, or the separations of public and private poems of other poets, represent less a total rejection of the public world than a sublimation of failed hopes, thwarted desires, and deep-seated fears by recourse to a realm of private life in which a greater integrity might be found. In this sense, the private poetry of the Metaphysicals —which is to say that of their poetry which is most essentially Metaphysical—is an alternative to public lives and represents a recoiling from public concerns either in revulsion or in times of failure in the world. Whatever their earlier hopes and whatever the nature of their earlier poetry, Crashaw and Herbert among the earlier poets and Vaughan and Traherne among the last of the Metaphysical race stayed most faithfully upon the private or retired path in which their poetry and their lives had entered. But Donne, King, Cowley, Cleveland, Marvell, and others reentered the public world, often with great personal success. Such success led them to cease to be Metaphysical poets or required a lapse from their public world for their composing private poems. As they became successes in the world, and to the extent that they continued to be poets, the Metaphysical poets found for the most part that they were exchanging the private gardens of Erato and Polyhymnia for the forum of the public Muses, Calliope and Clio. Metaphysical poetry is also an alternative in the sense that a poet might write not only in its pure styles, but also in public poetry, in poetry of middle esthetic distance, or in combinations like those favored by many Cavalier poets both in and out of "the line of wit."

Metaphysical poetry is after all but one, the private, aspect of the many-faceted larger Renaissance from Wyatt to Pope and Dr. Johnson. One aspect or alternative it may be, but in its own terms, which suffice to any reader, it is a private poetry with the spell of individual voices. It seems as we read it less a sublimation of public desires than a "naked, thinking heart." But in the best poetry the heart thinks in consciousness of the public world, and that is precisely one of its great strengths. Between the other, public world just beyond the Metaphysical poem, and the hither, private world which we see so closely, there is after a fashion a dialogue, a "dialogue of one," with the private world the speaker. The chief literary radical of Metaphysical poetry is, whatever the qualifications, its private mode.

II

FORMS OF PERCEPTION:
TIME AND PLACE

the tame Laws of Time and Place.

— Crashaw

SOME OF the most complex scientific or philosophical problems turn upon conceptions of time and space, and from Aristotle to Einstein major philosophical achievements have come with new insights into these two related subjects. Probably no seventeenth-century poem treats the matter at greater length than does Henry More's *Song of the Soul*,[1] a poem metaphysical and cloudy enough but not outstandingly Metaphysical in style or poetic in effect. Readers have understandably passed it by for Donne's lovers' seasons or Marvell's world enough and time. But it may be useful to tarry a moment with the scientific aspect of the subject before going on to the poetic.

The view of the world usually termed Ptolemaic conceived of a finite universe. With earth at the center, surrounded by spheres of the elements, "stars," and *primum mobile*, the universe hung from heaven by a golden chain. It was bounded below by hell, and around it was the not-quite-nothing of jarring elements or atoms constituting chaos. This view was of course challenged in numerous ways and by numerous writers. Aristotle was known to have held

[1] More's philosophical verse is discussed by John Tull Baker, *An Historical and Critical Examination of English Space and Time Theories from Henry More to Bishop Berkeley* (Bronxville, N.Y., 1930), pp. 6–13; and Marjorie Hope Nicholson, *Mountain Gloom and Mountain Glory* (Ithaca, N.Y., 1959; New York, 1963), pp. 130–40.

matter, and therefore implicitly space, to be infinite. Galileo, Kepler, Copernicus, and others had challenged the geocentric view of the universe and the finite, finished nature of the frame of things. In the seventeenth century, educated men knew very well of the challenge, if not necessarily at first hand, then in terms of more than a dozen theories of the universe—not just the "Ptolemaic" and "Copernican," each of which existed in several varieties. Educated men were also aware of the implications. They were aware of the numerous attempts to "save" or "solve" appearances. They were nearly giddy with the writings of the learned, with the thought of the world tossed about in a blanket, as Burton put it; and most of them appear to have taken one of three stands: agnosticism, use of two or more inconsistent interpretations, or the compromise of Tycho Brahe, who argued that a fixed earth at the center and a fixed *primum mobile* around the universe were boundaries between which the planets and stars took courses directed by God but not in the familiar old spheres.[2] The general effect appears to have been to instill in the minds of most educated men an idea of a very much less tidy, a perhaps enlarged, but a still finite universe. Since the view of time was a corollary of the view of space, what might be termed natural time (as opposed to the supernatural duration of God and the angels) was also finite. Only after the growth of a belief in what was called the plurality of worlds, or infinity of worlds, did a conception of a long future expanse of natural time emerge, and that but slowly and under considerable attack from the great majority of men, who held in one way or

[2] Perhaps the most interesting contemporary discussion of astronomical theories is Burton's *Anatomy of Melancholy*, ii, ii, 3; ed. A. R. Shilleto (London, 1896), ii, 58–96. Burton shows that cosmologies raised questions of man's situation, of the principles of coherence or structure, and of the meaning of things. In their poetic form, these questions provide the basis for the next three sections of this chapter.

another to the teleological and providential Christian time-scheme.[3] Very few Englishmen expressed doubt that the world was created some six thousand years before, or that it was subject at some date nearer or farther in the future to dissolution, probably by fire. There would then be created a new universe ("heaven and earth"), the millenium would come, and at last the Day of Judgment would bring a stop to time and usher in an eternity of bliss or punishment. The spatial universe was surrounded by a chaos at best neutral; natural time was surrounded by eternity, a time of grace with far happier possibilities.

The conception of space, however shaken by new ideas, was in any given theory tidier than conceptions of time. There was nothing outside the universe, heaven, and hell. At least few seemed to think that God had further designs to create. The distinctive feature of the conception of space is a peculiar transcendence that differentiated it from time. Spatial transcendence involved relations between man and the earth or man and the universe—microcosm and macrocosm—or between earth and heaven. The relation was, as it were, instantaneous and constant. Such a formal connection required no time for moving from heaven to earth—there was a king in both places—and that relationship abolished in one sense the distance between two very separated points. Space within the earth or the universe implied time unless it too was transcendental in correspondences. It is easy to see that, in Crashaw's terms, the laws of space

[3] In *Democritus Platonissans* (1646), later given as Part II of his *Song of the Soul*, More argued for "The Infinity of Worlds out of Platonick Principles" and for temporal as well as spatial infinity as attributes of God or spirit. In so doing, he was adapting Cartesian hypotheses to "Platonick" ends but not arguing for infinity of matter *per se* or of what I have called natural time. Most English writers before More were less enthusiastic about a plurality of worlds and what it implied, though Milton and Dryden were excited by the idea.

were tamer than the laws of time, which was obviously sequential. In "The Sunne Rising" Donne's speaker can abolish space by transcending it—both Indies lie next to him in bed in the figure of his mistress. His one little room is, as he puts it in "The good-morrow," an "every where." In the former poem he looks forward to the passing of the day just begun, in the latter to the past of his nonage and to the present world outside them. Many seventeenth-century writers wrote of moments that were transcendent of the present moment in other senses, usually those which began or would undo time—the creation, the millenium, or the day of judgment. As God incarnate, Christ had obviously joined eternity and time as well as God and man. But whereas space seemed to exist altogether at once—almost as if lying at one point simultaneously in the numerous correspondences between all parts of the creation—time was an irresistible sequence and a devourer of things, *tempus edax rerum*, as Ovid said.

It long seemed to Christians that time had not only sequence but also direction, and that the direction was downward in decay, since the fall of man, at least in the mutable spheres beneath the moon. Above the moon all remained constant, and one day the downward motion of time would be interrupted by the upward sweep of eternity. The theory of historical decay was challenged in the sixteenth century and weakened in the next,[4] but without upsetting the view that there was a sequential direction (up if not down) and without immediately challenging belief in a providential teleology. Most of Donne's writing supports the view of historical decay, and most of the later Metaphysicals either follow him or are ambiguous. For present purposes, we may say that the world in which Metaphysical

[4] See Victor Harris, *All Coherence Gone* (Chicago, 1949); Herschel Baker, *The Wars of Truth* (Cambridge, Mass., 1952).

poems are set is a world in which both space and time are bounded, space absolutely and time by eternity: a world in which space, being made up entirely of God's creatures in ordered hierarchies, is not restrictedly sequential or extended, since formal correspondences might instantaneously and constantly relate the corresponding parts of the separate units; and a world, too, in which the sequence of finite natural time (as opposed to eternity) leads either certainly or probably downward in historical decay. Man's hopes lay rather outside of time than in it, and it was to that happy end that the well-schooled Adam at the end of *Paradise Lost* learned to direct his hopes.

Although the inexorable sequence of time is as it were an axiom of human consciousness, the consciousness of sequence implies an ability to think back on what is past and forward to what is to come; in addition, man has conceived of a mode of timeless duration, or eternity. Four very well-known lines from Donne's "Valediction forbidding mourning" show how transcendentally space was conceived to be, and how such a view of space was held with a conception of sequential time:

> Moving of th'earth brings harmes and feares,
>   Men reckon what it did and meant,
> But trepidation of the spheares,
>   Though greater farre, is innocent. (9–12)

The comet beneath the moon, like the earthquakes near to hand, suggested by correspondence that similar unnatural upheavals would take place in the body politic or the body of man, whereas such seeming eccentricities as the "trepidation" of the spheres above the moon (one of the notions introduced to conform the geocentric universe with observation) was natural to them and portended no evil. Three lines (9, 11, and 12) are cast in the generalizing present

tense of immutable truth; one line (10) sets the physical
universe in the world of natural time: "Men reckon what
it did and meant." Man, in his moment of present consciousness, looks most naturally from it to the past and
thence to the future with an assumption of causation.

We do not find as much difficulty in conceiving what
may be termed the philosophical time sequence of Metaphysical poetry as we do its unsequential, transcendent
universe. But there is another kind of time in Metaphysical
poetry besides the philosophical; it may most readily be
called poetic, because it is based upon fiction. A play like
Antony and Cleopatra (Jacobean masques provide yet better
evidence) can be set in Rome at the dawn of the empire
and yet jump ahead across hours or years by a change of
scene and a phrase or two; or it may move forward in topical
allusions to the seventeenth century. A narrative poem like
The Faerie Queene can be set somewhere, sometime—at
once nowhere, never and everywhere, ever—in the world of
Arthurian faery, and by its allegory it can express at once
that which is timelessly, universally true and yet also that
which is also only intermittently true of the reign of Mary
Tudor or of Elizabeth. There are numerous other permuta-
tions of space and time possible to literature, but the Metaphysical poets chose rather to manipulate those mentioned
than to seek out others. They usually chose to root their
poems in the here and now or, more accurately, in either
the here or the now. That *here* was, until the mid-century
poetry of Marvell and Vaughan, normally within doors; that
now was usually an exalted moment, often pressed upon
by other temporal vistas ("What if this present were the
worlds last night?"), but always returning to, or seeking out,
a wondrous *now* ("Now in age I bud again"). There was
reason for Spenser to begin, "A Gentle Knight was pricking
on the plaine," using the narrative past tense without any

53

temporal implication, because the plain was as much the field of grace as the field of nature. But there could be no reason for a Metaphysical poet to begin thus, especially Donne, whose "dramatic" poetry implies characters realized in a definable time or place. If, as in *The Extasie*, he did anticipate his successors on occasion, giving his poem a more "narrative" cast by emphasizing a sustained sequence, he is still more careful to emphasize the here and now. The poetic view of time enabled Donne and his followers to do what their philosophical view did not much encourage: that is, to manipulate both the here and now in fictional or poetic ways varying from the ingenious to the breathtaking.[5] In this, as in much else, Donne often stands apart from his successors, but for them and him alike we can begin a consideration of the poetic treatment of time and place in terms of formal aspects of Metaphysical poetry under the heads of situation, theme, and transcendence.

i. Situation

Different situations, that is, different handlings of time and place, are possible to the various literary genres. When Dryden wrote *The State of Innocence*, a dramatic version of *Paradise Lost*, he was barred from showing the scenes in heaven or eternity. There are certain abeyances of time and changes of temporal scale possible in narrative poetry that

---

[5] Such manipulations of time and space are referred to as "drama" and set as a distinguishing criterion of European Baroque poetry by Lowry Nelson, Jr., *Baroque Lyric Poetry* (New Haven, 1961). See Nelson, pp. 121–37 for a discussion of Donne's poetry in these terms. The critic with interests most like my own in this matter is, however, Ellrodt, whose ideas about time and space in Metaphysical poetry may be found at the beginning of the Conclusion to *Les Poètes Métaphysiques Anglais*, i, Pt. 1, vol. ii, 400–10, although I myself prefer his less schematic discussions, for example of Marvell, 1, ii, 114–27. It will be clear to any reader how much I share with Professor Ellrodt and how far I disagree with his stimulating presentation.

are impossible in dramatic representation. To the extent that the poems of Donne or Herbert approached the dramatic, they were barred certain highly significant literary effects. Of course to say that Donne's poetry is dramatic is to speak metaphorically of effects rather than strictly of a genre. More than that, the "drama" of early Metaphysical poetry, and the "narrative" of later, are really two definitions of the private mode in terms of certain coordinates of time and space. Moreover, as a subsequent chapter will suggest, the major themes of Metaphysical poetry rise from lyric and satiric emphases, and both song and satire are freer as to form than drama or narrative. Much of the finest Metaphysical poetry is most quickly understood as the adaptation of "dramatic" or "narrative" situations to lyric or satiric themes.

What justifies our saying that Donne, Herbert, and Crashaw produce dramatic effects in their poetry is the fact that each creates situations with a clearly defined sense (if not always an actuality) of speaker and audience at a specified time or place. Again and again we are convinced that someone definite is speaking somewhere, sometime, to someone. It is a characteristic of Donne's that he commonly chooses to develop either time or place without bothering with the other. In "Twicknam garden," there is one explicit (l. 2) and one implicit (l. 10) reference to time—spring, but no more particular time within this season. On the other hand, the place is developed in highly significant detail. A fictional equivalent of the garden at the Twickenham seat of Lucy, Countess of Bedford, the place itself enacts the "dramatic" situation of a lover who creates his own misfortunes. The good place offers "such balmes, as else cure every thing," including, hopefully, the hurts of this neo-Petrarchan lover, "But"—

> But O, selfe traytor, I do bring
> The spider love, which transubstantiates all,
> And can convert Manna to gall,

And that this place may thoroughly be thought
True Paradise, I have the serpent brought. (5–9)

The place is paradise lost, because the speaker is his own
tempter. To be sure, much of this ingenious transformation
of poetic situation stems from the peculiar social situation in
which Donne found himself: he felt it necessary to pre-
tend to be a suitor utterly and hopelessly dedicated to the
Countess of Bedford, even while social and other considerations demanded that he make plain that his suit be taken as
no more than a general tribute. The final paradox makes this
clear:

O perverse sexe, where none is true but shee,
Who's therefore true, because her truth kills mee.
(26–27)

Many an earlier poet writing much more simply in the
Petrarchan mode to ladies of superior rank had faced Donne's
problem and had found their solution in a mild neo-
Platonism. In its very title, Drayton's *Idea* suggested the
method: if one woos the Idea of beauty, one's aims are
wholly innocent. In "Twicknam garden," Donne's solution
is to go down the scale of nature rather than up the Platonic
ladder. His images move from the animate souls of the
"spider" and "serpent" to the vegetative souls of "trees" and
beyond to no soul at all:

[Love,] let mee,
Some senselesse peece of this place bee;
Make me a mandrake, so I may groane here,
Or a stone fountaine weeping out my yeare.
(15–18)

There is a double wit in the movement of the poem. The
moving down from the rational to the animal to the vegetative soul and beyond is desired to escape grief, and yet even

his hope to end as a "senselesse peece" is defined in terms of grief. In addition, the problem presented by the place—the paradise made a kind of hell—is to be solved by a metamorphosis into some part of the place.

It is remarkable that another of Donne's best and most complicated poems, "A nocturnall upon S. Lucies day, Being the shortest day," possesses a very similar rhythm but that its dramatic situation is defined in terms of temporal rather than spatial transformation. Again, a hopeless lover laments his lot. Now, however, the obstacle is not the lady's just love for another person but her death (l. 28). Instead of a spatial transformation, into a "senselesse peece," there is a complex alchemic process transforming a time sequence of future-present-past-present:

> Study me then, you who shall lovers bee
> At the next world, that is, at the next Spring:
>   For I am every dead thing,
>   In whom love wrought new Alchimie.
>   For his art did expresse
> A quintessence even from nothingnesse,
> From dull privations, and leane emptinesse:
> He ruin'd mee, and I am re-begot
> Of absence, darknesse, death; things which are not.
>   (10–18)

This sequence in the second stanza explains the present agony of midnight on the night of vigil, so preparing for the temporal sequence of the remaining three stanzas. The third stanza is alchemical and deals with the past: "Oft a flood/ Have wee two wept . . ." (22–23). The fourth also has alchemical detail, now to convey the speaker's anguished present. A characteristic shift to a new audience—"You lovers . . ."—turns to their future and his own, closing with his present "Vigill" on this present "Eve." The poem had started and now ends on the selfsame hour—midnight on St. Lucy's Day (or the eve leading to the feast day). But it is also "the yeares midnight" and, as the poem shows us more and more, the doleful midnight of the speaker's life. There will come another year "at the next Spring," and that will bring "the next world" to lovers. But the speaker keeps his dark "houre her Vigill." It is of course an alchemy of woe that makes the one hour of his grief so much other than the hour itself, and it is the alchemy of time that transforms the woe into poetry.

Because such distinctive use of time and place is so obviously a feature of the situations of Metaphysical poetry, it hardly seems necessary to look at other poems in any detail. It may not be amiss, however, to remark upon the necessity for discrimination. Many occasional poems by poets of the Metaphysical race do indeed locate time and place squarely, whether in dramatic or narrative terms. Bishop King, the early Vaughan, and Donne himself provide numerous examples. But it is significant that the very titles of such poems are unknown to most readers today whereas "The Exequy," "The World," or *The Extasie* conjure realities that most of us feel and respond to as familiar experience. The significance is, of course, that occasional poetry—that is, public poetry— was largely contradictory of the private radical of Metaphysical poetry and that the poets did not write Metaphysical poetry successfully in that mode. It was not real times and real places rendered in a sense fictional that gave the times and places of their best poems, but fictional times and places rendered in a sense real. The two poems by Donne just discussed are notable exceptions to the usual process of rendering the fictional real, and other exceptions (e.g., *Goodfriday, 1613. Riding Westward*) may indeed be found. But each of the successful exceptions allows for the transformation of reality into private terms. The Metaphysical poet had to separate himself from the world, seek out his private integrity; he could not successfully regard himself, insofar as he retained that vision of experience we call Metaphysical, in terms of what he shared with other men. Other discriminations become necessary with later poets. Marvell, for example, is most the successful Metaphysical poet when dealing with place. He also handles time outstandingly well, but when he does so, it is in the Cavalier vein of transience and mutability as in *To his Coy Mistress* or in the public vein of *Upon Appleton House* and *An Horatian Ode*. The important exception to this rule in his canon is a curious poem, one of perhaps two successful Metaphysical poems combining pastoral, narrative, and lyric as also place and time. But *The Nymph complaining for the death of her Faun* will be the subject of lengthier discussion in a later chapter (see ch. v.). It is enough to say for now that Metaphysical treatment of time and place in situations is various within the limits of the private mode and of "dramatic" or "narrative" fictions for lyrics and satires.

ii. From Structure to Theme

The Anniversaries differ markedly from most of Donne's other best poetry in failing to establish either time or place as a significant continuing basis for drama or narrative. It may well be that this fact underlies the sense that in these two longer poems, and especially in the earlier, something has gone out of control. But not everything has, and I wish to argue that both *Anniversaries* use time as crucial themes as well as basic modes, and that the two poems differ not only from Donne's other poems, but also from each other, in their themes and modes. Having quite a large enough brief of my own in this, I am reluctant to enter upon the argu-

ments of others concerning whom or what these poems are
"really" about.[6] However, if the poems are in some major
sense about the Virgin Mary or Elizabeth I, the relation
between time and theme may differ from that obtaining if
the poem is about Elizabeth Drury and related topics, and I
fear that it is a problem that must be aired.

A great deal of fanciful criticism has been written about
Donne's lyrics, relating this to the mistress of wild Jack
Donne and that to the wife of the Dean of St. Paul's, when
in fact the circumstances of none and the dates of all but a
very, very few cannot be certainly known. The two *Anniversaries* are different. Not a great deal is known about them,
but what is known probably equals all that is known concerning the fifty-eight poems of the *Songs and Sonnets.*
Curiously, the main business of criticism of these two long
poems in our century has been to deny the relevance of what
is known when, in this case, it is known. Without going into
all the details or entering into speculation, we may rehearse
certain established facts. Elizabeth Drury was buried in the
Church of St. Clement Danes on 17 December 1610, some
two months before her fifteenth birthday. Donne had never
met her. *The First Anniversarie (Anniversary I)* appeared
with *A Funerall Elegie* of 106 lines in 1611. In November
Donne accompanied the Drurys to the continent. Whether
he began *The Second Anniversary (Anniversary II)* at
Amiens about the time of the actual first anniversary, as is

[6] In the Introduction to his edition, *John Donne: The Anniversaries*
(Baltimore, 1963), pp. 5–18, Frank Manley very usefully reviews interpretations about what the central subject of the poem may be, and on
pp. 18 ff. he offers his own. Most of the discussion has revolved about
the identity of the female person spoken of as she/shee in the two
poems. Some of the chief candidates are the Virgin Mary, Jesus Christ,
Astraea, the Logos, and Elizabeth I. Manley adds Wisdom. My own
opinion, which is now three and a half centuries out of date, will
emerge in what follows.

60

widely supposed, cannot be absolutely proved. But lines 511–18 show that the poem was completed in France, and it seems reasonably certain that it had not been begun before leaving. While Donne was still abroad, the poem was quickly printed. It was sent from France to London, where Joseph Hall added *The Harbinger to the Progres*, and both *Anniversaries* were printed with that tribute by early April.

Apart from Hall, none of Donne's contemporaries is known to have had a good word for the poems—although the patronage of the Drurys speaks for itself; and after Dryden's praise in the epistle dedicatory to *Eleonora*, the poem sank from attention. In the second half of the last century, however, there was a revival of interest; and in our own century the passage on the new science in *Anniversary I* and the line, "That one might almost say, her bodie thought" (*Anniversary II*, 246) have been referred to almost as much as the compass legs of "A Valediction: forbidding mourning" as indices of Donne's poetic sensibility. Everyone seems to agree that *Anniversary II* is the better poem, although there are some readers who regard the two poems as halves of a larger whole.

Because the meaning of the poems has often been questioned, their success doubted, and their connection with Elizabeth Drury disputed, it may not be amiss to take guidance from the poems' full titles.

The First Anniversarie. An Anatomy of the World. Wherein, By occasion of the untimely death of Mistris Elizabeth Drury the frailty and the decay of this whole World is represented.

[The Second Anniversary.] Of the Progres of the Soule. Wherein: By occasion of the Religious death of Mistris Elizabeth Drury the incommodities of the Soule in this life and her exaltation in the next, are contemplated.

Something has been made of the fact that Elizabeth Drury is not mentioned in the poems proper. She is obviously mentioned in their titles. Moreover, usual seventeenth-century practice in elegiac poems was not to mention the person's name within the poem, though a fanciful name might be used (e.g., "Lycidas"). Dryden's poems on the death of Oldham, Charles II, Anne Killigrew, or Purcell show how far this was the case. Donne's own epicedes and epithalamia show his intimate familiarity with the conventions. Something has also been made of different spellings in the poems, distinguishing between *she* and *shee*. To make the distinction valid, evidence is required that Donne read proof of his poems or left specific directions for printing. In the absence of such evidence, we can only conclude that the situation is like that with "A nocturnall upon S. Lucies day": there are different spellings of pronouns, and they are in principle attributable to the usual source of such variants in the century, the printer.

We may return to the titles. For *Anniversary I*, the death of the girl afforded an occasion to anatomize "the frailty and decay of this whole World." For *Anniversary II*, the anniversary of her death provided Donne with an occasion for contemplation on the soul's vicissitudes in this life and its exaltation in the next. The balance of subject in the titles seems just right. Elizabeth Drury is the formal subject and her death, or its anniversary, provides the formal situation. So the Drurys thought, so Jonson thought, so the witty lady friends of Donne thought when they objected to such praise of this girl. Similarly, Edward King is the formal subject of *Lycidas*. But anyone can see that Donne and Milton have as well certain other things on their minds, and in particular themselves in their worlds. In this second and larger concern of the poems, the formal subject is transformed into a kind of counterpart-image for the self, a symbol, or as Donne said, an idea of a woman. If this can be agreed upon, and I do not see that it inflicts any strain on the poems, then I do not see that the basic themes require attention to outside figures.

The structural time pattern of *Anniversary I* differs from rational or objective time in not having measured intervals, order, or consecutiveness. But there are a very great number of poems and many processes of human thought of which the same may be said. What Donne's poem possesses in relation to time is direction and causation. The direction is of course worsening, temporal pejoration, historical decay. The cause or causes of this worsening have been variously explained, and Donne's actual words as to what causes what allow a margin wide enough to include contradictions. Elizabeth Drury's death is the formal cause of all the problems and the worsening, and she is pretty much taken as the actual cause in the first 184 lines. Then, in ll. 190–204, the fall of the angels and of man is the cause: "So did the world from the first houre decay," which is the orthodox explanation. Immediately thereafter (205–18), it is "new Philosophy" that puts all in doubt, and whether cause or joint cause, or symptom, science is related to celestial and social breakdowns. In ll. 219–38 our formal cause returns in new guise—she might have saved the world, but she is dead. The next statement of cause (ll. 239–84) reintroduces science as the cause of disorder in the world. There are the "Copernicans" as we call them:

> They have empayld within a Zodiake
> The free-borne Sunne, and keepe twelve signes awake
> To watch his steps . . .   (263–65)

And there is the problem of the oblique ecliptic of the sun:

> nor can the Sunne
> Perfit a Circle, or maintaine his way
> One inche direct; but where he rose to day

He comes no more, but with a cousening line,
  Steales by that point, and so is Serpentine.   (268–72)

After this, the formal cause enters again (309–26); her
death is cause of the disproportion and disorder, because,
like the ark, she was a type of concord. The loss of attrac-
tiveness from the world (327–76) is similarly explained by
her death, since she gave things their beauty. In the last
section (377–434)[7] before the conclusion, we are told that
there has been a loss of correspondence between heaven
(where she now is, above time) and earth (which is de-
teriorating in time), preventing benefit from her virtues.
Through no fault of hers, she is unable to cause good effects
on earth after her death. The conclusion (435–474) suggests,
however (especially in ll. 455 ff.), that she still "workes"
upon man for good.

There is, then, in the poem's structural sequence a fluctuating attribution of causation or its lapse: the death of the
girl, the Fall, new philosophy, the girl, astronomy, her death,
the lack of correspondence between heaven and earth, and
her influence nonetheless. Although such causes are temporal
in accounting for the dire results that follow them (or the
good results that are prevented by the abortion of the
causes), their order in the poem is wholly unchronological,
repetitive, and therefore temporally static. Some people have
been upset even more by the fact that the causes that seem
to be introduced in parallel are not wholly parallel nor
seemingly logical in any other relation. There is scarcely any
logical relation (in the sense of cause and effect and therefore temporal connection) between the death of Elizabeth
Drury, the Fall, and new philosophy. True, they are all
considered disasters; equally, there is presumably an implied

---

[7] The divisions distinguished in my analysis are those of Louis L.
Martz, *The Poetry of Meditation* (New Haven, 1954), pp. 222–23.

chronology from the Fall, to the new philosophy, to her death. That is not, however, their order in the poem, because (other reasons apart) the panegyric purpose required that Donne speak first and last of his "blessed maid." She is brought into the poem repeatedly between these sections, but often Donne permits himself a move by associative processes to other causes. It is therefore necessary to understand that, in the poem, although it is clear that the Fall preceded the invention of the new science and the recent death of a girl, there is no *causal* relation between the three. There is possible only a sequential relation that may be abstracted from the poem by a reader. The poem itself offers none. The causes are, then, neither parallel nor sequential. They are, however, structurally alternative and they share a common effect (apart from the conclusion) of operating in the same direction, toward decay.

The thematic treatment of time is, therefore, much more simple than it appears at first to be. It involves only the direction of time—worsening, decay. It is as though each of several causes is a different hand giving the hoop yet a faster push down the hill to destruction. Only by accepting the strong, all but absolute sense of decay and worsening can we see why it did not much matter to Donne that one part of his praise should be that her death should be made the cause of "This great consumption" (19) of the world. So far is the worsening of the world presumed to be fixed. Because the direction is fixed, Donne allowed himself to play atemporally, unchronologically, with a number of other causes. The problem for most readers is that the death of a fourteen-year-old girl does not seem to rank as a cause with the fall of man or new assumptions about the nature of the world. But having chosen to raise these matters, Donne really had no choice other than the one he took: to make her an idea or symbol, a grand *exemplum* of causes operating in the world. Otherwise, there would have been a worse conflict between his despairing meditations and his necessity for praise. The girl and the other causes are brought together in despair and yet in hope for what might have been. She is a possible cause for good, but a cause forestalled by her death. Again, we can see that of his two major concerns with time—direction and causal sequence—direction was his chief concern, and to that he vigorously adhered. Aiming for a poem at once witty and eulogistic, he evolved paradox (not for the first time) and treated the causes as atemporal in their relation to each other but as temporal, each in itself, by each having the same general effect.

The only possible situation for the poem would seem to be its formal one—a voice mourns the death of the "rich soule," Elizabeth Drury. What is particularly noticeable is that this situation is, in most of the poem, almost lost sight of. That is a very strange poetic procedure for Donne. Yet so much else is talked about that we might forget the "blessed maid" altogether at times if it were not for that refrain line: "Shee, shee is dead," etc. The question requiring answer is whether that situation, slight as it is, is extended by "narrative" or intensified by "drama." The answer is that it is largely dramatic, though with a few narrative touches in individual passages. It could hardly be narrative in the large without some greater degree of sequence than it has. It is, however, dramatic in several ways implied by the use of that term in this book. It is concentrated upon an individual speaker rather than extended into the action of a character outside the speaker; its time scheme involves direction without consequential events or measured intervals. There is not even in most of the poem a fictional progression. For example, Donne does not tell us the history of what happened after the girl's death, as Dryden tells us what happened after the death of Charles II in *Threnodia Augustalis*. Nor do we

66

even get that passing of a day such as Milton gives us fictionally in *Lycidas*, and Donne himself in "A nocturnall upon S. Lucies Day." Once again, we can see how the *direction* of time is stressed, not only by the absense of "real" time but also by the absence of narrative time. The direction of time is made more thematic and tonal than temporal; it is more subjective and "dramatic." In a way the case is not very different from Donne's lyrics in that time as a mode is absorbed, or overwhelmed, by the situation; it must be admitted, of course, that in *Anniversary I* there is more overwhelming than absorption, primarily because the speaker of the poem is all voice and no role; like Othello, he finds his occupation (as anatomist) gone when disaster leaves only lament possible.

There are two sections of the poem, however, that function differently from what has been described so far. Both the introduction and conclusion show a sense of more natural, less subjective, time. The poem starts with a strong temporal emphasis in its sign-words: when (1), when (7), now (16). Or again, line 39 says, "Some moneths she hath beene dead." In like vein, the girl is addressed in the conclusion as if a saint:

> And, blessed maid,
> Of whom is meant what ever hath beene said,
> Or shall be spoken well by any tongue,
> Whose name refines course lines, and makes prose song,
> Accept this tribute, and his first yeares rent,
> Who till his darke short tapers end be spent,
> As oft thy feast sees this widow'd earth,
> Will yearely celebrate thy second birth,
> That is, thy death. (443–51)

Both at the opening and close, then, we have a natural order of time relating to the formal subject, Elizabeth Drury.

When she died, Donne begins by saying, there was grief; he ends by adding, I shall write such a poem each following year for her feast day. These sections of the poem are very much more definite, and they intensify the poem's dramatic character by relating "the idea of a woman" to a particular "blessed maid" dead a few months ago. This is the element of which Donne's scandalized patronesses and Ben Jonson were aware and which led Jonson to snort that "if it had been written of the Virgin Marie it had been some thing." To such readers—whom Donne had trusted for years to understand some of the most complex lyric poetry written in our language—Donne seemed to be saying that Elizabeth Drury has died, and this—its effect upon the world—explains its effect upon poor me. Donne's answer, that he was writing of the idea of a woman rather than of any individual, really does apply to the middle sections of the poem, the greater part of the poem, in fact, and it is these that lose his usual dramatic immediacy. On the other hand, his contemporaries were more conscious of the opening and close of the poem (and the middle in such a frame); and it did not occur to them that it was Astraea who had died a few months ago or Jesus Christ whom Donne promised yearly to celebrate for the Drurys.

The opening and closing passages of the poem intensify the dramatic situation, but they do so in such a way that they seem at times to be narrative. By stressing measured intervals ("moneths") and consecutive sequence (when ... when ... now), the Introduction raises narrative presumptions. Donne is, however, capable of absorbing these notes into his dramatic emphasis, and the real problem is that the formal situation is one related to the natural sequence of time as we know it in this world, whereas the thematic treatment of time involves causes temporally unrelated to each other and so rendered structurally parallel. The emphasis is upon worsening in time, and any interpretation of how well the thematic treatment sorts with the formal situation must concern the means of bridging the formal girl of the dramatic situation and the thematic temporal worsening. The crucial issue is not so much whether the "blessed maid" is also the Virgin Mary or Elizabeth I as whether the mixed causes in the middle sections of the poem relate satisfactorily to the formal situation. Donne must have realized that he had set himself a difficult task: to write, what he had never done successfully before, a long poem; to combine elegy and satire of the world; to speak both of a girl he had not met and of his experience of the nature of things. Perhaps he relished such difficulties and hoped that his great powers of wit had sufficient violence to yoke together such heterogeneous ideas. Any reader of the poem must grant at the least that the poem is witty, that it is frequently powerful in eloquence, and that it must have given the Drurys as much cause for pride as Donne's older friends reason for some envy.

The Second Anniversary is less witty and less daring in its handling of time. But it is also much more demonstrably unified. In fact it differs from *Anniversary I* in both its temporal structure and its temporal theme. As in the earlier poem, there is again an introductory (1–44) and a concluding (511–28) section, each of which stresses time, emphasizing in particular the passage of a year since writing the earlier poem ("a yeare is runne," 3) and the intention of continuing to write annual poems: "take this, for my second yeeres true Rent" (520). But other temporal concerns also arise. In the belief that "these Hymnes may worke on future wits," there is an attention to future natural time that has no counterpart in the earlier poem. In addition, in his expression of hope to write annual poems, Donne touches upon eternity in terms not emphasized in the earlier poem:

These Hymns thy issue, may encrease so long,
As till Gods great Venite change the song. (43-44)

The introduction of natural time and its effect on future
writers raises a public concern with history and what all men
may share, while the attention to the end of time and the
institution of eternal order raises time to its most sublime
Christian conception. In either treatment, the situation (the
annual song) is rendered thematic (that it is true till Christ's
judgment), or is made at least agreeable to thematic development.

The six main sections of the poem [8] show what the development consists in—how a certain temporal situation
might be structurally disposed to convey a temporal theme.
These sections comprising the body of the poem (45-510)
bring back to Donne's poetry the dramatic *audience* of the
lyrics, and especially of a poem like "The Indifferent," where
the technique is (as we have seen) very subtle. The speaker
now addresses his Soul, almost as if she were another character, commenting in a *contemptus mundi* vein on the
things of this world and contrasting them with the joy that
she (the Soul) may anticipate finding in heaven. Such a
description fails to account sufficiently for the considerable
change in tone in *Anniversary II*. It rejects "this rotten
world" as firmly as the earlier poem had, but the assurance
that the girl is in heaven directs attention there, bringing an

[8] Again, the sections distinguished by Martz, *The Poetry of Meditation*, p. 236-37. In his very valuable book, *The Enduring Monument*
(Chapel Hill, 1962), pp. 176-177, O. B. Hardison severely questions
Martz's divisions but without, to my mind, disproving them. The fact
that in his *Eleonora*, which is an elegy-*cum*-panegyric, Dryden clearly
echoes a number of passages from those called eulogistic by Martz, and
those only, seems to me a very unusual kind of corroboration of Martz's
analysis. (See my *Dryden's Poetry* [Bloomington and London, 1967],
ch. vii.)

optimism unknown before with a new conception of space and time:

> Looke upward; that's towards her, whose happy state
> We now lament not, but congratulate.　　(65–66)

The optimism is founded upon a double comparison that provides the whole poem with its theme and the main central sections of the poem with their structure. In each section, the soul is assured that the inadequate sinful *now* will yield to a joyful *then*. Thus far the poem is of course completely orthodox, even biblical in theme, as can be seen by comparison with Donne's well-known Easter Day sermon, 1628, preached on the text, "For now we see through a glass, darkly; but then face to face." Donne also goes on, however, in what is his main panegyric emphasis in the poem, to say that those joys which the soul will taste then, what it will know, have been pretasted now by the girl on earth, even before she died. The former theme is led into by the Introduction and its talk of "Gods great Venite"—God will welcome home the blessed. Both the introduction and the body of the poem are concerned with the theme of temporal contrast—Now and Then. This contrast implies a temporal direction, not the decay of the world as in *Anniversary I*, but the good soul's progress to its reward. In one passage (263–89), Donne contrasts earthly knowledge with divine. In the earlier poem, new knowledge seemed to put matters in doubt, but now there is a vision of what may be seen from high heaven's ramparts:

> 　　　　　　small things seeme great,
> Below; But up unto the watch-towre get,
> And see all things despoyld of fallacies:
> Thou shalt not peepe through lattices of eies,

71

Nor heare through Laberinths of eares, nor learne
By circuit, or collections to discerne.
In Heaven thou straight know'st all, concerning it,
And what concernes it not, shall straight forget.

(293–300)

The panegyric theme, which praises the dead girl for having known in this life what the speaker's soul may joy to know in the next, employs the same contrasts of Here and There, Now and Then. It is appropriate that in the conclusion of the poem (511–28) the speaker should turn from address to his soul to address to that of Elizabeth Drury. In effect she is a saint (see the wit of ll. 511–18). Her role as "a patterne" (524) explains how she could have been here and then what he tells his soul it will be there and then. (Donne of course addresses his soul throughout as if it is feminine, a conventional designation based on the Latin gender of *anima*.) Essentially we are given two parallel time sequences: for the dead girl, then and now; for the speaker's soul, now and then. The girl's then was the past, her life on earth; her now is the life of her soul in heaven. His soul's now is life on earth; its then is life in heaven. But her then of the past is also equivalent to its then in the future, because in this life Elizabeth Drury foretasted the joys his soul can expect.

The fuller title of *Anniversary II—Of the Progres of the Soule*—also suggests the greater spatial and temporal emphasis of the poem. The progress suggests movement in space, movement in time, and a direction—all to what is better. The imagery of space provides another major difference between this and the earlier poem. It begins in the dramatic situation of the poem, the speaker's address to his soul, because the charge to "Looke upward" implies space as well as quality. The finest sustained imagery, the best poetry,

72

is indeed that emphasizing space and spatial movement, beginning in the second main section (85–156) and continuing through the third (157–250). In the second, the speaker charges his soul to imagine its deathbed and burial. How particular the imagery of place becomes can be judged by the very effective opening:

> Thinke then, My soule, that death is but a Groome,
> Which brings a Taper to the outward roome,
> Whence thou spiest first a little glimmering light,
> And after brings it nearer to thy sight.   (85–88)

Here plainly we have the drama of the lyrics. It is curious how the deathbed scene brings back the "sad friends" of the opening stanza of "A Valediction forbidding mourning":

> Thinke thy frinds weeping round, and thinke that thay
> Weepe but because they goe not yet thy way.
> Thinke that they close thine eyes . . .
> Thinke that they shroud thee up . . .   (107–13)

The scene is not only dramatic but also structural in function and thematic in import. Its drama provides the means of getting from the poem's here and now to its then and there. Once the body is buried, the soul sleeps out its "saint Lucies night" (120) before going to heaven. What is meant is not that the soul sleeps till judgment day but that it stays with the body while the last "rite" is performed, a sleep best imaged by the longest night of the year in conventional reckoning, but only a "night" till the burial rites are complete. That this is the case is shown by the third section, in which the soul begins her progress to heaven upon the body's dying.

The scene of the soul's journey from earth to heaven in this section is narrated in the central progress piece promised by the poem's title. The progress is one of Donne's sublimest

73

passages and is written as only he could. The soul flies through the "Ptolemaic" universe, sphere by sphere, with the speaker (though not the soul) concerned over such contemporary questions as that whether the element of fire existed; and the whole passage is cast in classical terms unusual in their detail for his poetry. The soul:

> staies not in the Ayre,
> To looke what Meteors there themselves prepare;
> She carries no desire to know, nor sense,
> Whether th'Ayrs middle Region be intense,
> For th'Element of fire, shee doth not know,
> Whether she past by such a place or no;
> She baits not at the Moone, nor cares to trie,
> Whether in that new world, men live, and die.
> Venus retards her not, to'enquire, how shee
> Can, (being one Star) Hesper, and Vesper bee;
> Hee that charm'd Argus eies, sweet Mercury,
> Workes not on her, who now is growen all Ey;
> Who, if shee meete the body of the Sunne,
> Goes through, not staying till his course be runne;
> Who finds in Mars his Campe, no corps of Guard;
> Nor is by Jove, nor by his father barrd;
> But ere shee can consider how shee went,
> At once is at, and through the Firmament. (189–206)

This progress bridges earth and heaven, now and then, the more effectively because the deathbed scene of the second section (85–156) leads so naturally and directly to the progress piece in the third (157–250). Except for the fact that the poetic high point of the poem comes before the work is half done, the poem is admirably put together, structurally and thematically.

It is remarkable that what can only be called the narrative of the death and progress of the soul—especially stressed as it is by a situation, a closely described scene, and a spatial progress—does not swallow up the drama of the poem. The fact that the narrative does not dominate the poem is due to the strength of the poem's basic contrast between earth and heaven, now and then. It is also true that the rehearsal of the contrast in each section and the interruption of these meditative contrasts by eulogistic passages result in a repeated, cyclical emphasis that is more static, more stanzaic one can say, than the progress motif by itself would seem to imply. In other words, the poem is essentially dramatic in spite of a very exciting narrative interval in two of the seven sections of the body of the poem. The basic dramatic emphasis is one shared with *Anniversary I* and with Donne's most familiar poems. Perhaps the drama originates in part in Donne's inclination to think in terms of thematic dualities—body and soul, here and there, now and then, earth and heaven. Christianity provided the explanation as to how these dualities might be bridged, and the death of Elizabeth Drury provided the situation, indeed the moment as well, at which the Christian soul might cross the bridge. By holding both halves of his dualisms so intently before his mind, Donne insisted upon the reality of both, a fact which contributes greatly to the integrity of his vision, but also a fact that helps explain his particular intellectual drama, not of conflict but of contrast. Since *Anniversary II* is Donne's most successful sustained poem, it is more than a little interesting to observe that his success comes from his having written his lyrics large. There is a speaker and an audience (or rather more than one audience, primarily his soul and the "Immortall Maid," addressed chiefly in the Introduction and Conclusion). The stanzas have become repeated sections. The wit has become a seemingly outrageous panegryic. The drama is given a structure of ideas contrasted in thematic terms of time and place.

75

iii. Transcendence of Time and Place

Although much shorter than *The Anniversaries*, *The Extasie* is in some ways more difficult, as the controversy surrounding it has shown. My present concern with this fascinating poem is of course with its use of time and space, a matter rarely discussed before in relation to this poem, and it is my aim to show that its use is one that combines drama and narrative, one that prefigures later Metaphysical methods of reducing the preponderance of drama and increasing that of narrative, and one that allows in this shift for a transcendence in the treatment of time and place. In these terms, the poem is unusual, perhaps unique, in Donne's canon by its specification of place, outdoors, after a dramatic fashion and then its development of action in the manner of narrative.

After the initial specification of place on "A Pregnant banke," there is a narrative of ecstasy, a literal *exstasis* of the souls from their bodies:

> Our soules, (which to advance their state,
> Were gone out,) hung 'twixt her, and mee.
>
> (15-16)

Having "gone out" from the bodies left behind "firmely cimented" together in place, the souls enact a narrative of their "propagation" (l. 12). As bodies (that is, man without the rational soul but including the vegetative and animal) can "beget," so do the (rational or intellectual) souls beget an "abler soule," a single "new soule" that can speak a united "dialogue of one" that is audible to "any, so by love refin'd,/That he soules language understood" (21-22). The major narrative of the poem consists in this going out of the rational souls, their propagation, their single or joint dialogue, and the acquisition of new knowledge by the abler soul:

> This Extasie doth unperplex
> (We said) and tell us what we love,

76

> Wee see by this, it was not sexe,
>   Wee see, we saw not what did move.
>
> (29-32)

Since narrative of any kind is unusual in Donne's lyrics, that in *The Extasie* deserves some stress.

In fact the dialogue of one continues through the rest of the poem (49-76). There is a problem, however, in interpretation here, with many people arguing that there is a shift from a concern with spiritual to a concern with physical ecstasy:

> But O alas, so long, so farre
>   Our bodies why doe wee forbeare?   (49-50)
> To our bodies turne wee then, . . .   (69)
>
> Let him [some lover] still marke us, he shall see
>   Small change, when we'are to bodies gone. (75-76)

The dramatic emphasis is obvious. Whether or not a seduction is being urged, it is clear that in the second half of the poem a drama is enacted. It cannot be denied that there is diction and imagery suggestive of sexual matters, as many have shown; and it is true that the "persuasion to enjoy" is very like that in seduction poems, down to a similar use of rhetoric and dialectic. At the same time, it must be remembered that the speaker of the last half of the poem is ambiguous. Is it the male lover alone, as most sexual readings presume, or is it the joint abler soul, man and woman, speaking together? To my mind, the latter is by far the more natural possibility (and the phrase "dialogue of one" comes in the last line but two); I think that the poem makes best sense if considered as a serious parody of the seduction poem, with both parties speaking *in unison* to themselves considered separately.

The element of parody can be understood from the

77

resemblance of this poem in certain particulars to Donne's witty love poems. As in "The Indifferent" and "The Canonization," there is an audience apart from the two lovers. The effect of this listener and observer is to render the narrative more dramatic:

> If any, so by love refin'd,
>> That he soules language understood,
> And by good love were growen all minde,
>> Within convenient distance stood,
>
> He (though he knew not which soule spake,
>> Because both meant, both spake the same)
> Might thence a new concoction take,
>> And part farre purer than he came.   (21–28)

The first stanza given here has the technique of Donne's lyric drama; the second moves back to the narrative line, extending the moment to a possible future, so harmonizing the dramatic intrusion with the narrative line of the first half of the poem. The listener is passive (unlike Venus in "The Indifferent," he has nothing to say or do but to listen, understand, and depart). But his presence emphasizes the importance of the soul's union and the transcendence of separate individuality in ecstasy.

The corresponding section in the dramatic second part of the poem is the last stanza:

> And if some lover, such as wee,
>> Have heard this dialogue of one,
> Let him still marke us, he shall see
>> Small change, when we'are to bodies gone.
>>>>> (73–76)

Before, the passive audience had introduced a dramatic moment into a narrative time flow. Now, with the consideration of past ("Have heard"), present ("Let him still marke us"), and future ("he shall see"), a temporal review of the whole poem is introduced, and with it there enters an element of narrative in the dramatic section of the poem. (There is a similar narrative touch in ll. 53–55.) By giving the narrative intrusion the same condition of entry as the dramatic intrusion in the narrative first part—that is, a presumed exterior audience—Donne goes very far toward harmonizing his two modes of relation and his two conceptions of ecstasy. The harmony depends upon qualification and what might be called parody, since in each section there are instances of the narrative imitating drama or the drama narrative; similarly, in the first part souls have shown their ability to propagate, an activity normally restricted to bodies. Now, in the second half, the abler soul urges itself/themselves to submit to the religion of the body:

> To'our bodies turne wee then, that so
>   Weake men on love reveal'd may looke;
> Loves mysteries in soules doe grow,
>   But yet the body is his booke.   (69–72)

The particular mystery being urged is incarnation. As God became man in the Christ, so the single abler soul may reveal its separate individuals in the two bodies—which yet have the capacity for their own physical union, their ability, as the Bible puts it, to become one flesh. Love is revealed in bodies; therefore, the bodies are the Bible of the religious mysteries of the soul. Ecstasy and union continue.

There is a further connection between the two parts of the poem in that the second half parodies the "propagation" of the first. Strictly speaking, as we have noted, the propagation of souls is a serious neo-Platonic parody of physical propagation. But since the soul's propagation is given first in the poem, the physical version becomes in effect a parody of the parody. By turning to bodies it is possible, in the physiology of the day, that the united blood may labor "to beget" / Spirits, as like soules as it can" (61–62). These spirits were thought a middle nature between soul and body:

> Because such fingers need to knit
> That subtile knot, which makes us man:

> So must pure lovers soules descend
> T'affections, and to faculties,
> Which sense may reach and apprehend,
> Else a great Prince in prison lies.   (63–68)

This passage is by all odds the most difficult in the poem. The familiar difficulty of identifying the "great Prince" may be deferred for a moment to consider a more immediate question: what do the bodies beget? The souls had begot an abler soul. Do the bodies beget a better body, another human being? If so they either create, or aid in creating, another rational soul.

In the eighteenth Meditation of *Devotions upon Emergent Occasions,* Donne treats a question much debated in the century: the origin of rational or intellectual souls, whether by one or both parents in the act of procreation or by divine infusion. (He also toys with metempsychosis in *The Progres of the Soule.*) Donne speaks of the begetting in *The Extasie,* by blood, of the "Spirits" of middle nature between bodies and souls. The aim is to make the bodies as spiritual, as soul-like as possible, even as the soul is maintained in itself and may find its fulfillment unimpeded by the body: "Soe soule into the soule may flow, / Though it to body first repaire" (59–60). It is possible to read the second half of the poem purely in such terms, and this reading has been put very concisely and persuasively: "The blood strives to produce the spirits, or powers of the soul, which are necessary to unite the intellectual and corporal in man. Conversely souls must descend to the affections and

80

faculties of the body in order that man's sense organs may become rational." [9] It is in light of this reading, I think, that Dame Helen Gardner emends the text of l. 67 from "Which sense may reach and apprehend" to "That sense may reach and apprehend." Her alteration suggests that souls must descend to inferior faculties "in order that . . . sense . . . may become rational." I should be happier if the interpretation depended upon the text rather than *vice versa*. The reading of the 1633 edition and the manuscripts suggests a different meaning:

> So must pure lovers soules descend
>   T'affections, and to faculties,
> Which sense may reach and apprehend,
>   Else a great Prince in prison lies.

This means that souls must descend to those faculties under the command of sense (the vegetative soul and the animal soul).

We are finally to the crux of the matter, what is meant by "Else a great Prince in prison lies." It is well enough established that Donne uses the metaphor of the prince for the soul; and in *Anniversary II*, addressing his soul, he charges her to "Thinke in how poore a prison thou didst lie" (173) before death freed her. So the body may be a prison for the soul in denying it full realization. The question comes down to whether that Prince is the rational soul of each of the lovers requiring bodies for its operation; or whether that Prince is the rational soul which will be created by procreation. Dame Helen Gardner's emendation supports her reading along the lines of the former possibility; the unemended text more nearly suggests the latter possibility. It

---

[9] Helen Gardner, ed.. John Donne, *The Elegies and The Songs and Sonnets* (Oxford, 1965), p. 187; see also her closely argued Appendix D, "The Ecstasy," pp. 259–65.

is the latter interpretation that I favor, partly because it requires no emendation to support it, and partly because, as we have seen, the structure of the poem in other respects is highly complementary. What I am suggesting is that the propagation by souls in the first part of the poem strongly suggests the likelihood of a propagation by souls-in-bodies (whole human creatures) in the second. In the earlier half of the poem, the lovers are first said to have "Sat" on "A Pregnant banke," a posture not as suggestive of love-making as the place of sitting might suggest. A few lines later, they are lying side by side, but as if dead: "Wee like sepulchral statues lay," saying "nothing, all the day" (18–20). In the latter half of the poem, the souls depend upon the bodies to bring them together (53–54), to function, and (if the usual text of the line be accepted) to create or assist in God's creation of a new rational soul. What gives the poem its unity is partly a contrast of complementaries, but further the fact that the souls can participate, as the bodies cannot, in ecstasy in both the physical and the spiritual senses. This is one reason why there will be "Small change, when we'are to bodies gone" (76).

With this reading, we see Donne moving from an almost complete emphasis upon a narrative technique to narrative and drama combined. The two modes are complementaries in *The Extasie*, and both (like soul and body) seem to depend upon each other. Of course the narrative is what is special, given Donne's usual practice, but the combination of the two modes produces some surprises. The narration of the souls' ecstasy, of their going out and of the propagating an abler soul, reveals a kind of transcendence of the material world that will become more and more important in Metaphysical poetry. The drama of the soul/souls seeking to convince itself/themselves to return to bodies is an undoing, or promises an undoing, of the transcendence, a return from that going out or ecstasy. And yet the poem is not anti-climactic, because of the irony that the return from transcendence has been parodied in advance by the souls (in their propagation) and now parodies their ecstasy with the bodies' ecstasy, in which the souls may nonetheless share in a united way (53–55, 59–60). It is not necessary to accept all the details of this interpretation to regard *The Extasie* as one of Donne's greatest poems; but it is an interpretation that accounts for perhaps the largest number of elements in the poem and one, moreover, which in its emphasis upon certain matters may take us to the temporal and spatial modes of later Metaphysical poets.

The poem usually compared with *The Extasie* is Lord Herbert of Cherbury's *Ode upon a Question moved, Whether Love should continue for ever?* That fine poem is truly dependent upon Donne's in conception, but it is otherwise wholly free. Its ending is at once Metaphysical and of a purity of tone Donne did not seek:

> So when from hence we shall be gone,
>   And be no more, nor you, nor I,
>   As one anothers mystery,
> Each shall be both, yet both but one.
>
> This said, in her up-lifted face,
>   Her eyes which did that beauty crown,
>   Were like two starrs, that having faln down,
> Look up again to find their place:
>
> While such a moveless silent peace
>   Did seize on their becalmed sense,
>   One would have thought some Influence
> Their ravish'd spirits did possess.   (129–140)

One can see the increased emphasis upon narrative as a vehicle for conveying ways of transcending time and place.

Death will bring one kind of transcendence, and the peace of their love even now ravishes them. The situation is like Donne's, but there is little dramatic counterpart to the narrative, and the ecstatic transcendence is far less complete. For the poem closest to *The Extasie*, though wholly independent in its poetic achievement, we must turn to one of Marvell's most admired poems, *The Garden*.

Marvell's poem resembles Donne's in its emphasis upon creation and in its serious parody of usual erotic conventions. There are efforts to create outside the garden (1–24) and inside (25–56); the efforts may be those of a single soul in a garden (25–56) or of two souls in a Paradise (57–64). Unlike Donne, Marvell comes down quite unambiguously in favor of one side of each contrast, and yet more unlike Donne, he makes little effort to accommodate the contrasted parts. Marvell's wit, which manages to exert the maximum pressure with the least force, in this poem is largely linguistic and imagistic, directed to the end of showing the superiority of the rational soul in its garden.[10] The first two stanzas show the retired, contemplative life to be as superior to the active as the opening of the *Horatian Ode* on Cromwell shows the active to excel the contemplative. The third and fourth stanzas introduce a considerable eroticism, which is parodied by the wit. Green (rather than the usual red and white for feminine beauty) becomes "am'rous." The speaker declares to the trees that he will carve no woman's name on their bark:

[10] What the garden implies in terms of the tradition of *hortus conclusus* and the Canticles is examined at length by Stanley Stewart, *The Enclosed Garden* (Madison, 1966). Stewart's very valuable study seems to me to overlook the importance of the secular traditions of Horatian retirement and of neo-Epicureanism so well discussed by Maren-Sofie Røstvig. *The Happy Man*, 2 vols. (Oslo and Oxford, 1954), vol. 1. Donne's phrase, "it was not sexe," applies to Marvell more than to himself, and that it is also true that Marvell takes some of the imagery and some of the significance of Canticles without their physical rapture.

> Fair Trees! where s'eer your barkes I wound,
> No Name shall but your own be found.   (23–24)

Marvell only says so much, and it is just right. We are left
to apply the wit and turn it rather into a joke, with "Beech"
carved on a beech, or perhaps, as it were, "A. M. loves
Beech." The wit of the next stanza—"*Apollo* hunted *Daphne*
so, / Only that She might Laurel grow" (29–30)—lies somewhere between the earlier wit and the joke, probably because
Marvell wishes to set up a contrast with the delicate touches
to follow.

The crucial section of the poem (stanzas v–vii) recounts
the speaker's experience of the garden, where to some extent
he becomes its lover (v), a component part of it (vi), and
a resident of it (vii)—a sequence that turns out to be exactly right. The fifth stanza gives us, in Donne's terms, an
ecstasy of the body, of the inferior souls with their "sense"
and "faculties":

> What wond'rous Life in this I lead!
> Ripe Apples drop about my head;
> The Luscious Clusters of the Vine
> Upon my Mouth do crush their Wine;
> The Nectaren, and curious Peach,
> Into my hands themselves do reach;
> Stumbling on Melons, as I pass,
> Insnar'd with Flow'rs, I fall on Grass.   (34–40)

The close but not rigid parallelisms, the end-stopped lines,
and the increased use of internal pauses all contribute to
the vision of plenitude in the imagery. It is indeed a
"wond'rous Life" in the garden, and Marvell somehow
manages to suggest such full sensuous satisfaction that we
believe that the garden is "am'rous" and that "Love" here
has found "his best retreat." But Marvell has not descended
to sexual detail. Perhaps the fruit imagery (within the Gar-

den context) directs us with some assurance to the Canticles, and perhaps in itself and in such direction it carries an erotic aura. But it is direction rather than directive, and what is "am'rous" is far too refined for erotic paraphrase.

What all these quotations have shown is that, above all, place is at the center of *The Garden*. This is true even more of this poem than of *The Extasie*. We shall have occasion subsequently to observe that between Donne and Marvell there is an increasing tendency to lose the poetic sense of place in Metaphysical poetry and instead to develop temporal situations, structures, and themes. The poetry with a sense of place had become the possession of Cavalier poets (Metaphysical prose poetry like Traherne's provides exceptions), and the loss of a sense of place led to a loss of drama; or rather, the emphasis upon time led to narrative and meditation. Marvell's keen sense of place is partly expressed by sensuous imagery, partly by movement within an area. Spatial movement inevitably implies temporal movement, but in fact Marvell has taken great care to suppress temporal narrative. The verb tenses are, for example, unusually equivocal. Stanza I, present; II, present, perfect, present; III, past, present, future; IV, present, perfect, past; V, present. There is indeed a basic sense of having moved from something inferior before to something superior now. But such a temporal, "narrative" sequence is greatly modified in the early stanzas by apostrophe, by talk of gods and goddesses in a remote place, and by address. Similarly, the even stronger spatial sequence is resolved largely into a contrast between men in the outside world (I), or gods chasing goddesses elsewhere, somewhere (V), and the speaker in the garden (II–III, v ff.). What motion there is leads to a fall, a cessation of motion in a symbolic physical ecstasy. To this point, we have had some sense of narrative to heighten a sense of drama, and the combination in the first seven stanzas is so natural, so smooth ("artificial" would have been the seventeenth-century word) that Donne's labors in unifying the two halves of *The Extasie* seem by comparison to be of a strenuous kind indeed.

The high point of Marvell's poem is of course the incomparable sixth stanza, and its placing in the poem seems more natural than Donne's ecstasy of soul in the first third of *The Second Anniversary*. Marvell begins:

> Mean while the Mind, from pleasure less,
> Withdraws into its happiness.   (41–42)

"Mean while"—the Body is in its ecstasy during this time —the idea suggests both narrative and drama. But the crucial word is probably "Withdraws," a spatial concept used for a mental process, a motion implying transcendence of the points crossed. Just as the enclosed garden is a traditional emblem of the contemplative soul, so now spatial and physical imagery will be used to describe, in a creation metaphor, the perceptions and apperceptions of the mind:

> The Mind, that Ocean where each kind
> Does streight its own resemblance find.
>
> (43–44)

As the ocean was thought to have every type of creature found on land (sea-horses, sea-lions, perhaps mermen and mermaids), so the mind was believed to have its mental correspondences in thoughts for all that is in the material world. The mental Ocean at once ("streight") makes the connections. What is so extraordinary is that the mind "creates" in an ever-extending series of correspondences, "transcending these / Far other Worlds, and other seas" (45–46). The mind (that is, the rational, or intellectual, soul) is a sea that imagines a land; that imagined land has its sea, which imagines its land with its sea.

By the time we have gone as far as our minds are capable of taking us, we have left the original physical world and place far behind us. In the poem, the garden becomes an idea of an idea of an idea—in a process:

> Annihilating all that's made
> To a green Thought in a green Shade.
>
> (47–48)

The greenness of thought is a quality suggestive of the mental procreativity of the mind, and indeed what is left is precisely the "green Thought" itself. Marvell is also careful to say where it is left—in "a green Shade." In the terms of this stanza alone, the green Shade is a creative world in which the resembling creative thought exists to create another green Shade with its green world-thought. But "a green Shade" also has a larger context. Without dropping the immediate context as its main predication, the image also reminds us that we are in a "real" garden. The next stanza beautifully harmonizes this possible dissonance. It treats the separation of soul and body as an accomplished, final, and normal fact. The soul becomes a bird of rare plumage—a plumage of thought and sheer quiet, that is, of light and green shade. The bird of the mind, "till prepar'd for longer flight, / Waves in its Plumes the various Light" (55–56). Time is introduced as something almost to be waited for, and the transcendence of physical place by a self-transcending mental place ends in a chiaroscuro, a flickering of thought-place. The temporal narrative has been subdued by transcendent, thematic place, and the activity is at once so surpassingly peaceful and so procreative of itself that we can scarcely call it narrative or drama or anything other than (to alter one word in Lord Herbert of Cherbury's phrase) a moving silent peace. That this is so may best be judged from the last stanza of one of the greatest of modern lyrics:

> Once out of nature I shall never take
> My bodily form from any natural thing,
> But such a form as Grecian goldsmiths make
> Of hammered gold and gold enamelling
> To keep a drowsy Emperor awake;
> Or set upon a golden bough to sing
> To lords and ladies of Byzantium
> Of what is past, or passing, or to come.

Yeats' energy and his sense of being ill at ease contrast markedly with the Marvellian lightness of touch and the mental repose gained by thought itself. Marvell seems very much more sure of himself.

The comparison with "Sailing to Byzantium" is not all in Marvell's favor, however. In total movement, Yeats is superior, and in particular, he ends with the lines quoted— he ends with perfect justice. To put it bluntly, Marvell's eighth stanza, and therefore regrettably the ninth as well, mars the tone and mode of the poem. The function of the last two stanzas is to return us from the mental and physical ecstasies to the natural garden without shock. But shock there is. After the fine and scrupulous narrative of transcendence with touches of drama, the poem suddenly shifts over to narrative as the dominant mode; it pushes us without a by-your-leave to another place; and it indulges in some now not very funny jokes. Once Yeats went as far as his bird, he stopped. Marvell prepares himself as a bird for flight to eternity and then suddenly changes the subject. He does have a verbal transition:

> Such was that happy Garden-state,
> While Man there walk'd without a Mate:

After a Place so pure, and sweet,
What other Help could yet be meet!   (57–60)

We shift to a pun (Mate, Help-meet), the past tense, and
a simile. The stanza plays with the old idea that Adam was
androgynous and that sexuality was the result of the Fall.
But all this forgets that there has been a fall of a different,
good kind in an earlier stanza and that throughout sexuality
has been, in serious parody, a major means of conveying the
ecstasy of the body and the mind. At this stage, we are in
no mind to have Pan chasing Syrinx merely to get a reed
for his pipe, or for carving the names of trees in their own
bark. Moreover, the androgynous Adam sorts very ill with
the amorous piety attributed to the Canticles, where the
Beloved is sick with love (in the passage from which the
fruit imagery derives) and the divine Lover contemplates
the physical beauty of his spouse. Finally, what does this
stanza mean? The simile indicates that, just as Adam had
paradise before he had Eve, so the speaker has his paradisical
garden while he is alone in it (actually, the sisters, Peace
and Solitude, seem to have been somewhere in the garden—
stanza II). Does someone come into the garden and disturb
him? Does he leave it? If so, for where? Does he stay?
Marvell might well have followed his former progress in
reverse, having the mind return to body, both to appreciation
of the garden, and then perhaps both back into the world.
Or he might have stopped where Yeats did. Unfortunately,
the rapt soul-bird ecstatically but peacefully pluming its
wings for flight to eternity yields to a pedantic joke.[11]

[11] I hope that my enthusiasm throughout this book for Marvell will
win my strictures on one stanza an open hearing. It is perhaps significant that in The Happy Man, I, 256–61, Maren-Sofie Røstvig found
traditional analogues for all stanzas but the eighth (I, The Denuncia-
tion; II, The Dedication; III-IV, The Liber Creaturarum; V, The Earthly
Paradise; VI, The Concentration; VII, The Ecstasy; and IX, The Divine
Hieroglyph). My position is that the poem would read better without

The last stanza (IX) has similarly little connection with VIII. In fact it follows VII much more naturally than does VIII, because its past tense ("How well the skillful Gardner drew") (65) does not imply, as does the comparison with Adam, a full involvement with place on the part of the speaker. The ensuing present tense takes us to the "real" garden—with the sun, the bee, the dial, and flowers—with great naturalness. This stanza, following upon the seventh, would not have given the shock that does the eighth, but for Metaphysical poets it was obviously no less difficult to return from "extasie" than it was to lead up to it or celebrate it.

Time and narrative are important to the *Anniversaries* and to *The Garden* alike, but in all three the effect of drama is in some ways more important than narrative—and place than time in Marvell's poem. What the three share with much of the best Metaphysical poetry written between Donne and Marvell is the transcendence of man's present world or time to another. (That such transcendence also led to a good deal of very dull writing only confirms how important and widespread was this single treatment of time.) What intervening poets came less and less to share with Donne (and with the Marvell of *The Garden*) is the dramatic fiction, and especially a dramatic fiction rooted in place. The general, although by no means absolute, tendency after Donne is for time gradually to replace place as the basis of situations and, thereafter, for narrative to replace drama. In his other more Metaphysical poems, Marvell's tendency is very similar. Perhaps one should say that he attempts to recapture, as it were, some of Donne's drama within a general narrative scheme. The creation of place in

---

the eighth stanza. My fellow admirers of Professor Røstvig's work will know, and perhaps regret with me, that she omits this analysis in the second edition of vol. I (1962).

his other poems (e.g., the Mower poems, "The Gallery," "The Picture of little T. C. in a Prospect of Flowers," *Upon Appleton House*) is usually directed to narrative and transcendent ends; it does not itself become a narrative/dramatic transcendence as in *The Garden*, where place and mind become one in "a green Shade." Why Marvell and other later Metaphysical poets turn to narrative is a question difficult to answer in terms of biography or of individual poems. But it seems most likely that the impulse came from a source not Metaphysical at all, but immediately Cavalier—the concern with time, transience, and mutability that runs as one of the great themes from Elizabethan to Victorian poetry, strangely bypassing Donne and his earlier followers. Donne's speakers in seduction poems are not obsessed by time as are those of the Cavaliers' (in that respect showing where Marvell's debt lies in *To his Coy Mistress*). The simplest reason for the increasing concern with time over place is, therefore, that it was a theme that Metaphysical poets found useful in contemporary poetry written in styles different from their own. It is also true that Cavalier poetry often concerned place—as topographical poems show very well. The concern with place in poems like Jonson's "To Penshurst" or Denham's *Cooper's Hill* is, however, of a public nature unsuited to Metaphysical poetry. In *The last Instructions to a Painter*, Marvell (if he is, as many people think, the author) showed his command of public treatment of place in the very memorable scene of De Ruyter's sailing up the Thames. In *The Garden* he chose rather "a fine and private place" better suited to contemplation soaring from a garden and yet transcendentally the garden itself. Aware as I am that my adverse criticism of the eighth stanza is not likely to be shared by some readers, I may add that I also think it true that in *The Garden* Marvell came as close as anyone is ever likely to to beating Donne at his own game, even while—in those incomparable three stanzas (v–vii) setting a combined standard of wit and delicacy of style of that no one else has rivalled.

iv. The Shift from Dramatic to Narrative Treatments of Time and Place

Herbert and Crashaw continue Donne's "dramatic" effects, but usually in ways less specific of time and place. Place especially weakens as a felt poetic reality. In "The Quip," Herbert goes some way toward place: the "merrie world" with "his train-bands and mates . . . meet together, where I lay" (1–3). And in "The Collar," we learn at once:

> I struck the board, and cry'd, No more.
> I will abroad.

There is some suggestion of location in these poems, but the suggestion has little felt presence. (Is "the board" a desk, a floor, an altar? It *is* indoors.) We do not even have the suggestion of Donne's elegies and other secular poems that we are in the town. Almost all we know is that we are where a specific speaker is.[12] And yet it is that felt speaker (and the illusion of speech in questions, imperatives, apostrophes) who contributes very greatly to the sense of drama in much of Herbert's poetry. Perhaps the best illustration to begin with can be taken from a somewhat less familiar poem. "Artillerie" begins with a brief narrative of the situation, with a somewhat general specification of time and of place, and with relation of an action:

[12] There is of course another aspect of place and time in *The Temple* considered as an integrated poetic sequence. The sequence of worship beginning with the entry from "The Church Porch" and ending with the exodus of the Church Militant involves a time-span of worship and often specific places within the "temple." Stanley Stewart has explored this aspect in "Time and *The Temple,*" *Studies in English Literature,* vi (1966), 97–110. See also Martz, *The Poetry of Meditation,* Ch. viii.

As I one ev'ning sat before my cell,
Me thoughts a starre did shoot into my lap.
I rose, and shook my clothes, as knowing well,
That from small fires comes oft no small mishap.

(1–4)

Here we see Herbert's extraordinary simplicity in handling complex matters in such a way that their complexity seems simple and his simplicity seems complex. Soon, indeed "suddenly," the narration of the strange evening scene yields to a yet more astonishing drama. The angel of this shooting star—the "intelligence" believed to direct each heavenly body—speaks directly and ironically to the speaker:

Do as thou usest, disobey,
Expell good motions from thy breast,
Which have the face of fire, but end in rest.

(6–8)

The next stanza turns once more to narrative emphasis—but then again to dialogue, now the speech of the speaker to God occupying the rest of the poem:

I, who had heard of musick in the spheres,
But not of speech in starres, began to muse:
But turning to my God, whose ministers
The starres and all things are; If I refuse,
Dread Lord, said I, so oft my good;
Then I refuse not ev'n with bloud
To wash away my stubborn thought:
For I will do or suffer what I ought. (9–16)

The remaining two stanzas continue the address to God and develop the imagery suggested by the title ("Then we are shooters both," l. 25). It is certainly a very strange conversation, but it is undeniably characteristic of the poet and dramatic in its effect:

94

Then we are shooters both, and thou dost deigne
To enter combate with us, and contest
With thine own clay. But I would parlay fain:
Shunne not my arrows [prayers], and behold my breast.
   Yet if thou shunnest, I am thine:
   I must be so, if I am mine.
   There is no articling with thee:
I am but finite, yet thine infinitely.   (25–32)

Such a shift from narrative to drama, from a time sequence
to an open confrontation at a moment, is very common with
Herbert. He appears to have found it easiest to develop
dramatic situations by leading up to them with narrative.

Such an emphasis in a relatively unfamiliar poem may be
confirmed by attention to another poem that is highly
esteemed and of course well known, "Love (iii)," the last
poem in *The Temple* proper. Its three stanzas may be given
in full:

Love bade me welcome: yet my soul drew back,
   Guiltie of dust and sinne.
But quick-ey'd Love, observing me grow slack
   From my first entrance in,
Drew nearer to me, sweetly questioning
   If I lack'd any thing.

A guest, I answer'd, worthy to be here:
   Love said, You shall be he.
I the unkinde, ungratefull? Ah my deare,
   I cannot look on thee.
Love took my hand, and smiling did reply,
   Who made the eyes but I?

Truth Lord, but I have marr'd them: let my shame
   Go where it doth deserve.
And know you not, sayes Love, who bore the blame?

95

My deare, then I will serve.
You must sit down, sayes Love, and taste my meat:
So I did sit and eat.

The first and last lines are rather narrative in character, suggesting a little story of welcome, a sequence of protest, reply, urging, and acceptance. But the effect is dramatic. The dialogue which gives the poem much of its character is most important for the dramatic effect, but the dialectic of argument also gives an immediate rather than an extended pressure. There is also the conflict of drama, unusual as it is, in the confrontation of Love, or Christ, and the beloved who is conscious of his guilt.

There is also in Herbert's drama a kind of narrative and transcendence in which he outshines the other Metaphysical poets. To take the narrative first: within the larger form and movement of *The Temple*, the worshipper has been directing his attention all along toward the loving Christ. "Love (III)" follows "Heaven" and so half suggests that Man is being welcomed by Christ to eternity. That is true, but in a special sense. Man partakes of eternity from Love in the sacrament of the Eucharist, which is finally and specifically taken in *The Temple* only here, in its last poem. Given the context, we have of course a special place, the Church, and a special time in divine service. The drama is, then, the climax of a narrative. What bridges the taking of the Eucharist and the entry into heaven is the biblical passage alluded to, the return of the prodigal son, which was traditionally glossed as the return of the penitent Christian to forgiveness—Love's "meat," the fatted calf, was a type of Christ crucified and of the Eucharist.[13] In the suggestion of entry into heaven, in the taking of a sacrament which is a mystery of the

[13] Luke 15. Cf. *Biblia Sacra cum Glossa Ordinaria* (Douai and Antwerp, 1617), 6 vols., v, 893–904. See below, ch. v, n. 14, on my use of this splendid Bible.

Church, and indeed in the capacity for man to talk with
God we find a transcendence as undeniable and as moving
as it is also dramatic and superficially simple.

Herbert maintains, in whatever altered form, that situa-
tional rather than extended use of time and place which
Donne had developed to give his lyrics their dramatic effect.
Crashaw is less consistent, and in his poems we see the beginning of the end of drama as the central feature of Metaphysical poetry. In fact he wrote narrative poetry in the strict
sense—*Sospetto d'Herode* contains some 528 lines. It is no
task to prove such poems narrative, and I wish rather to show
briefly the kind of dramatic effect that Crashaw was capable
of creating. The poem endeavoring to persuade the Countess
of Denbigh to become a Roman Catholic begins with a clear
situation:

> What Heav'n besieged Heart is this
> Stands Trembling at the Gate of Blisse:
> Holds fast the Door, yet dares not venture
> Fairly to open and to enter? [14]

There is something more like a place than not in such a passage, and something more like a dramatic effect than anything else. Later lines heighten the drama by implying action
and tension in address—"Ah! linger not, lov'd Soul" (7)—
and sometimes, as in the concluding lines, by attending to
time:

> Disband dull Feares, give Faith the day:
> To save your Life, kill your Delay.
> 'Tis Cowardice that keeps this Field;
> And want of Courage not to Yield.
>   Yield then, O yield, that Love may win
> The Fort at last, and let Life in.

[14] Following the "letter" text in L. C. Martin, ed., *The Poems . . .*
of Richard Crashaw, 2nd ed. (Oxford, 1957), pp. 348 ff.

Yield quickly, lest perhaps you prove
Death's Prey, before the Prize of Love.
This Fort of your Fair Self if't be not wone,
He is repuls'd indeed, but You'r undone. (81–90)

The argument towards the end is akin to that of *carpe diem*; such touches, like the erotic imagery and diction earlier in the poem (e.g., 7–10, 46–48 [Venus' doves], 69–74 [Canticles]), show that the poem is a sacred parody of the seduction poem. The parody is adapted to suit the tradition of Christ ("Love") wooing his Church, but it is also adapted so that the speaker of the poem presents his "persuasions to enjoy," as Carew puts it, on behalf of someone other than himself, that is, God.

Crashaw is much given to sacred parody—of erotic love in poems like that urging the Countess of Denbigh or in others on mystics like St. Theresa, but also of such other secular forms as the love elegy, the epitaph, and even the pastoral. Sometimes Crashaw invents a style (which is usually not very successful) that can be termed neither dramatic nor narrative, because it has no situation or specifiable actors to give its intensity a dramatic effect, nor yet any discernible sequence to give its details narrative succession. Such a poem is the hymn, *To the Name Above Every Name, the Name of Jesus*, whose two most specific lines as to what Crashaw elsewhere calls "the tame laws of Time and Place" are hardly specific at all. He is speaking of "each severall kind / And shape of sweetnes":

. . . they convene & come away
To wait at the love-crowned Doores of
This Illustrious DAY.   (37–43)

One is tempted to say that a person who can visualize that can visualize anything. It should be recognized, I think, that Crashaw's effort to transcend often left behind the details of time and place, the effects of drama or of narrative, and sometimes poetry itself. But so closely are Crashaw's faults involved with his virtues that the same kind of abstracted transcendence can also evoke his fullest poetic power, as for example in the concluding lines of his *Answer for Hope* to Cowley's *Against Hope*:

> Though the vext chymick vainly chases
>> His fugitive gold through all her faces;
> Though Love's more feirce, more fruitlesse, fires assay
>> One face more fugitive then all they;
> True hope's a glorious hunter & her chase,
> The GOD of nature in the feilds of grace.   (45–50)

Our first impression is of second-rate Donne, and of action, if it is action, transpiring at no definable place or time. Then the last line but one quietly turns us about to face that kind of perfection that Crashaw alone knows how to create. Indeed the conceit of the last two lines, paralleling the desperate pursuits of the two preceding couplets, is a very striking and daring metaphor. In lines like these, Crashaw does not raise either narrative or drama to transcendent heights. Rather, he has been at those heights all along, and at these moments he descends to time and place. He does not come down the whole distance, or he would have said "The God of grace in the fields of nature." But what he says is better and theologically as true. Passages like these, and they are not rare in Crashaw, reconcile us to his style. They almost make us think that he always could *see* what we often can only read. His consistent problem as a poet was one that Donne in *The Extasie* and Marvell in *The Garden* faced only in those poems—how to return to "the tame laws of Time and Place" after the liberties of ecstatic rapture.

v. Alteration of Time

In some ways the most fascinating decade for poetry in the seventeenth century is the as yet insufficiently explored period from about 1645 to 1655. These ten years or so are a micro-cosm of the entire century, and no one poet writing at that time can be said to be wholly Metaphysical, Cavalier, Resto-ration, or anything else. Always of course with the proviso that Milton is entirely himself. Henry Vaughan is especially useful among these poets, both because he is authentic in many poems as a poet and as a Metaphysical, and also be-cause he shows how in the special circumstances of mid-century that kind of poetry was possible only by emphasizing certain tendencies that had been strongly present but not uppermost before. His death within five years of Dryden's should not obscure the fact that he was writing many of his poems even as Cowley was writing many of his. In fact, he began a few years before Marvell. But the poems he was writ-ing at that time were Cavalier rather than Metaphysical, and he is probably the single important example of a poet who began in another style and then turned Metaphysical. (The reverse is common enough.) Herbert probably wrote secular poems that have not survived, but it is likely from what he says in his "Jordan" poems that they were Metaphysical. Vaughan began with Cavalier poetry—lyrics and public po-etry—buttressed by translations. The verse of his early stage appeared in the *Poems* of 1646 and was followed by the verse in *Olor Iscanus*, whose Dedication dates from 1647, although the volume did not appear until 1651.

It would have required great percipience in reading these volumes to foretell that Vaughan would become a major fig-ure among Metaphysical poets. But just about this time he was busy on the poems in *Silex Scintillans*, which in 1650 preceded *Olor Iscanus* into print. The fluidity of poetic styles in the century is suggested by such dates and is confirmed by *Thalia Rediviva*, a collection Vaughan mentions as being in hand in 1673, though it was not published till 1678, when it appeared probably as a compilation of early and late poems by a hand other than the poet's. Often in this last volume we sense that elements from Metaphysical poetry combine with elements from Cavalier to produce one of the notes of Restoration poetry. We may take "To Etesia parted from him, and looking back":

> Hath she no *Quiver,* but my Heart?
> Must all her Arrows hit that part?
> *Beauties like Heav'n, their Gifts should deal*
> *Not to destroy us, but to heal.*
> Strange *Art* of Love! that can make sound,
> And yet exasperates the wound;
> That *look* she lent to ease my heart,
> Hath pierc't it, and improv'd the smart.   (7–14)

Here we have the dialectic, conceits, wit, questions, and exclamations we believe to be Metaphysical techniques. And so they are, but the poem has a social rather than a private tone—the italicized lines have not only the very cadence of a second-rate Restoration song but also the first person plural of the public world.

Like other major mid-century poets (Charles Cotton may be mentioned with Marvell, Cowley, Waller, and others), Vaughan is Janus-faced, looking before and after. But there is also a true Metaphysical vein in Vaughan's poetry, and a special realization in it of poetic tendencies begun much earlier. The often-quoted acknowledgment in the Preface to *Silex Scintillans* (2nd ed., 1655) suggests the direction to look: "The first, that with any effectual success attempted a *diversion* of this foul and overflowing *stream* [of secular poetry], was the blessed man, Mr. *George Herbert,* whose holy *life* and *verse* gained many pious *Converts,* (of whom I am the least) . . ."[15] There is much in Vaughan's best Meta-

[15] *The Works of Henry Vaughan,* ed. L. C. Martin, 2nd ed. (Oxford, 1957), p. 391.

physical poetry that is owed ultimately less to Herbert than to Donne—splendid dramatic outbursts, a witty dialectic, and certain kinds of concern with time. But the debt is owed directly to Herbert and, we observe, is expressed both in terms of "holy *life*" and of *"verse."* The combination of these two in poetry of course has its biographical implications, but the literary result is an approach primarily devotional. What I am suggesting is that Vaughan represents one version of the last phase of Metaphysical poetry and that this may be characterized, again in an adapted sense like my "drama" and "narrative," as "meditation." [16] The meditational approach sometimes has an element of drama, usually when it is a colloquy between man and God or Body and Soul. Sometimes it has concern with a place that is meditated on, or a time of meditation, or time as a subject to be transcended. But the dominant effort is toward a raising of musing and colloquy to exclamation or apostrophe, to that spiritual ecstasy which has led many people to speak of Metaphysical poetry, and especially that of Vaughan, as mystical. The meditative mode almost never sustains such flights and usually returns to drama or narrative in rather diffuse versions. But whereas Crashaw seems to have difficulty in touching earth, Vaughan struggles to stay in flight.

Such flights suggest what is certainly true, that like all else of importance in Metaphysical poetry, the *fons et origo* of meditation is to be found in Donne. At their best, his divine

[16] Martz, Dame Helen Gardner in her edition, John Donne, *The Divine Poems* (Oxford, 1959), and others show how varieties of the formal religious mediation were drawn upon by different poets, both as general models and, at times, for formal division. My usage will be clear from the rest of the paragraph but it obviously includes the technical as well as a more general application. As late as Traherne, formal religious mediations were being written. See *Meditations on the Six Days of the Creation*, ed. George Robert Guffey, Augustan Reprint Society, no. 119 (1966).

poems admit the maximum amount of meditation possible with drama. Both elements may be focused on time ("What if this present were the worlds last night"), on place ("At the round earths imagin'd corners, blow / Your trumpets, Angells"), or on time and place both ("This is my playes last scene, here heavens appoint / My pilgrimages last mile"). Indeed time and place, with that wonderful immediacy of address of which Donne is master, combine to subsume a dominant dramatic cast. On a few occasions, the meditational mode does dominate in Donne. "A Litanie" is a good example:

> Father of Heaven, and him, by whom
> It, and us for it, and all else, for us
> Thou madest, and govern'st ever, come
> And re-create mee, now growne ruinous:
> My heart is by dejection, clay,
> And by selfe-murder, red.
> From this red earth, O Father, purge away
> All vicious tinctures, that new fashioned
> I may rise up from death, before I'am dead. (1–9)

There is here no sense of functioning time and place, and drama has turned to musing prayer, a combination of "holy *life* and *verse*."

Herbert, who is all but entirely a devotional poet, is of course more often meditational (in my sense) than Donne. Herbert is, as we have seen, often dramatic, and his dramas often have narrative frames. But frequently Herbert is as fully meditational as any of the Metaphysicals; that is, he will be found speaking and thinking but not at a dramatic time and place or in a narrative sequence. This aspect of Herbert's poetry can be shown by a couple of stanzas from "Grace":

My stock lies dead, and no increase
Doth my dull husbandrie improve:
O let thy graces without cease
  Drop from above! . . .

The dew doth ev'ry morning fall;
And shall the dew out-strip thy Dove?
The dew, for which grasse cannot call,
  Drop from above.   (1–4; 9–12)

One cannot say that there is no drama here, or that such meditation in other poems excludes narration in the sense of strongly implied sequence. But it is a drama of prayer, not a drama enacted at a time or place. There is also something akin to drama in the constant pressure toward transcendence —of place to heaven, of time to eternity, and of ordinary drama to union. Herbert's ability to do this is clear enough in many poems, but "The Temper (1)" is especially useful for illustration and its possibilities for making discriminations:

How should I praise thee, Lord! how should my rymes
 Gladly engrave thy love in steel,
  If what my soul doth feel sometimes,
   My soul might ever feel!

Although there were some fourtie heav'ns, or more,
 Sometimes I peere above them all;
 Sometimes I hardly reach a score,
  Sometimes to hell I fall. . . .

Whether I flie with angels, fall with dust,
 Thy hands made both, and I am there:
 Thy power and love, my love and trust
  Make one place ev'ry where.   (1–8; 25–28)

The distinction between the dominant meditation here and a dominant drama in Donne can be quickly understood by setting beside the last stanza four lines from Donne's "Good-morrow":

> And now good morrow to our waking soules,
>   Which watch not one another out of feare;
> For love, all love of other sights controules,
>   And makes one little roome, an every where. (8–11)

Donne's language is not more particular than Herbert's, and the concluding concept is essentially the same. But there is this difference that we feel and that evokes in us a very different response: Donne's "one little roome" is a chamber, a curtain-bed, in which the two lovers awake and find in their joy that all they desire is right there. It is, then, a specific, felt place at a specific, felt time, and the urge to transcend rather transforms the time and place than aspires for that which is beyond. Herbert is thinking of some of God's attributes—omnipotence, immanence, and love—and it is not so much the speaker's one place and time that is important as, so to speak, God's eternity and ubiquity. Both share a rapture, but with Herbert it is Vaughan's meditative combination of "holy *life*" ("How should I praise thee, Lord!") and of "*verse*" ("my rymes").

What Herbert frequently does, Vaughan almost always tries for in *Silex Scintillans*. He is uneven, as a meditative poet is apt to be. He has very, very few poems that sustain their best effects; but what is equally important, he has in this collection very, very few poems that are untouched by his best meditative mode. He seems far more aware of time and place than Crashaw, but because he is aware, he seeks to transcend them in flight, whether in time or place or in occult musing. "Childe-hood" treats a favorite subject, and it might therefore be thought to provoke a thematic use of time contrasting the present and the past. That is indeed what the poem comes to, but it is not that with which it begins:

I Cannot reach it; and my striving eye
Dazles at it, as at eternity. . . .
Quickly would I make my path even,
And by meer playing go to Heaven.

Why should men love
A Wolf, more then a Lamb or Dove?
Or choose hell-fire and brimstone streams
Before bright stars, and Gods own beams? (1–2; 7–12)

It may seem that a passage like this one—so lacking in wit, conceits, strong lines, and other ordinary criteria for defining Metaphysical poetry—is simply not Metaphysical. Of course the label is not as important as the poem. But I think that somewhat similar passages from an earlier and a later poem will suggest that in Vaughan's poem we do have something different, and that what is different is something that we may as well call Metaphysical, since it is to be found to a smaller or larger degree in poets usually given the name. In the sixth stanza of Milton's *On the Morning of Christ's Nativity* (1621) we have stars as emblems of providence, as in Vaughan's poem, and a threat against that providence, also as in Vaughan:

The Stars with deep amaze
Stand fixt in steadfast gaze,
      Bending one way their precious influence,
And will not take their flight,
For all the morning light,
      Or Lucifer that often warn'd them thence;
But in their glimmering Orbs did glow,
Until their Lord himself bespake, and bid them go.
                                        (69–76)

The differences are remarkable. Vaughan's speaker is isolated in a retreat from a sorry world, musing on God's goodness to man. Milton (here at age twenty-one) shows an intimate familiarity with the larger reaches of the universe, and to his lyric gives an essentially heroic narrative. A different example may be found in the conclusion to Dryden's *Hind and the Panther* (1687):

> For now the streaky light began to peep;
> And setting stars admonish'd both to sleep.
> The Dame withdrew, and, wishing to her Guest
> The peace of Heav'n, betook her self to rest.
> Ten thousand Angels on her slumbers waite
> With glorious Visions of her future state.
>
> (III, 1293–98)

Here we have true narrative rooted in time and suggestive, with divine providence, of eternity. There is no personal distress, but rather a vision of the Catholic Church as bride of Christ: the stars are part of the narrative scene (in an allusion to the *Aeneid*) and by association link to their intelligences, the angels that post divine guard. What Milton and Dryden do not possess is most readily specified as the private mode, and particularly a privacy suggesting a direct intimacy between the speaker and God, as well as a privacy expressing a shrinking from the world. Only apart from the world, only by oneself, may one muse, may one's heart be lifted up in the silent call of prayer; and, to these poets, only in such private musings was the surge of exaltation possible.

Everyone familiar with Metaphysical poetry is familiar with Vaughan's breathtaking beginning of "The World": "I Saw Eternity the other night. . . ." This, which is thought the finest part of the poem, shows time transcended by eternity, place by the totality of the universe—in the musing of a private speaker. The force of the musing is often augmented in Vaughan's poetry by symbols—eternity is a ring and is suggested by light—that have been variously called emblematic,

Hermetic, and otherwise. "Cock-crowing" and "The Water-fall" are often given as examples of such thought. In fact, there was a very great rise during the 1640's and the 1650's in numerous forms of occultism, typology, perennial symbolism, "natural magic," and suggestive lore. Those who would deny such elements in Vaughan, and those also who would insist that they *must* be called Hermetic, should compare the opening of "Cock-crowing" with the opening, and the notes on the opening, of the first fable in John Ogilby, *The Fables of Aesop Paraphras'd in Verse*, 1651 and several times reprinted.[17] The point is that Vaughan's allegiance to the Metaphysical race is not due to the "mystical," "occult," or "Hermetic" lore he shared with numerous contemporaries but to his exploration of the meditative strain in Metaphysical poetry. Almost always his poems rise and fall as he seeks to intensify his *"verse"* by meditations of a "holy *life.*" Perhaps the best example of this mode is in one of his finest and most characteristic poems, "They are all gone into the world of light!"

[17] Ogilby treats the cock's seed, its ray, the hurt to lions, and other old topics he discusses in terms both of the fabulists and the philosophers, particularly the Pythagoreans and Epicureans. Few subjects seem to me more in need of desimplification than the current one of scientific vs. "occult" thought in the seventeenth century. The evidence shows that Dryden's poetic and intellectual stand antedates in important ways Milton and Donne's (see, besides my *Dryden's Poetry*, ch. v and pp. 273–83, the numerological analysis by Alistair Fowler and Douglas Brooks, "The Structure of Dryden's 'Song for St. Cecilia's Day,' " *Essays in Criticism*, XVII [1967], 434–47). No discussion of the literary effects of science can afford omission of the extraordinary transformation of Samuel Butler's Sidrophel from interregnum astrologer to virtuoso of the Royal Society; see *Hudibras*, Pt. II, canto iii and the following "An Heroical Epistle of Hudibras to Sidrophel." Vaughan, Henry More, Dryden, and, for that matter, Isaac Newton believing in astrology, secretly practicing alchemy while Master of the Mint, and interpreting the prophecies of Daniel are much more like each other than one could guess from the usual attempts to make bogeyman and destroyers of "sacramental" thought out of Bacon, Hobbes, and the Royal Society.

They are all gone into the world of light!
    And I alone sit lingring here;
Their very memory is fair and bright,
    And my sad thoughts doth clear. . . .

I see them walking in an Air of glory,
    Whose light doth trample on my days:
My days, which are at best but dull and hoary,
    Meer glimmering and decays. . . .

Dear, beauteous death! the Jewel of the Just,
    Shining no where, but in the dark;
What mysteries do lie beyond thy dust;
    Could man outlook that mark! . . .

Either [, God,] disperse these mists, which blot and fill
    My perspective (still) as they pass,
Or else remove me hence unto that hill,
    Where I shall need no glass.
                    (1–4; 9–12; 17–20; 37–40)

As so often, in Metaphysical poetry, the musing takes on the quality of address, and the grammatical modes are more often than in most other styles the less ordinary: interrogative, imperative, and vocative. Fourteen of the poems in *Silex Scintillans* begin with an "O . . ." (Similarly, eighteen of Herbert's poems begin in such fashion; in all Dryden's canon, only three.) The impulse behind meditation, like its private character, is something shared with the other dominant structures—the dramatic and the narrative. The meditative does not create the intense scene of the dramatic nor work as directively as the narrative, but it does seek intensity and movement. The effort toward transcendence is, then, a common motive in Metaphysical poetry, and the meditational structure hovers or muses over a subject until, or as long as, it proves capable of rapture. Obviously, this is the hardest structure to sustain, and Vaughan, who is the most given to meditation of all the major Metaphysical poets is, with Crashaw, the most uneven. "The World" begins in glory, falls to sinful earth, and rises at its end once more to glory. We do not much mind Vaughan's irregular falls when we come to know with full assurance that he will rise, and rise yet again. Indeed, as "The World" and certain other of his poems show, he often incorporated dramatic and narrative elements into his meditational structure. Perhaps the real truth is that a given narrative structure by Vaughan is remembered for its meditative moments. In *Thalia Rediviva* there are some poems that are almost wholly meditational, and they are not nearly so satisfactory. This tendency toward meditation alone is to be found in its most advanced state in Traherne. Traherne has a few fine poems but none that one feels rise to greatness, and most of them are less effective than his prose-poetry. One would rather have a writer over-praised than undervalued. But with Traherne one main line of Metaphysical poetry was at its end. New experience, and new styles answering to that experience, had intervened. As Traherne shows, one could now be a Metaphysical only by an actual separation from the world. Donne, Herbert, Crashaw, Marvell, and Vaughan very well knew the world they fled, and that is one reason why their private mode has the integrity and intensity it does. To be a Metaphysical poet as late as Traherne, one had to meditate alone, almost nowhere, almost at no time. Drama was past, and narrative was past. After musing there was silence—or the social voice and argument of "almost the last of that race," Cowley.

Abraham Cowley has been as undervalued in our time as Traherne has been over-rated. It is true that in his famous review of 1921 T. S. Eliot said that Cowley ("at his best") possessed that sensibility which he found wanting in Milton and Dryden. Certainly Cowley is the best mid-century poet after Marvell, and is, in a few respects, not very far after. The two share a number of qualities, but in some ways Cowley is more like Donne than is Marvell. It will be recalled that in his *Life* of Cowley, Dr. Johnson took examples of Metaphysical techniques and faults (there was not always a difference, to Dr. Johnson's mind) almost equally from Cowley and Donne. But one is entitled to think both Dr. Johnson and T. S. Eliot wrong, and there are perhaps not a few people who think that Cowley is in no meaningful sense a poet in "the line of Donne"; and others that he is, but that his poems are inconsiderable. It is the first question to which I should like chiefly to address myself, because though it is no real answer to the second, the presence of Cowley in my discussion implies an estimate of his worth as a poet.

Cowley is sometimes more Cavalier or even more proto-Restoration than he is Metaphysical. His anacreontic verse follows Cavalier values, and his ode to the Royal Society fits Restoration values. Sometimes Cowley is wholly Metaphysical and not very poetic, or at least not very successful. Dr. Johnson found the second stanza of "The Innocent Ill" especially Metaphysical and especially bad:

> Though in thy Thoughts scarce any Tracks have been,
> So much as of *Original* Sin,
> Such Charms thy *Beauty* wears as might
> Desires in dying confest *Saints* excite.
> Thou with strange *Adultery*
> Dost in each breast a *Brothel keep*;
> *Awake* all Men do *lust* for thee,
> And some *enjoy* thee when they *sleep*.
> Ne'er before did *Woman* live,
> Who to such *Multitudes* did give
> The *Root* and *Cause* of *Sin*, but only *Eve*.

It would be difficult to frame a description of Metaphysical poetry that would include Donne's secular poems and exclude this stanza, as Dr. Johnson unerringly recognized. But something has gone wrong. Donne is occasionally blasphemous and often outrageous. But his poems retain either a morality more basic than conventional moralism or leave us with the conviction that what they say is appropriate for such a speaker on such an occasion. Cowley's poem is obviously private, and it will be found to suit with the discussion of wit or of themes in the ensuing chapters. But there is in this poem a lack of conviction, and it may be got at most readily in the terms of this chapter, formal procedures.

This seems the most revealing, as well as the most difficult, approach. Some of Cowley's poems are different, but the stanza just given is nonetheless symptomatic in lacking drama, narrative, and meditation. Of those three, Cowley is most skillful with narrative, but the poems one is most readily inclined to call Metaphysical are often like the stanza from "The Innocent Ill." One feature, a negative one, is a tendency to abstraction implied by his very titles. Although *The Mistress* would be as good a title for Donne's *Songs and Sonnets* as for the collection of Cowley's most Metaphysical poems, individual titles are less happy: "The Innocent Ill," "The Soul," "The Passions," "Wisdom," and "The Despair." The abstraction seems to me a symptom of the removal from time and place in these poems. But if the poems neither cohere about a dramatic center nor develop along a narrative line, in what does their structural coherence lie? I think that it lies in what may be called "argument." As in Donne (and, it must be admitted, in Suckling) so in Cowley there is almost always a man addressing a woman or some other presumptive audience. The man and his audience are specifiable, even if their time and place are not. And the nature of the address is argument in the sense both of the dialectic discussed in the next chapter and of the pursuit with urgent show of language of whatever point the poem sets out to make. This explains why the woman herself innocent of any ill may keep a brothel in each breast, why she is a greater cause of sin to multitudes than any since Eve. What many people were formerly pleased to find in Donne is what I often find in Cowley: quaint hyperbole, and not so much of language and imagery, though of them certainly, as of thought. This is part of the argument, too, as if by calling a rise in the ground a mountain one may get agreement that it is a hill.

The exaggeration seems to me a symptom of a lack of conviction related to the absence of time and place coordinates in the poems. Too often Cowley does not know where such experience exists. He knows all the forms very well indeed, and the techniques lie ready to hand. But the woman, and the experience of love, have to be conjured into being by strong measures and held before the mind by a degree of argument louder than Donne or other Metaphysicals of stature equal to Cowley found necessary. What we see in Cowley is, I believe, what we see in other terms in Vaughan and Traherne. The private mode is growing more and more marginal. It had begun as a revulsion from the Elizabethan court and had found conviction either in anonymous urban privacy or in private prayer. Whatever the cause—the Civil Wars and the following strain on English life—by the middle of the century it was hard to keep a balance between the private world and the public. Nothing could better indicate Marvell's poise than just such an achievement (in separate poems). But writers like Vaughan were driven farther inward to isolation and musing, beyond even the private mode (Vaughan so often sounds a note as of one left behind), and that brooding is reflected in the very structure of their poems. Cowley, on the other hand, is torn between the public and the private worlds. And I believe that his Metaphysical poetry is a compromise between the two. It retains the private character and the wit of Metaphysical poetry, but it introduces a special social tone unknown before in Metaphysical poetry.

The same vacillation between the active and the retired life will of course be found throughout the century. But it is less often found explicitly in poetry than in prose. (Marvell solved the problem by advocating the contemplative life in *The Garden* and the active in the *Horatian Ode*.) Cowley's essays, which possess an ease and quiet charm not always found in his poems, explicitly deal with the question, and they usually answer it by arguing the case for the retired life in the new social voice of the English Gentlemen (whose birth can almost be dated from those essays). Somewhat similarly, the argument of the poems has a strong social tone, because Cowley uses his hyperbole, at least as Eliot says, "at his best," as a form of gently mocking humor. "The Innocent Ill" is a kind of loudness no gentleman (in theory) could be guilty of. But the same tendency to argument, pursuing a point with a show of logic in talking with a woman, the same argument and the social tone, can be seen in a poem like "Inconstancy":

> Five Years ago (says *Story*) I lov'd you,
> For which you call me most *Inconstant* now;
> Pardon me, Madam, you mistake the *Man*;
> For I am not the same that I was then . . .
> My *Members* then the *Father Members* were,
> From whence *these* take their Birth, which now are here.
> If then this *Body* love what th'other did,
> 'Twere *Incest*; which by Nature is forbid.   (1–4; 11–14)

"Pardon me, Madam"—there is a note not heard before in Metaphysical poetry, though the disingenuous sly mockery *was* known to Suckling and other Cavaliers. The scientific premise of the poem and the sexual detail build up the argument around a single line of argument: inconstancy is change; I am changed; therefore I am not what I was; therefore I am not inconstant. What this poem also shows is that

Cowley could be playful, invoking history (*"Story,"* *storia*) with a light touch.

The more one reads Cowley, the more one is drawn into liking him, because one begins to detect a note of shyness or hesitation under the show of argument, and one begins to suspect that his poems are exaggeratedly fictional so that he can avoid seeming to talk about the subject that really interests him, himself. Again and again the argument directed toward the woman or other audience turns out to be a transparent way of talking about his sexual passion ("The Innocent Ill"), his own bewildering alterations ("Inconstancy"), or, in a different tone, of his integrity ("All over Love"):

> Whatever *Parts* of me remain,
> Those *Parts* will still the *Love* of thee retain;
> For 'twas not only in my Heart,
> But like a *God* by pow'rful Art,
> 'Twas *all* in *all*, and *all* in *ev'ry Part.*
>
> *My' Affection* no more perish can
> Than the *First Matter* that compounds a Man.
> Hereafter if one *Dust* of Me
> Mix'd with another's *Substance* be,
> 'Twill *leaven* that whole *Lump* with Love of Thee.
>
> (6–15)

In a sense not altogether different from its applicability to Donne's poems, the phrase "dialogue of one" also applies to Cowley's approach. In Donne, however, there is such greater certainty as well as greater consciousness of the self that he can, in good faith, count his "five gray haires" and think the number says something (allowing the requisite humor) about human experience. Cowley seems to find it necessary for either social or poetic convention to address "The Mistress," perhaps because he lacks the conviction that his private experience is wholly valid.

Cowley's argument, like Vaughan's meditation, is, then, a means of discovery and of expression. But structurally the two poets work in contrary terms. Vaughan meditates on a topic, rising and falling in flights of rapture. Cowley pursues a straight line of argument, with the points of logic and the conceits marking stages of the journey. In this he resembles Donne much more than do Vaughan and Traherne, as may be seen at once by a comparison of Donne's "Blossome" with Cowley's "Welcome" to his errant heart:

> Go, let the *fatted Calf* be kill'd;
>   My *Prodigal's* come home at last,
> With noble Resolutions fill'd,
>   And fill'd with Sorrow for the past.
>   No more will burn with *Love* or *Wine*,
> But quite has left his *Women* and his *Swine*.
>
>   (1–6)

It is a pity that Cowley did not always write so directly about himself (or a poetic speaker like himself). But there is another vein in which his tendency to abstraction produced a kind of poetry which is no doubt somewhat tenuous, yet which is also possessed of real integrity. Both "For Hope" and "Against Hope" are poems of that kind. And there are also his elegies, on Crashaw and Hervey, that are among his finest poems. They are also among his best known, and my aim has been to revive the lyric, Metaphysical Cowley in whom we may discover one of the last phases of the revolution begun by Donne. The manifesto of that revolution had been an exploration or a dramatizing of time and place as part of lyric experience, with meditation and argument as means of sustaining the illusion that a speaker and audience were present at that time and place. In poets following Donne, narration comes to replace drama, and place gradually fades. Except for Marvell, Metaphysical poetry in its

116

last phase had neither world enough nor time, and what was left was a sustaining of the private mode in meditation or in argument. Poets before Cowley and poets after him knew how to argue. Donne and Dryden are masters of the art. Dryden does not concern us (much as there is of the Metaphysical in him), because the radically public nature of his poetry marks its division from the radically private nature of Metaphysical poetry. But it is obvious that argument is, in some sense, an element in a great deal of poetry from Donne to Cowley, and it is also obvious that argument somehow involves that wit which, from Dryden on, critics have associated with Metaphysical poetry.

≥ III «

WIT: DEFINITION AND
DIALECTIC

Whose DEFINITION is a doubt
Twixt life & death, twixt in & out.

— Crashaw

IF ANY feature of Metaphysical has seemed to be its prime characteristic, that has been wit. To Carew, Donne had ruled, as no one else might have, *"The universall Monarchy of Wit"* and to Dryden he was "the greatest Wit, though not the best Poet of our Nation." [1] Dr. Johnson regarded wit as the chief feature distinguishing poets who might be termed Metaphysical and advanced the subject considerably by locating wit in a process of thought: "The most heterogeneous ideas are yoked by violence together." [2] Although Johnson spoke of ideas and did not restrict wit to images, it has since become common to think of wit in terms of conceits, and Donne's "stiffe twin compasses" have become the archetype of all Metaphysical imagery and wit. Certainly images are often yoked to ideas—Donne's use of public language and imagery for private experience was remarked on in an earlier chapter and may serve again for example. But Dr. Johnson meant ideas, that Donne had thoughts and used them (whether with imagery or without) strikingly, often bizarrely or distastefully, but always conspicuously. Both the use of

[1] Carew, *An Elegie upon . . . Dr. John Donne*, l. 96. Dryden, epistle dedicatory to *Eleonora*, 3rd paragraph.
[2] Johnson, *The Lives of the English Poets*, ed. G. B. Hill, 3 vols. (London, 1905), I, 20.

ideas and the strikingness or novelty of their use were important meanings of "wit" in the century. Of the two, the use of the intellect was the more dominant sense of the word. Dryden was yet more particular. Donne, he said, "affects the Metaphysicks, not only in his Satires, but in his Amorous Verses, where Nature only shou'd reign; and perplexes the Minds of the Fair Sex with nice Speculations of Philosophy, when he shou'd ingage their hearts, and entertain them with the softnesses of Love." [3] Dryden's usual critical sense deserts him at the end of this passage, leading him to think that a love poem is less a poem than a real stage in wooing. But he is certainly right in finding ideas in Donne's love poems as well as in his satires and to suggest that they come from metaphysics and from science ("Philosophy"). Philosophical divinity and theoretical science *are* sources of Donne's ideas and they *are* unusual in love poetry. But such ideas, like their equivalents in the other Metaphysical poets, are also witty in the freshness of their application and valuable for the way in which they arc set to work poetically.

If we might summon up a sixteenth- or seventeenth-century schoolboy and ask him to identify the arts teaching how ideas are used and put to work, he would not have spoken of philosophy and psychology as we know them today, but of logic and rhetoric. Anyone who has looked at the old logics and rhetorics that were memorized by, or beaten into, a schoolboy three or four centuries ago is apt to regard the lad with a sigh and heaviness of heart. Homozeuxis and homozeugma are not calculated to touch modern hearts very deeply, and the differences between Aristotle, Cicero, Quintilian, and Ramus in matters rhetorical likewise do not seem matters of very pressing poetic interest. What two central arts of the Renaissance and the seventeenth century have less

[3] Dryden, *Discourse Concerning Satire, The Poems of John Dryden,* ed. James Kinsley, 4 vols. (Oxford, 1958), ii, 604.

119

relevance to our familiar experience? What, we are inclined to ask, do such "predicaments" as "substance," "accident," or "quantity" have to do with *us*? Or with our understanding of Metaphysical poetry? On the other hand, if Donne's "Communitie" assumes the form of an exact complex disjunctive syllogism, the fact is a fact. It is difficult to construct a modern parallel, since the comparable logic today is so mathematical that it has little connection with poetry. But what if all our poets had been taught at school and at the university to memorize William Empson's *Seven Types of Ambiguity*, to analyze writing in terms of each type along close lines by attention to the "grammar" of Kenneth Burke and the "genres" of Northrop Frye, and to compose constantly with the alternatives in mind? Then should a critic three centuries hence be expected to know what all this is about?

The equivalent questions have been raised by some of our students of Metaphysical poetry, and some very different answers have been given, sometimes with a vigor approaching vehemence. Obviously, a major difference of opinion is involved, not just of fact or of critical method, but of how poetry should be, or how poetry in fact is, read. The late Rosemund Tuve advocated one major position, arguing at length and in thick detail, that both Elizabethan and Metaphysical imagery (as she categorized the subject) grew from the same systems of logic and rhetoric. In other words, the same poetic principles underlay the work of a Spenser and a Donne; we must approach contemporaneous writers with broadly the same expectations.[4] To this proposition of fact,

----

[4] Rosemund Tuve, *Elizabethan and Metaphysical Imagery* (Chicago, 1947). I have found two articles along similar lines very useful: Elizabeth Lewis Wiggins, "Logic in the Poetry of John Donne," *Studies in Philology*, XLII (1945), 41–60; and Thomas O. Sloan, "The Rhetoric in the Poetry of John Donne," *Studies in English Literature*, III (1963), 31–44. The former is especially detailed and informative. It may be

others, notably the very subtle and cogent William Empson, have responded with a proposition of literary effect—that Spenser and Donne are palpably different in their poetic feel.[5]

Abstracting such central propositions from their entanglements in other arguments, we must, I think, admit that both sides are right on their own grounds and that they are talking at cross purposes. The Tuves think of the mental training and disposition to certain forms of expression in writers; the Empsons think of the very different effects of differing poets on readers. The question is how we can use both propositions to advance our understanding and appreciation of Metaphysical poetry, that entity quarreled over but lying, *Ding an sich*, between the propositions of the Tuves and the Empsons. It must be said at once that Spenser and Donne *are* different in poetic effect and, indeed, in their drive toward what is important in human experience. But I do not think that anyone has even really doubted that. I think it is also true, on the other hand, that most people who have read poetry carefully over that century and a half running from Spenser to

---

added that a recent book has, as it were, brought D. W. Robertson's Chaucerian views into Donne criticism; see *John Donne: Conservative Revolutionary* (Princeton, 1967), in which N. J. C. Andreasen argues that Elizabethan Christian morality must be taken to Donne's secular poems, so that there is a kind of comedy in which most of the lovers look idolatrous and foolish. My view is that criticism and literary history need a better balance between what can be discerned as views contemporary with the poet and as views relevant to the poem in terms of the experience of our own day.

[5] The most useful proponent of this view is William Empson: see "Donne and the Rhetorical Tradition," *Kenyon Review*, xi (1949), 571–87. One wishes that he had commented on the view of medieval Donne, as in John Hayward, ed., *John Donne* (London, 1929), p. xiii. Of yet another extreme view, Helen White commented in the right tone in *The Metaphysical Poets* (New York, 1936), p. 30: "So we find the strange vogue of John Donne as a 'modern,' an interpretation . . . that is likely to prove congenial enough at a time of confusion to last for some years more."

Dryden would agree that it is distinguished by its learning, and that to all the important poets ideas passionately mattered. As for Donne, many of his best critics have recognized that there is in his poetry an element variously characterized as scholastic or medieval, or represented in terms of philosophy, dialectic—or, indeed, as Dryden put it three centuries ago, "Metaphysicks." But it will be remembered that Dryden declared that Donne "affected" metaphysics, and it is true that to Spenser, Milton, or Dryden the ideas themselves mattered more in their poetry than they did in Donne's, whose poetry may be said to *concern* ideas. To him, the ideas were outward signs of inward states—or even, sometimes, sheer fun, as in the *Paradoxes and Problemes.* But as that work as well as the poems show, Donne calls upon the resources of his whole education, upon the seven arts of *trivium* and *quadrivium,* with certain religious and literary accessions as well.

The problem in approaching this large subject is that to study it we would need to become schoolboys again. I shall return at the end of this chapter to historical questions in order to seek to explain how such interests may have developed in Donne and to discriminate between those of his techniques that were put to work by subsequent Metaphysical poets on the one hand, and similar but basically different techniques employed by non-Metaphysical poets on the other. The concerns that one needs to set before himself, it seems to me (or at least what I find most workable), are certain poetic features of Metaphysical wit that will serve, in spirit if not in letter, to embody the propositions of the Tuves and the Empsons and the poems themselves. In other words, what we seek are features that stress the logical and rhetorical nature of Metaphysical poetry emphasized by Rosemund Tuve and others and that also enable us to explain the very distinct effect that William Empson properly discerned Met-

aphysical poetry to have. One such feature is certainly analogy. Argument or proof from analogy is notoriously the most
prone to error and the most natural to the mind, especially
if the mind is one composing poetry. Donne's arguments
from analogy are very thickly sown, and "The Flea" may
serve as one example among many. Another aspect of his use
of analogy is the employment of the simile. For some reason,
his very frequent use of this figure has never had the attention it deserves (probably because the simile, like allegory,
has had a bad press for some time), although Donne uses
it for precisely its distinctive feature, its directive force, a
feature in which it excels other figures. It should be evident
that a directive figure (like the simile employed in the opening stanza of "A Valediction forbidding mourning") has the
air of being more specific, of being logical, that is especially
useful to witty writers. Investigation would discriminate between numerous kinds of similes, from casual, simple examples on to extended, complex forms. We have learned in
another connection that "composition by similitude" is one
possibility in the formal religious meditation drawn upon by
Donne for his divine poems. This feature is enormously important, if for no other reason than that figurative language
is often so crucial to poetry. But I find myself unable to pursue it in this book, because I am unable to prove to my own
satisfaction that these techniques outlasted Donne in Metaphysical poetry. In this, Donne and Dryden resemble each
other more than they are resembled by Herbert and Marvell.
My purpose is, therefore, to explore two logical-or-rhetorical
techniques, of a simple kind, for the uses of criticism, even
as the poets had done for the uses of poetry. These techniques
may be called definition and dialectic.

Such a discussion can best begin with stress on one word
of Dr. Johnson's comment that in the wit of the Metaphysicals the most heterogenous *ideas* are yoked together by vio-

lence (the yoking will subsequently take us to definition, and the "violence" or steady force of thought to dialectic). I stress this because there is a peculiar idea abroad that Metaphysical poetry is somehow quintessentially witty (in a sense not true of other poets) for its imagery. But the distinction between air and angels in Donne's poem of that title is not primarily one imagistic at all, but intellectual. To be sure, that distinction is more the poetic basis than the poetic texture. But what of that poem, "Breake of day," which is especially interesting for its use of a woman as speaker?

> Must businesse thee from hence remove?
> Oh, that's the worst disease of love,
> The poore, the foule, the false, love can
> Admit, but not the busied man.
> He which hath businesse, and makes love, doth doe
> Such wrong, as when a maryed man doth wooe.
>
> $(13-18)$

There is hardly an image in six lines, and the simile at the end is without imagistic content. (No doubt one would have to consider a pun on "businesse"—affairs and sexual intercourse.) And yet the ideas sparkle as they move. So with Marvell:

> Therefore the Love which us doth bind,
> But Fate so enviously debarrs,
> Is the Conjunction of the Mind,
> And Opposition of the Stars.
>
> ("The Definition of Love," 29–32)

It may be that "bind" and "debarrs" are attenuated images, but it is the use of "Conjunction" and "Opposition" that carries the wit. What is necessary is, as these passages show, that the poem show that the ideas are in use, that a mind is demonstrably at work—or at play.

A close look at either of these examples suggests that a fundamental way in which the ideas work in Metaphysical poetry is through "definition," or "identification": the technique of saying of *x* that it means thus-and-so, sometimes that it is identical to *y*, and often by "dialectic" or argument that it means *a, b, c,* and therefore *d.* Business—"that's the worst disease of love"; our love "Is the Conjunction of the Mind, / And Opposition of the Stars." If our two souls "be two, they are two so / As stiffe twin compasses are two." Or, as Herbert asks in "Jordan (1)," "Is it no verse, except enchanted groves / And sudden arbours shadow course-spunne lines?" The examples are chosen to illustrate various processes of definition, to suggest the continual effort in Metaphysical poetry to make logical propositions, to make images define abstractions or abstractions images, to bring ideas to mean what they had not earlier meant (and hence produce wit), or to pursue identities between unlike things (the operation of Fancy in faculty psychology, and hence to produce conceits). Whether with ideas alone, with images, or with the two mixed, definition is the commonest Metaphysical way of making single and dual ideas work.

To the examples given may be added others in a descending order of obviousness as to the fact that they are poetic versions of definitions. One of Donne's familiar Holy Sonnets begins, "I am a little world made cunningly," a definition of man that is used more often in his poetry than any other, though seldom as explicitly as here. In another he begins, "What if this present were the worlds last night?" The grammatical mode has shifted from declarative to interrogative, but the thrill comes from acceptance of the definition. So far the examples have employed the copula, but other less obvious means are common. "Busie old foole, unruly Sunne" is undeniably witty, precisely because it defines the sun as a busy old fool. Yet it should be observed here, since it is typical of Donne, that the logical process is not mere statement or apposition substituting for the copula. If it were apposition alone, the "unruly," which plays so large a part, would need to belong syntactically and logically with the preceding phrase: busy old unruly fool, you sun. There has been a kind of leakage from one term of the definition to the other. Rather than proceed now into such complex examples or to multiply examples from Donne, however, it will be more helpful to establish the use of simple definition in longer examples and in a limiting case, from another poet, in order to go on to the more complex extension of definition into working dialectic.

A thoroughgoing use of strict, brief definition will be found in Herbert's sonnet, "Prayer (1)," from which the opening and close may be quoted:

> Prayer the Churches banquet, Angels age,
>> Gods breath in man returning to his birth,
>> The soul in paraphrase, heart in pilgrimage,
> The Christian plummet sounding heav'n and earth; . . .

> The milkie way, the bird of Paradise,
>> Church-bels beyond the starres heard, the souls bloud,
>> The land of spices; something understood.

There is not, of course, a finite verb in the poem. The logic implied is that prayer is $a, b, c, d, \ldots n$. The n is "something understood," one of those lovely simplicities of Herbert's complex mind and one which, in this case, is tantamount to saying what the absence of the verb has perhaps already implied: that in the end the full meaning of prayer cannot be defined. Definition is shown to be impossible only after its resources are fully exhausted. (Herbert's "H. Scriptures" and Vaughan's imitation with the same title are longer but less successful exercises in simple definition.) A partially similar technique of ransacking the resources of definition is to be found in Crashaw's much less successful, even ludicrous poem, "The Weeper":

> Hail, sister springs!
> Parents of sylver-footed rills!
> > Ever bubling things!
> > Thawing crystall! snowy hills,
> Still spending, neuer spent! I mean
> Thy fair eyes, sweet MAGDALENE!
>
> > O cheeks! Bedds of chast loves
> By your own showres seasonably dash't
> Eyes! nests of milky doves
> In your own wells decently washt,
> O wit of love! that thus could place
> Fountain & Garden in one face.   (1–6, 85–90)

No doubt we are tempted to respond in Herbert's terms, too little understood, and too much said. But the definition, the wit—exceeding the bounds of decorum—and in short the yoking together of heterogeneous ideas with violence is certainly there. The best source for a "limiting case"[6] to show the nature of definition in Metaphysical poetry is a poet whose verse is only partly in the Metaphysical line and whose most Metaphysical image is agreed upon. There may be argument whether Lovelace's "Grasse-hopper" is entirely a Metaphysical poem, but all have agreed that if there is anything in the poem answering to the name it is the well-known image, "Poore verdant foole! and now green Ice" (l. 17). A shift in the poem from summer to autumn and winter is of course involved, but the technique is the same kind of definition in apostrophe as in "Busie old foole, unruly Sunne."

---

[6] I take the term from J. B. Leishman, *The Monarch of Wit*, 6th ed. (London, 1962). Since I have found Leishman the most congenial of Donne's critics, I must add that he preferred "dialectical" and that he doubted that "Metaphysical" had any utility.

Anyone with the works of the Metaphysical poets on his shelf or in his memory can quickly multiply examples of the purer or simpler forms of definition. What the limiting case of Lovelace demonstrates is therefore of more immediate utility. It shows that the use of definition is more than characteristic; it is also a means of discriminating what we feel to be Metaphysical from what we feel to be different. (Analogous practices in earlier poets will be discussed later.) It gives a specific formulation of what we more commonly speak of in terms of the characteristic wit or imagery of this poetry by telling us of their logical, modal expression.

The use of definition in longer passages often involves varieties of figurative language because, as has been shown, definition is often the basis of witty Metaphysical imagery. The kind of figure involved may be the simile, the most explicit and directive form of imagery, as is shown by a passage Dr. Johnson found objectionable in Donne's elegy, "The Comparison":

> As the sweet sweat of Roses in a Still,
> As that which from chaf'd muskats pores doth trill,
> As the Almighty Balme of th'early East,
> Such are the sweat drops of my Mistris breast,
> And on her necke her skin such lustre sets,
> They seeme no sweat drops, but pearle carcanetts.
>
> (1–6)

The lover goes on in a similar vein to contrast with his girl's sweet perspiration that "sweaty froth [which] thy Mistresse's brow defiles." The effort is to define the differing character of the two mistresses in terms of their attractive or repulsive sweat, with the similes carrying the role of definition, and a logical extension of definition into "dialectic," as we shall see in a moment. Underlying the similes is a further tacit identification in synecdoche of the mistresses' totalities with their differing perspirations. In a somewhat similar fashion, the most famous Metaphysical metaphor of all begins as a simile and advances to a metaphor for "two soules therefore, which are one":

> If they be two, they are two so
>> As stiffe twin compasses are two,
> Thy soule the fixt foot, makes no show
>> To move, but doth, if the'other doe. . . .
>
>> (25 ff.)

In these and the next eight lines of "A Valediction forbidding mourning" the imagistic vehicle of the metaphor is seized upon and worked out in logical extension. If we are like "stiffe twin compasses," then the identity must extend to feet, motion, and activity. What is tentatively directed by the simile is thereafter assumed a proven identity.

Other kinds of figures that may be involved are shown by Vaughan's best known poem, "The World":

> I Saw Eternity the other night
> Like a great *Ring* of pure and endless light,
>> All calm, as it was bright,
> And round beneath it, Time in hours, days, years
>> Driv'n by the spheres
> Like a vast shadow mov'd.   (1–6)

Again we have the directive figure, the simile, defining two abstractions," Eternity" and "Time," as "light" and "shadow." The technique is more complicated of course, because the ring image is an emblem for eternity and the light image is a symbol, as the rest of the poem shows. Vaughan is quite capable of using the same symbol of light for eternity without definition: "They are all gone into the world of light!" And the result is a poem less strikingly Metaphysical.

The more emblematic poems of Donne and Herbert commonly set forth an image in the title and go on to define it in varying degrees of explicit connection, much after the manner of Herbert's "Prayer (1)" when most explicit, much more like the compass image in "A Valediction forbidding mourning" when less so. In poems like "The Blossome" and "The Primrose" Donne assumes the definition—that the heart is a blossom, for example—and proceeds to work out the implications of the unspecified definition. In "The Blossome" he begins, "Little think'st thou, poore flower," continuing to speak through the first stanza as if only with a blossom as subject but with enough conventional *sic vita* overtones to suggest that more is meant. The suggestions become very nearly explicit at the beginning of the second stanza, "Little think'st thou poore heart," with the rigorous rhetorical and even rhyme associations (cf. ll. 5 and 13, "bough . . . bow") to define implicitly the heart as the blossom. Thereafter Donne addresses the fated flower-heart, leaving the title to carry the force of the emblem. In "The Primrose," the emblematic image is worked out with greater detail and the use of definition is more thoroughgoing. Each assists in keeping the other in business, as the last stanza shows:

> Live Primrose then, and thrive
> With thy true number, five;
> And women, whom this flower doth represent,
> With this mysterious number be content;
> Ten is the farthest number; if halfe ten
> Belonge unto each woman, then
> Each woman may take halfe us men,
> Or if this will not serve their turne, Since all
> Numbers are odde, or even, and they fall
> First into this five, women may take us all.

From the identification of women in the flower emblem, Donne proceeds to the number of its petals and a complicated series of numerological definitions.

More truly and more frequently emblematic in his poetry, Herbert often works by positing in his title that which must be defined, more closely than does Donne, in the body of the poem. In a sense such shaped poems as "The Altar" and "Easter-wings" define the meanings of their titles partly by shape as well as by words, but the emblematic technique is more subtle and satisfying in such less formally emblematic works as "The Pulley" and "The Collar." Like the Jordan poems in their obscure way, "The Pulley" defines the image and idea of the title by working out a lyric narrative which in its totality defines the concept of the title, although without using (as Donne does) images which themselves explicitly define the title concept. God's creation of man, or such images as that of the glass of His blessings, or even the crucial concept of rest, have no overt defining connection whatsoever with the emblematic title:

> When God at first made man,
> Having a glasse of blessings standing by;
> Let us (said he) poure on him all we can:
> Let the worlds riches, which dispersed lie,
> Contract into a span.
>
> So strength first made a way;
> Then beautie flow'd, then wisdome, honour, pleasure:
> When almost all was out, God made a stay,
> Perceiving that alone of all his treasure
> Rest in the bottome lay.   (1–10)

It is the fourth stanza that shows how such varied ideas and images define the pulley emblem. God is speaking:

> Yet let him keep the rest,
> But keep them with repining restlesnesse:
> Let him be rich and wearie, that at least,
> If goodnesse leade him not, yet wearinesse
> May tosse him to my breast.   (16–20)

As is proper in an emblematic poem, only its totality defines the significance of the emblem, or "hieroglyph," which is in this case of course an image or concept expressed in the title rather than in a picture such as was favored by Francis Quarles. A somewhat comparable pulley emblem can be found in Quarles's *Emblemes*, Bk. I, emblem iv, but there is this difference in technique. Whereas Quarles and other emblem writers usually "read" or define the significance of each detail in the picture, Herbert chooses to define a single concept—"The Pulley"—by talking of nothing that has to do with pulleys. In one sense his is a species of witty yoking exceeding Donne's conceits in "violence." Moreover, what is true of the single emblematic poem in *The Temple* is true of the whole collection. As Louis L. Martz has shown in *The Poetry of Meditation*, the separate poems of *The Temple* are so ordered as to be integrated into a sequence based upon worship: the separate poems constitute in part a definition of the title of the collection. "The Collar" is as it were midway between the technique of "The Pulley" or of *The Temple* as a whole and the technique of Donne's emblematic poems, in that while keeping the whole poem as the proper definition of the emblematic title, Herbert uses as well a number of images conveying, however ironically, the sense of restraint implied by the title. The images of "lines" (l. 4), of "cage" (l. 21), or "rope of sands" (l. 22), of "Good cable" (l. 24), and of "tie up" (l. 29) which the speaker rejects in his rebellion are not precisely like Donne's sub-images in being subordinate features of the defining image but rather parallel imagistic equivalents for the collar of the title. Herbert is more given to the emblematic, Donne to the dialectical.

Although the origins and specific poetic features of Metaphysical dialectic will be discussed subsequently, something by way of introductory description is necessary here. Dialectic is a form of logical argument. In the sixteenth and seventeenth centuries there was a strong tendency in Protestant countries to accept the conflation of logic and rhetoric into dialectic that had been advocated by Peter Ramus (i.e., Pierre de La Ramée). Since poetry is not a species of either philosophy or oratory but its own species, it necessarily used logic and rhetoric to its own purposes, that is, more rigorously and purely as poetry, less rigorously and purely as logic or rhetoric. But men trained in the tradition of Quintilian and Aquinas or excited by Ramist dialectic were well able to use these arts in a speech like Hamlet's "To be, or not to be" soliloquy or in Antony's praise of Caesar in *Julius Caesar*. What is remarkable about Metaphysical poetry is that it brought to lyric poetry a dialectic that had been known before only in the more extended forms and, lyric poetry being what it is, that it used the dialectic in ways at once psychological and epistemological. In Metaphysical poetry, dialectic means most characteristically a motion of ideas toward determined ends in such a way that an air of logic is maintained in order to persuade. It can be seen that poetic dialectic is likely to be a logical or rhetorical process drawing upon definitions, analogies, similitudes, arguments, and "proofs." When definitions (or other logical resources) are employed—not singly or even in isolated and therefore static parallels—but in sequence and therefore in kinetic fashion, then we have the dialectic of Metaphysical poetry. It is this motion, this dialectical ordering and liveliness in the whole, that distinguishes the *use* of Metaphysical definitions from Petrarchan. We can readily grasp the process by looking at Donne's poem, "The Flea," and by somewhat simplifying its definitions for the sake of clarity:

> Marke but this flea, and marke in this,
> How little that which thou deny'st me is;
> It suck'd me first, and now sucks thee,

And in this flea, our two bloods mingled bee;
Thou know'st that this cannot be said
A sinne, nor shame, nor losse of maidenhead,
 Yet this enjoyes before it wooe,
 And pamper'd swells with one blood made of two,
 And this, alas, is more than wee would doe.

(A. *Negative Definition.* The Flea's enjoyment before wooing proves that our enjoyment before wooing would not
 be: sin, shame, or loss of virginity.)

Oh stay, three lives in one flea spare,
Where wee almost, yea more than maryed are.
This flea is you and I, and this
Our mariage bed, and mariage temple is;
Though parents grudge, and you, w'are met,
And cloysterd in these living walls of Jet.
 Though use make thee apt to kill mee,
 Let not to that, selfe murder added bee,
 And sacrilege, three sinnes in killing three.

(B. 1. *Postive Definition.* The Flea is: You, I, our marriage
  bed, and marriage temple.
 (2. *Definition Necessarily Following.* Given B. 1., to kill
  the Flea is to commit: suicide, murder, and sacrilege.)

Cruell and sodaine, hast thou since
Purpled thy naile, in blood of innocence?
Wherein could this flea guilty bee,
Except in that drop which it suckt from thee?
Yet thou triumph'st, and saist that thou
Find'st not thy selfe, nor mee the weaker now;
 'Tis true, then learne how false, feares bee;
 Just so much honor, when thou yeeld'st to mee,
 Will wast, as this flea's death tooke life from thee.

(C. 1. *Concession of Faultiness of B. 2. to prove A.* You
disprove B. 2. by killing the Flea, showing that to kill
it is not to destroy ourselves, etc.

  (2. Exactly. Therefore our enjoyment before wooing (A.)
is no less of honor.)

Donne's dialectic is complicated and amusing in equal
proportions. But his is not the only version. Herbert's "Jordan
(1)" offers another version of the dialectical process. Its three
stanzas are tissues of definitions, but those are so obvious as
not to need specification. Unlike Donne's, they have an appositive, static, repeated quality, and the actual logical movement (as the summary arguments supply) is much less para-
doxical:

> Who sayes that fictions onely and false hair
> Become a verse? Is there in truth no beautie?
> Is all good structure in a winding stair?
> May no lines passe, except they do their dutie
>   Not to a true, but painted chair?

(A. *Interrogative Definition 1.* Is poetry something served
only by falsehood, deviousness, and pretense?)

> Is it no verse, except enchanted groves
> And sudden arbours shadow course-spunne lines?
> Must purling streams refresh a lovers loves?
> Must all be vail'd, while he that reades, divines,
>   Catching the sense at two removes?

(B. *Interrogative Definition 2.* Is verse (a) only romantic
gilding of trivial and ill-treated subjects; or is it (b)
something obscure in obliqueness?)

> Shepherds are honest people; let them sing:
> Riddle who list, for me, and pull for Prime:

135

I envie no mans nightingale or spring;
Nor let them punish me with losse of rime,
    Who plainly say, *My God, My King.*

(C. 1. *Declared Definition.* Simple poets (like me) are
    honest.

  (2. *Concessive Definition.* I will allow fancy poets to be
    poets.

  (3. *Conclusive Definition.* But I am equally or more
    wholly a poet for speaking simple truth in simple
    ways.)

Such abstraction of the arguments of Donne's and Herbert's poems cannot substitute for the total poetic effect, but
study of the dialectic suggests something of the skeleton, if
not the fair flesh, of Metaphysical poetry. And an examination of the difference between Donne's degree of paradox
and air of proof and Herbert's laying down of axioms suggests much of the difference between the two poets.

The dialectical usage of definition can be followed in poem
after poem. A few less minutely pursued examples will serve
to show some alternative versions of the technique. Donne's
"Autumnall," on middle-aged beauty (often thought that of
a patroness, Magdalene Herbert), follows a very sinuous,
even tortuous, dialectical line, sometimes employing a definition as proof of a dialectical process involving subsidiary
definitions. That is the nature of the case in the following
passage, coming after praise of middle-aged, autumnal
beauty:

But name not *Winter-faces,* whose skin's slacke;
    Lanke, as an unthrifts purse; but a soules sacke;
Whose *Eyes* seeke light within, for all here's shade;
    Whose mouthes are holes, rather worne out, then made;
Whose every tooth to'aseverall place is gone,
    To vexe their soules at *Resurrection;*

Name not these living *Deaths-heads* unto mee,
  For these, not *Ancient,* but *Antique* be.   (37–44)

To the extent that wit involves the ingenious (as the Latin sense of that word may be taken to suggest), it is commonly found in Donne to be based on such logical hair-splitting, which is precisely a chop-logic over definition and an arguing (that is, rhetoric) presented as a reasoning process (that is, logic): a dialectic.

"Aire and Angels" provides a more serious example. Its dialectical distinctions are inherent in the definitions proffered by the first stanza, as a few lines show:

> Still when, to where thou wert, I came,
> Some lovely glorious nothing I did see,
>   But since, my soule, whose child love is,
> Takes limmes of flesh, and else could nothing doe,
>   More subtile then the parent is,
> Love must not be, but take a body too.   (5–10)

Both the use of definition and the dialectical motion are evident, but there is a larger dialectical process in the whole poem which becomes clear in the definitions of the last eight lines:

> For, nor in nothing, nor in things
> Extreme, and scattring bright, can love inhere;
>   Then as an Angell, face, and wings
> Of aire, not pure as it, yet pure doth weare,
>   So thy love may be my loves spheare;
>   Just such disparitie
> As is twixt Aire and Angells puritie,
> 'Twixt womens love, and mens will ever bee.   (21–28)

Although there has been debate over the conclusion, the common interpretation that "womens love" is defined as the "lovely glorious nothing" of "Aire" and of "mens" as the greater "Angells puritie" seems accurate. An initial recondite distinction between two things highly similar but different is employed to make the poem's slight but meaningful distinction between the loves of which the two sexes are capable. The poem marches through subordinate definitions to the climactic definitions of its last three lines.

Since Crashaw was given as an example of Metaphysical addiction to definition at its worst, it must in fairness be shown that he also uses it at its moving best. In his hymn, "In the Holy Nativity of Our Lord God" (that very unusual though not unique thing, a Metaphysical pastoral), Tityrus and Thyrsis seek to set forth the nature of one of the mysteries of the Church, the Incarnation, stressing the Nativity, as is usual with Catholic poets. The two shepherds disagree about the fitting circumstances for the great mystery, Tityrus arguing that decorum calls for a contention among the world's powers to render the birth glorious. Thyrsis replies that such rivalry is wide of the mark, defining God's love as expressed in the Incarnation in various images and coming to a final climax identifying love as itself.

> Proud world, said I; cease your contest
> And let the MIGHTY BABE alone.
> The Phaenix builds the Phaenix' nest.
> Love's architecture is his own.   (44–47)

There are few more beautiful, more sublime lines in Metaphysical poetry than the last. Its logic is akin to that of Herbert's "Prayer (1)," which concludes, after all, that prayer is "something understood." Ultimately, human power must fail in its attempt to define mysteries and can only affirm that Love's architecture is—its own.

Marvell's "Definition of Love," which acknowledges the technique in its title, does not employ definition extensively in the simple sense of positing a meaning for love. Rather,

like Donne in some poems, he chooses to develop a dialectical treatment of conceits and, like Herbert, he uses the
whole poem as a means, although without an emblematic
approach, to convey what the title promises. He begins by
defining in terms of the rhetorical "places" of origin and
ancestry:

> My Love is of a birth as rare
> As 'tis for object strange and high:
> It was begotten by despair
> Upon Impossibility.

He goes on (ll. 9–16) to speak of the fatedness of his love
and to explain (ll. 17–28) that fatality in astronomical, car-
tographical, and geometrical conceits, gradually becoming
more explicit in his use of definition:

> As Lines so Loves *oblique* may well
> Themselves in every Angle greet:
> But ours so truly Paralel,
> Though infinite can never meet.   (25–28)

The role of definition in the violent yoking together of the
Metaphysical conceit emerges very clearly in those lines, and
the last stanza gives us the formal definition promised by
the title:

> Therefore the Love which us doth bind,
> But Fate so enviously debarrs,
> Is the Conjunction of the Mind,
> And Opposition of the Stars.

What requires emphasis is the fact that the element of logic
and rhetoric—of wit—is something larger than the last
stanza. It is found in details of conceits, and it is subsumed by
the dialectical movement of the whole poem. Marvell's central aim is to define love, this love, as one by birth or origin

fated to perfection and frustration. The origin, the wondrous perfection, and the frustration alike are sometimes conveyed by defining images and sometimes by means not in themselves involving definition. To speak of Marvell's definition is, therefore, to speak of detail, of conclusion, and of a central conception worked out in dialectic. Both superficially and profoundly it rules the poem, and there is real significance in the fact that "The Definition of Love" has seemed to most readers Marvell's most Metaphysical poem because, for all its other important elements, it exemplifies in simple and complex ways the tendency to definition and dialectic in Metaphysical poetry from Donne forward.

The tendency expresses itself in various forms, revealing certain larger characteristics of this branch of seventeenth-century poetry. For one thing, the secular poems usually employ more startling definitions than do the religious. It is noteworthy that Dryden thought Donne affected the metaphysics too much in love poetry, and that Dr. Johnson's examples of Metaphysical passages are exclusively taken from secular poems.[7] Occasionally among the best poets, and usually in Crashaw, one may find exceptions, but religious subjects normally restrained ingenuity. They imposed a kind of decorum upon those witty poets. This tendency is only a tendency, but it finds its characteristic expression in Herbert, as his quietly beautiful "Vertue" shows. In it there is a sequence of definitions—of a sweet day, a sweet rose, a sweet spring, and a sweet and virtuous soul. The dialectic involves a double process. On the one hand it argues that sweet days

[7] A good deal may still be gleaned from Dr. Johnson's *Life* of Cowley, as I hope to show a bit later in this chapter. I may say here that, as far as his examples go, Johnson's "Metaphysical race" consists of Cowley (twenty-seven passages in the section characterizing the "race"), Donne (sixteen), and Cleveland (two); that no divine poems are included; that Cowley's poems quoted are chiefly from *The Mistress*; and that Donne's are chiefly those that Grosart termed "verse-letters" and "funeral elegies," in which the Metaphysical styles do not show to best advantage.

plus sweet roses equal (as it were) sweet spring, though virtue must be added to make a truly sweet soul. On the other hand it argues that the sweet day, sweet rose, and sweet spring are mortal, but that the sweet (definition: virtuous) soul lives chiefly when all else dies. The addition of virtue is, as the title suggests, the crucial and unifying element for the two arguments. Herbert's own sweetness or gentleness of manner is such that the dialectical processes are more readily felt than described:

> Sweet day, so cool, so calm, so bright,
> The bridall of the earth and skie:
> The dew shall weep thy fall to night;
> > For thou must die.
>
> Sweet rose, whose hue angrie and brave
> Bids the rash gazer wipe his eye:
> Thy root is ever in its grave,
> > And thou must die.
>
> Sweet spring, full of sweet dayes and roses,
> A box where sweets compacted lie;
> My musick shows ye have your closes,
> > And all must die.
>
> Onely a sweet and vertuous soul,
> Like season'd timber, never gives;
> But though the whole world turn to coal,
> > Then chiefly lives.

To say that there was less ingenuity in the religious poetry is not to say that there was little, and to say that because the process of definition in the religious poetry brought together less disparate things is not to say that it therefore altogether lacked a violence in yoking together. The identification of religious ardor with sexual ecstasy or violence in Crashaw and Donne is ample reminder. Yet even such identifications are mellowed by tradition, and it will usually be found that the yokings in religious verse have the sanction of tradition in one form or another.

If we take Donne at his most sublime, we can see this to be the case: "What if this present were the worlds last night?" The logic is that of hypothesis or question but the process is that of definition, and a thrilling one to anyone with the slightest eschatological interest. Yet the idea is itself familiar, and the beginning of a poem with such an equation of times is part of the meditational procedure of "composition of place," as Louis L. Martz has shown.[8] Other seemingly extreme yokings possess the sanction of the emblematic tradition, as Herbert's "Pulley" and "Collar" show. The secular poems, chiefly on love, had a freer decorum permitting such witty excursions as Donne's "Flea" and, perhaps more importantly, allowing poets to introduce into private experiences a full panoply of learning and "universal" experience. Death, the constitution of the universe, eternity, and religious mysteries were but a few of these larger subjects absorbed into the personal and secular. Such definition of the limited private experience in terms, so to speak, of unlimited public universals is in fact a chief resource of Metaphysical poetry.

Another important feature of definition in Metaphysical poetry is, as has been observed, its tendency to become dialectic. That is probably what Dryden meant by saying that Donne affected the metaphysics and Dr. Johnson by his term "scholastick." Some modern critics, notably J. B. Leishman, have chosen "dialectic" partly because they think it more accurate than "Metaphysical" as a label for the "Donne tradition," and partly because the alternative term, rhetoric, has had a mixed critical reception in our day. More fundamentally, critics have traditionally recognized that logical process and intellection prior to feeling are characteristics of

[8] *The Poetry of Meditation* (New Haven, 1954), pp. 27 ff.

the poetry. (Critics of the past few decades are exceptional in thinking that the thought and feeling are simultaneous.) What makes this so seems to be the fact that the normative definition in Metaphysical poetry is witty—it is slightly askew, oblique; it is usually after but not in the manner of strict definition. With his usual penetration, and not infrequent prejudice, Dr. Johnson got at the matter in relation to metaphor: "The fault of Cowley, and perhaps of all the writers of the metaphysical race, is that of pursuing thoughts to their last ramifications. . . . Thus all the power of description is destroyed by a scrupulous enumeration; and the force of metaphors is lost when the mind by the mention of particulars is turned more upon the original than the second sense, more upon that from which the illustration is drawn than that to which it is applied." [9]

In modern terms, the Metaphysical poets were more interested in the vehicles than in the tenors of their metaphors. What is especially acute in the judgment is its perception that the two elements of metaphor are held at once apart and together, with a pursuit of "thoughts to their last ramifications" often emerging from the tension. Or, in the terms of ideas as well as metaphor, definition often becomes dialectic because of the poets' exploration of the gap between that which is defined and that which defines it, with most attention being given to the latter. Basically, the identification resides in a conceit which, as its seventeenth-century meaning implies, is not necessarily imagistic.[10] But it does

[9] *The Lives of the English Poets*, ed. G. B. Hill, 3 vols. (London, 1905), I, 45.

[10] For example, see the last line of Donne, "The triple Foole," "Who are a little wise, the best fooles bee." The twentieth-century bias for images has too often obscured the logical and rhetorical pleasures of writers as different as Donne, Dryden, and Pope. (See also Leishman, *The Monarch of Wit*, pp. 201–202.) There are few more thrilling lines in Donne than the unimagistic "Nothing else is" of "The Sunne Rising."

define one element in terms of another which is different, often seemingly opposed. Sometimes the poet takes the defined elements in the conceit (whether imagistic or not) no further and simply passes on to another. But often a dialectical development follows, and it is convenient to distinguish two kinds of dialectic: extension and development. The extended definition is most familiar in the extended imagistic conceit, and that in Donne's compass image for parted lovers in "A Valediction forbidding mourning." Here, truly, the process is the pursuit Dr. Johnson recognized, to the last ramifications. Dialectical development, on the other hand, has the air of logical argument, of demonstration, of proof, either that the definition or other logical process is true or that some conclusion inevitably follows, or commonly both. Most of "Aire and Angels" functions to develop in "scholastick" terms the definitions of "womens love" with air and "mens" love with angels. Poems like *The Extasie*, "The Definition of Love," or "To his Coy Mistress" are far more complex in marshalling a highly involved dialectic with subordinate definitions towards a final proof. The ingenuity, or wit, is often prodigious, whether in the unextended definition, or the extended, or in the sustained dialectic, explaining why Dryden might term Donne "the greatest Wit, though not the best Poet of our Nation." The presence of such complexity is not open to dispute, however it be evaluated, so that its norms of working should claim our attention.

The norms can perhaps best be understood in terms of a further general observation on the characteristic processes of definition in Metaphysical poetry. In any event, it is convenient to distinguish between a procedure of assimilation of disparate elements in explicit or implicit definition—given the faculty psychology of the day, this is wit of fancy or imagination. There is also a discrimination of either similar or opposed elements—a wit of judgment or reason.[11] Assimilation, or "Fancy" wit, is an easily recognized procedure. The definition of lovers as saints in "The Canonization," of women's love with air or men's with angels in "Aire and Angels," or of many parallel images for "the merrie world" in Herbert's poem "The Quip" or in Vaughan's "The World" come at once to mind. But equally important in these very poems is a process of discrimination, of "Judgment" wit, since a definition must distinguish what something is not as well as what it is, and it often distinguishes between things apparently alike. Herbert and Vaughan distinguish the sinful world from sinless eternity or the resolved religious soul from created pleasure. The distinctions of "Aire and Angels" have already been sufficiently emphasized. "The Canonization" distinguishes between the love of the saints and the corrupt world of what Donne elsewhere calls (in a similar distinction) the laity, as also between the love of the saints in their golden age and that of lovers in inferior subsequent ages when invocation of those saints will be necessary. Marvell's "Definition of Love" and Donne's *Extasie* maintain a most difficult balance of assimilation and discrimination involving kinds of love or, in Donne's case, of bodies and souls, to the point of considerable disagreement among the poem's interpreters.

[11] My distinction between wit of Fancy and wit of Judgment is not, as far as I know, one made before the middle of the seventeenth century. In *Leviathan*, i, viii (1651), Hobbes remarks under the head of intellectual virtues and, in particular, wit, that "In a good poem, . . . both judgment and fancy are required." The year before, in his *Answer* to Davenant, Hobbes had remarked more specifically that "Judgment begets the strength and structure, and Fancy begets the ornaments of a poem" (*Critical Essays of the Seventeenth Century*, ed. J. E. Spingarn, 3 vols. [Bloomington, 1963], ii, 59). In the Account prefixed to *Annus Mirabilis* (1667), Dryden gives a more complex discussion of the relation of the faculties of the mind to literary composition.

For wit, as for other central features of Metaphysical poetry, Donne is the Grand Master of the race. He is the most often witty, and the most often profoundly witty. His poems most often depend upon wit for their impact, and they employ it most complexly. If I may summarize in the terms of this chapter, it is he who most forcefully uses definition and dialectic, the wit of Fancy and the wit of Judgment. Various as he is, however, his varieties are not infinite, and he did not preempt all the possibilities, as Marvell alone shows. Moreover, certain patterns are discernible in the wit of all the Metaphysical poets. Most of the witty definitions are examples of Fancy wit, of finding resemblances in ideas or things which are dissimilar or even quite different. Most examples of dialectic, on the other hand, are those using Judgment wit. Commonly the two processes are combined, definition to provide the initial surprise and shock of wit, dialectic to provide the witty structure or development of the poem. In *The Comparison*, we are astonished to find a lover defining his mistress in terms of her sweat, however sweet, and his acquaintance's mistress in terms of her sweat, however rank and frothy. But the poem is worked out by discriminations of the Judgment (i.e., reason) in differentiating between things apparently like: two sweaty mistresses. Similarly in "Aire and Angels," if we accept the usual reading, women and their love are defined as air, men and their love as angels. But the dialectic discriminates between these two insubstantial substances. Donne uses this combination frequently, and it is one on which much of his best wit depends. Sometimes, however, he and the other poets will use wit of Judgment briefly, locally, and wit of Fancy for extension. Negative definitions, such as we have seen in "The Flea" or in "Jordan (1)" show how skillfully the discriminations of Judgment might contribute to basic distinctions of poetic wit. As a counterpart, the extended conceit is a sustained flight

of Fancy wit in "pursuing thoughts to their last ramifications," as Dr. Johnson put it. Donne's compass image, Herbert's "Prayer (1)"—and, as the last chapter of this book will
show, preeminently Herbert's longish poem, *The Flower*—
sustain the central conceit to great lengths.

I am aware that this discussion has left, and no doubt too
far behind, the logic and rhetoric learned by Donne and the
other poets in their schools. Not Aristotle, nor Quintilian,
nor Aquinas—not even Ramus—reduced the arts to such
simplicities. In both the art of the closed fist of logic and
that of the open hand of rhetoric there was so much more
detailed concern and conceptualization. Figures and schemes,
colors and figures, syllogisms and enthymemes played roles
incomparably more complex and specific than those I have
assigned to definition and dialectic. It is possible that close
application of the famous dichotomies and hierarchies of
Peter Ramus would gloss poems like "Aire and Angels" in
minute detail. But, equally, I doubt the meaningfulness of
such glossing to readers in this century. The important thing
is rather to understand the principle: the poets used the arts
of logic and rhetoric as poets had not used them before, to
witty ends; but they also used them as the logicians and
rhetoricians did not, namely as poets. As Dryden said of
Donne, these poets "affect the Metaphysicks"; they seize
the principles, sometimes the techniques, and usually the air
of logic and rhetoric for their properly poetic ends. What is
witty about such ends is, in Dr. Johnson's term, "violence,"
or surprise, brillance, and a rigor of thought unusual in lyric
poetry. When Donne, for example, fancifully defines *a* as *b*,
we are surprised and pleased. When he also fancifully defines
c as *d* we are further astonished and pleased. And then,
when *a* and *c*, and also *b* and *d*, turn out to be so like that
the Judgment is required dialectically to distinguish and
argue the differences in the terms of each pair, we are yet

further astonished and pleased. That is the process and the effect of "Aire and Angels." Herbert's approach in "Prayer (1)" is different, but it too can be represented as it were algebraically. Prayer turns out to be defined as a and a^1 and a^2 and a^3 and a^4—and so on in a breathtaking sequence. I am not offering algebra (certainly not my algebra!) as a substitute for logic and rhetoric, much less for poetry. But I am certain that both the sudden and sometimes sustained identifications of what had seemed different and the brilliant discriminations or developments of what had seemed alike or simple provide the processes of Metaphysical poetry that may most readily explain to us today the nature of Metaphysical wit. Some poems possess little of these techniques, but they will also be found to possess little wit and are usually those which cause the most embarrassment to anyone seeking to define Metaphysical poetry. Donne's "Song"—"Sweetest love, I do not goe"—is an example. Of such a poem one can only say that it lacks some features we commonly associate with Metaphysical poetry, but that it retains others (e.g., the private mode, drama). The exceptions in Donne's case are partial, in another poet like Cowley so important as to lead us to say that the degree justifies our placing the poem in another line. The best Metaphysical poems, however, and those which therefore we like to think as characteristic of the race, vary in their wit without becoming less witty in their essences. Sometimes the approach is simple, as in Herbert's "Prayer (1)," and sometimes it is mixed and very complex, as in Donne's "A Valediction forbidding mourning." The example of Traherne is probably sufficient to show that if it was not necessary for a poem to be witty to be Metaphysical, it was necessary to be witty to be a great Metaphysical poet.

Such generalizations imply that definition and dialectic in their various forms are so important to Metaphysical poetry that they must have grown from real experience and from familiar ways of thought. The lack of real experience or any felt necessity to think in dialectical terms vitiates the Metaphysical poems of even such talented men as Cleveland and Cowley. Donne is another matter, and for him there is relatively abundant information early and late. A few sentences from "A Defence of Womens Inconstancy" in *Paradoxes and Problemes* will suffice to show that ingenious definition is as much a part of his prose thinking as his poetic:

> *Inconstancy* is a most commendable and cleanly quality . . .

> For as *Philosophy* teacheth us, that *Light things do always tend upwards*, and *heavy things decline downward*; Experience teacheth us otherwise, that the disposition of a *Light* Woman, is to fall down, the nature of women being contrary to all Art and Nature.

> To conclude therefore; this name of *Inconstancy*, which hath so much been poysoned with slanders, ought to be changed into *variety*, for the which the world is so delightfull, *and a Woman for that the most delightfull thing in the World.*[12]

The second quotation shows in addition that Donne imbibed the importance of definition, as well as many definitions themselves, from "Philosophy," as he and Dryden put it, from Dr. Johnson's "Scholastick" tradition, chiefly of Aristotle and accretions upon his method. As Donne himself says by way of justifying his numerous citations in that definition-riddled work, *Biathanatos*, "I did it the rather because scholastique and artificiall men use this way of instructing." [13] The definitions of ends, causes, and the rest, like the logical

[12] John Hayward, ed., *John Donne . . . Complete Poetry and Selected Prose*, 4th impression (London, 1946), pp. 336, and 337.
[13] Hayward, ed., pp. 424–25.

dialectic supporting them, were part of men's training in the old philosophy. And if at some moments the new philosophy seemed to call all in doubt for Donne, it was perhaps as much because of the alteration from familiar modes of thinking as because of a change in particulars of thought.

A related origin in Donne's background is the dialectic of logic and rhetoric, which had been clearly distinguished in antiquity and the middle ages but which were often confused in the Renaissance.[14] Certainly they tend to merge and even to become something other than themselves when they are made into a poetic argument or, as Leishman rightly put it, into dialectic. Once these necessary things are said, it remains true that Donne was aware that he had learned his ways of expression out of the books of the rhetoricians and logicians. In "An Essay on Valour" he says: "indeed it is cunning Rhetoricke to perswade the hearers that they are that already, which he would have them to be." [15] In its context the passage is itself "cunning Rhetoricke," and its witty awareness of definition is explicitly related to rhetoric. Donne had not been at Hart Hall and Lincoln's Inn to no purpose. If the expressive forms of logic and rhetoric, their rules and distinctions, seem sterile and overwrought today, they were absorbed as a system and made an integral part of the traditional ideas which their traditional modes expressed. In no area is this as true as in religion, and it is probably the logical and rhetorical procedures of theological writing that affected Donne most deeply. When Dr. Johnson spoke of the "scholastick" element in Donne, he was no doubt thinking gen-

---

[14] See Wilbur Samuel Howell, *Logic and Rhetoric in England, 1500–1700* (Princeton, 1956), especially Chaps. IV and V. In spite of his frequent dichotomies and his striking use of "invention," Donne seems to me to exhibit not Ramist but traditional thought, modified no doubt by the contemporary confusion between logic and rhetoric occasioned by Ramus and by his own needs as a poet.

[15] Hayward, ed., p. 418.

erally of the Aristotelian methods of Aquinas and his followers, in which "Philosophy," dialectic, and doctrine are
equally involved. The "Questions" of Aquinas and the "Problemes" of Donne are far apart in time and tone, but their
methods are very like.

The problem of definition and of meaning, both in particular words and in modes, was of course peculiarly acute in
the post-Reformation period. The Bible required interpretation, whether by Church, bishop, or inner light. Controversies
over modes of meaning and over the definition of crucial
words and phrases occupied the best minds of the day to a
far greater extent than did the problems of science. To
Donne, born a Catholic in a Protestant country of rival
Establishment and reform factions, the crisis of conscience
was in no small measure a question of defining religion aright,
as a few quotations from *Satyre III* reveal:

Is not our Mistresse[,] faire Religion . . .   (5)

Seeke true religion. O Where?   (43)

                doubt wisely; in strange way
To stand inquiring right, is not to stray.   (77-78)

That thou mayest rightly'obey power, her bounds know;
Those past, her nature, 'and name is chang'd; to be
Then humble to her is idolatrie.   (100-102)

Defining religion aright itself involves definition, as the last
two quotations make especially clear, because religion in its
civil "power" must be distinguished in its proper degree,
beyond which submission to the civil powers of religion is,
as Donne defines it, "idolatrie." The tendencies raised by
the general religious problem were enforced by the religious
genre most familiar to an Englishman: the sermon. Exposi-
tion of the text by definitions and paraphrase was not new,
but it became more crucial—as Donne's own sermons were

to show—in an age of conflicting religious systems and of crises of conscience in the necessity of choice between them. If "Philosophy" and "Rhetoricke" helped form the dialectical character of a good deal of Donne's poetry, religion made it natural and inevitable.

In addition to these nonliterary sources of ways of thought and expression, earlier Renaissance poetry was greatly influential upon the Metaphysical. Donne's poetry is often said to be anti-Petrarchan, which is true enough, although it is commonly not realized how different his anti-Petrarchan stance is from an un-Petrarchan, as the love poetry of, say, Prior would show. The poetry that developed in England out of the Petrarchanisms of Wyatt and Surrey is the trunk from which Donne's fruitful and unusual branch grows. The similarity of the offshoot to the parent is so marked that the task is not so much to show that the two shared conceits, definitions, or conventions as to discriminate between them.[16] Wyatt's familiar sonnet, "The lover compareth his state to a ship in perilous storm tossed on the sea," is an extension of parallel marine conceits for the lover's tortured state. The

---

[16] In what immediately follows, the discussion will again focus upon the way in which definition is basic to the conceit, whether that of Wyatt or of Donne. To some readers it may seem that definition is in a sense basic to all poetic metaphor and that it is therefore no surprise to find Donne and his followers using it. To this I would rejoin two things. First, that my use of the term implies verbal, syntactic, or dialectical processes of defining in the poem, not just in metaphor as an entity. Second, against the examples I give of definitions in poets before and after Donne may be placed the great bulk of familiar English poems. Anyone inspecting as a rude test the beginnings of *The Canterbury Tales, The Faerie Queene, Paradise Lost, The Rape of the Lock, The Prelude,* and other major works characteristic of other styles will find that what is common and characteristic in the Metaphysical poets is rare in the others. Of all important poets outside the Metaphysicals, Dryden probably approaches them more nearly in this, as indeed in certain other respects.

conceits are, in fact, a series of definitions, with related psychological phenomena being given definition by related marine phenomena—"And every oar a thought in readiness," for example.

The resemblance between Petrarchan and Metaphysical poetry in this respect is clear, but there are three important differences. To begin with, definition is more characteristic of the later poets because it is more frequent and because it is a norm (as are also such other features as use of the private mode) in their kind of poetry. More importantly, Metaphysical definitions usually employ a dialectic relating and directing definitions and other logical features to a rhetorical end and a greater continued violence in their yoking of elements. This is true not so much because the yoked ideas of the Metaphysicals are more heterogeneous but because, as Dr. Johnson observed in his way, the Metaphysicals pursued the vehicle of the metaphor at the seeming expense of the tenor—what was defined commonly seemed to be lost sight of in the pleasure of defining:

> Call us what you will, wee'are made such by love;
>   Call her one, mee another flye,
> We'are Tapers too, and at our owne cost die,
>   And wee in us finde the'Eagle and the dove;
>   The Phoenix ridle hath more wit
>   By us, we two being one, are it.

In this famous and much analyzed passage (ll. 19–24) of "The Canonization," Donne comes close to the parallel development of conceit found in Wyatt and other earlier writers. It would be hard to say that his insects or birds are much more violently yoked to their ideas than Wyatt's marine images are to theirs. The significant difference is that the vehicles of Donne's images lead him on, both for their

153

own sake and for a dialectic, and that in his usual way he begins with an imperative (sometimes an interrogative) version of definition and only ends with a declarative.

The third difference grows from the second.[17] Metaphysical definitions have more movement. Those of the Petrarchans appear to have been worked out in advance or to be static for such other reasons as that their conventional nature stirs little energy. The Metaphysical process possesses more movement because of the rapidity with which differing conceits are introduced, or because of the dialectical development of related images, or both. The earlier style lasted on, retaining its workability and beauty, as the last stanza of "Her Triumph" in Jonson's *Celebration of Charis* shows:

> Have you seene but a bright Lillie grow,
>   Before rude hands have touch'd it?
> Ha'you mark'd but the fall o'the snow
>   Before the soyle hath smutch'd it?
> Ha'you felt the wooll o'the Bever?
>   Or Swans Downe ever?
> Or have smelt o'the bud o'the Brier?
>   Or the Nard in the fire?
> Or have tasted the bag of the Bee?
> O so white! O so soft! O so sweet is she!

The movement towards the concluding definitions has something of the quality of Metaphysical dialectic, but the vigorous syntactic and verbal parallelisms of every other line are essentially static in effect. Moreover, as Dr. Johnson would have put it, the definitions stress the importance of the

---

[17] I am aware of numerous other differences—as for example that between the social and private worlds of the two poetic lines—but these lie outside my purpose here. I should also add that I am aware of what has been claimed for Donne's continental sources by Mario Praz and others but that, without wishing to debate them, I simply wish to insist upon the importance of native development.

secondary sense more than the original (as in that "bag of the Bee"), emphasizing the tenor more than the vehicle, which is for the most part of a more acceptably "poetic" kind. Yet the area of Jonson's choice of imagery resembles Donne's in the passage quoted from "The Canonization." It is the handling that differs. The explanation of literary and other causes that might account for such differences in handling is very difficult to discern in the last decade of the sixteenth century, when there was such a remarkable swelling of poetic achievement in numerous styles and when the circulation of manuscripts or of tides of influence is most difficult to distinguish. About all that can be said is that in their differing ways Shakespeare and Sidney in their sonnets, like Ralegh, Fulke Greville, and Donne in other lyric forms, brought, at about the same time, a greater intellectuality into poetry and that Donne carried the development furthest in terms of wit and witty handling of imagery. Sidney, Fulke Greville, and Ralegh make use of greater intellectual reasoning than earlier poets, and without recourse to definitions that are at once clear and striking in their pursuit of the vehicles. They lack Donne's commitment to Dr. Johnson's secondary sense. Shakespeare must be distinguished on other grounds. He often uses definitions, most strikingly perhaps in Sonnet 129: "Th' expense of spirit in a waste of shame / Is lust in action. . . ." What differentiates such definitions from Donne's is simply what Dr. Johnson would term their naturalness and justice. The primary and secondary senses are at one with each other and the experience created. In the terms introduced earlier, his definitions assimilate, but their terms are elements very like, or made to seem very like; and within a given pattern of definition, as in Sonnet 129, the discrimination is intellectual and moral rather than radically witty. The fact that Shakespeare does not strike us as an essentially witty writer suggests in part that his use of definition, striking images, and a dialectic of ideas has a naturalness, a justice in the yoking that sets him off from the Metaphysical poets.

The balance, the sanity, and the justice of Shakespeare's use of words and ideas assist, however, in the major literary miracle of the language, and it will not do merely to compare the Metaphysical poets unfavorably to him. To do so would be merely to repeat T. S. Eliot's mistake in a new guise by attributing a dissociation of sensibility to Donne instead of to Milton and Dryden, as Eliot did, in a projection of his own post-eighteenth-century difficulties in ordering his world. It may well be true, as Dr. Johnson said, that the wit of the Metaphysical poets errs in some austere sense by overemphasis upon the primary sense of images, on the vehicle, rather than on the secondary sense, or tenor. By the same austere standard, poets from Dryden to Dr. Johnson himself increasingly err on the other side by emphasizing the secondary sense, the tenor, the tulipness rather than the streaks of the tulip. Each emphasis implies a conception of poetry, a type of intellectuality, and a special embodiment of feeling. In the best (which is not all) of Shakespeare and, I believe, in the best of such other authors as Chaucer and Dickens, a steadier balance is maintained. But the lack of balance of this kind is not in itself a sign of dissociation of sensibility or of an impairment of poetry. The wit of the Metaphysical poets may indeed explore, as Dr. Johnson had it, the primary sense of images to their last witty ramification. But it is an exploration to the end of understanding the secondary sense, of arriving at a view of life. Such themes will be touched on in the next chapter, but it may be said at once that the wit of a Donne is far from precluding feeling or a sense of wholeness of experience within his definition of his world.

The wit of Dryden sometimes (and the wit of Johnson nearly always) offers a counterpart to the wit of Donne by seeming to withhold the primary sense in favor of the secondary. *Absalom and Achitophel* steadily keeps the evaluative biblical story in view, but a man would be certifiably mad to think that it has no particular personal relevance to Dryden or to his time. Similarly, *The Vanity of Human Wishes* plays off the tenor, Johnson's age, and a suppressed vehicle or primary sense, Juvenal's Rome. Any careful reader of the two poems will see how far Dr. Johnson's somber, dignified, and Christian stoicism differs from the explosive, vehement anger of Juvenal. It is in some sense true, then, that such masters of their styles, such influential creators of visions of experience for their age as Donne and Dryden, are witty precisely for emphasis upon opposed literary features. But it is equally true that they are masters of their styles, and that their styles are significant, because the emphasis and the withholdings in each case are witty, not because what is suppressed is not there, but precisely because, being suppressed, it may be released with a more bounding energy.

The suppressive forces vary somewhat between Donne and Dryden and yet more between Donne and eighteenth-century poets. For Donne and the others of the Metaphysical race, that force is a wit embodying logical and rhetorical procedures in poetic adaptation. What is suppressed varies considerably, because the private world of the Metaphysicals differs so much from the public world of Dryden and of the Augustans. The wit is, after all, closely related to the worlds of experience created in their poetry, and Donne as well as Dryden outlined for two generations or more the worlds that they and their followers might explore. Their important followers are followers in the sense that they accept the essential terms of their wit and the means of conveying a view of life. And the followers are important in the sense that they modify the revealing wit and the revealed experience in ways undeniably their own. Cleveland is often so poor a Metaphysical poet precisely because his wit is unrevealing, because (in his Metaphysical poems) he has expressed chiefly language and images, and far less ideas or a view of life. No sensibility and no image in itself could make up for the fact that his conception of life, in such poems, sometimes borders on the trivial.

There is sufficient evidence to show that Donne had his predecessors or, in any event, his contemporaries who were, like him, busy devising styles at variance from the received. In particular it may be recalled that Jonson and Donne have between them poems whose authorship has long been disputed. But to his contemporaries as well as to us, it was to Donne that might be attributed the role of fashioning an armory of techniques for private poetry that was to be useful for five or six decades and thereafter was to be employed at times by Dryden and even by Pope. The resemblances between Donne, Cowley, Jonson, and Dryden—in some of their poems—are ample reminder that concern with definition and dialectic has limits in assisting our understanding of the particular nature of Metaphysical poetry. But this concern, I hope, offers some advance over consideration of wit purely in terms of the imagistic conceit. The point is not that Metaphysical poetry is comprised of definition and dialectic any more than Tudor poetry consists of Petrarchanism or Restoration poetry of satire. All are merely features of some prominence among others. One may say with strict accuracy, however, that the poetry most commonly thought to be Metaphysical does use a dialectical process giving a motion to ideas, and in that motion resides the wit of the poetry. And it may be added, in both the historical and the descriptive senses, that it was Donne who gave definition to much of the poetry of the seventeenth century.

IV

THEMES: SATIRE AND SONG

Thus strangely will our difference agree,
And, with our selves, amaze the world, to see
How both Revenge and Sympathy consent.

— King

To MANY people Metaphysical poetry provides the finest English example of lyric poetry, at least of that kind of lyricism in which passion is articulated by thought. To this element of articulate feeling, of lyric affirmation, must, however, be added a very nearly contrary element of dialectical wit, of satiric antagonism, of a multiple and commonly ironic consciousness. Very little need be said to define the quality of Metaphysical lyricism, since it is so widely accepted. But since satire is less often associated with the Metaphysical race, it may be said at once that "satire" is meant both in the strict sense of poems that are satires in whole or in part and in the sense of satiric attitudes influencing poems that are not primarily satiric. To take Dryden as an example, we may speak of satire in the strict sense in relation to *MacFlecknoe* and *The Medall,* and in the tonal sense in relation to *Absalom and Achitophel* and *The Hind and the Panther,* which are not (to my mind) satiric in genre but satiric in a significant part of their outlook. In less obvious (or familiar) ways, satiric denial functions with lyric affirmation as a polar charge in Metaphysical poetry. In what follows, I shall try to present a simple proposition concerning "satire and song" in Donne, and then refine it and extend it to later poets.

The factor of greatest importance to the admission of satiric energy in Metaphysical poetry was that of most signif-

159

icance for lyricism: its private nature. The lyric affirmation of private integrity, of the joy of lovers' nights, or of the soul's traffic with God implied the inferiority of all else; therefore, that which was not public but private, that which questioned intimate love with the world's "businesse," or that which was ritual rather than experience in religion was so inferior or such a threat as to require resistance. In reacting in such ways, these private poets presented the obverse of Dryden in his public poems. To him, what men shared was important, what each held privately was eccentric; the business of the world was threatened by private indulgence, and what was merely individual in religion was dangerous. The fact that Donne could also write social, and Dryden personal, poems manifests the fact that although each made a different characteristic choice, each also to some degree comprehended the choice of the other.

More simply, the finest Metaphysical poets are given to turning from what they affirm and from what impels them to song to what they cannot abide, to what threatens their values and must therefore be denied. Such consciousness of the other side to things, of what others probably wrongly think, and indeed of oneself, is shot through Metaphysical poetry. The ironic habit of mind commonly attributed to the poets is founded upon a self-consciousness combined with a consciousness of that outside the self, upon a dissatisfied perception of the world with a remarkable degree of apperception. Most of the best-known Metaphysical poems are therefore poems of a double energy: of lyric affirmation and satiric denial. Donne often turns smartly upon the customary world with exasperation in order to justify a private world:

> For Godsake hold your tongue, and let me love,
> > Or chide my palsie, or my gout,
> My five gray haires, or ruin'd fortune flout,

With wealth your state, your minde with Arts improve,
   Take you a course, get you a place,
   Observe his honour, or his grace,
Or the Kings reall, or his stamped face
   Contemplate, what you will, approve,
   So you will let me love.

               ("The Canonization," 1–9)

The satiric energy is precisely what gives life and spice to such poems. The energy springs from self-consciousness and even defensiveness ("My five gray haires, or ruin'd fortune"), revealing a significant consciousness of the public world and one's relation to it.

Wit of course assists in providing the poets with their satiric force. It is unnecessary to go the whole way with Freud and hold that wit is necessarily inspired by antagonism, but there is no question that with the self-consciousness and with the pursuit of dialectic as an end in itself, the wit often does take on satiric overtones. Another of Donne's familiar poems, his "Song" ("Goe, and Catche a falling starre"), provides a convenient example. Suppose it after all possible to find one woman "true, and faire":

If thou findst one, let me know,
   Such a Pilgrimage were sweet,
Yet doe not, I would not goe,
   Though at next doore we might meet,
Though shee were true, when you met her,
And last, till you write your letter,
      Yet shee
      Will bee
False, ere I come, to two, or three.   (19–27)

Of course the satiric element in this "Song" is very much qualified by the humorous lyric self-approval. The tones *are* mingled, lyric *and* satiric. The "Song's" familiarity may dull our sense of the satiric, but the tone is recognizable on moderately careful reading, and at once in less familiar poems:

> Can men more injure women then to say
> They love them for that, by which they're not they?
> Makes virtue woman? must I cool my bloud
> Till I both be, and find one wise and good?
> May barren Angels love so . . .
>
> ("Loves Progress," 19–23)

Much that is affirmative appears in Metaphysical wit, not to mention in its other poetic elements, and very often the poets finely mingle the positive and the negative. Only a few poems may be called simply or purely satiric. But a very large number of poems possesses an astringency of wit, incursions and minglings of satire. It is very noticeable that the quality of most Metaphysical poetry depends as much upon its potential for satiric antagonism as for lyric affirmation. Herbert shows as much positively in religious poetry; Crashaw shows negatively the risks of unqualified affirmation; and Traherne shows how quickly a pall of dullness came when the satiric brightness had been forgot.

Satire possesses as well a major historical place in Metaphysical poetry. It was in satire that Donne, with Hall and Marston, nursed Metaphysical poetry and in satire that Marvell ended it. Poets in between (and Donne and Marvell as well) gave satire a role, not alone in poems called satires, but in avowed hymns, songs, and meditations. Just as those lyrics have satiric infusions, so notably do the satires at times (though less often) turn lyric and affirmative:

> Is not our Mistresse faire Religion,
> As worthy'of all our Soules devotion,
> As vertue was to the first blinded age?
> Are not heavens joyes as valiant to asswage
> Lusts, as earths honour was to them?
>
> (Donne, *Satyre III*, 5–9)

Even in *Satyre* V ("Thou shalt not laugh in this leafe, Muse"), we find one of Donne's favorite satiric images, of flood, given an attractive guise:

Alas, no more then Thames calme head doth know
Whose meades her armes drowne, or whose corne o'rflow.
(29–30)

A yet better instance may be found in a poem usually thought Marvell's, *The last Instructions to a Painter*, in which the merciless satire yields to a lyrical description of the Dutch admiral de Ruyter's invasion of the Thames and Medway (523–60) and again to a touching eulogy of Archibald Douglas (649–96).[1] The examples show that lyricism may be combined with satire, as well as the reverse, though the combination of satire with lyricism is much more frequent. It is also true that the satiric force is weaker in the second generation of Metaphysical poets (especially Crashaw, but also Herbert) than it is in the first (Donne) and third (e.g., Cowley, Vaughan, Marvell). The differences may be put another way. Satire grows weaker, though it does not disappear, in religious poetry and is stronger of course in secular. In his best poems, Crashaw is much the least satiric of the best Metaphysical poets; in their best poems Donne and Marvell are most.

Donne's satiric preoccupation shows itself most evidently of course in his satires. They share with the satires of Joseph Hall and John Marston an irrepressible outburst against the world and a ragged, hard-hitting style. But they also exhibit

---

[1] The passages referred to in *The last Instructions* will be dealt with in more detail later in the chapter to help discriminate Marvell's attitudes from those of other Metaphysical poets. This is a good place to note that after this chapter was written I found, and not for the first time, upon rereading Dame Helen Gardner's edition of the *Elegies and Songs and Sonnets* that she had been over ground before me. Having worked out in my mind Metaphysical tendencies I characterize as satire and song, I was taken up short to read (p. xliv) of "the satiric edge that [Donne] gives to even his gayest songs."

a greater capacity to create the detail of a bustling, corrupt scene and the presence of an outraged satiric observer. Donne excels because he is a finer formal satirist,[2] but just as his individual observer tells us something of his capacity for dramatic effects, so his telling detail suggests a failed lyricism. The development of a passage on the constantly talking lawyer in *Satyre II* will show how these elements work:

> And to'every suitor lye in every thing,
> Like a Kings favourite, yea like a King;
> Like a wedge in a blocke, wring to the barre,
> Bearing like Asses, and more shamelesse farre
> Then carted whores, lye, to the grave Judge; for
> Bastardy'abounds not in Kings titles, nor
> Symonie'and Sodomy in Churchmens lives,
> As these things do in him; by these he thrives.
> Shortly' (as the sea) hee'will compasse all our land;
> From Scots, to Wight; from Mount, to Dover strand.
>
> (69–78)

What seems at the outset a conventional satire of a conventional satiric victim, the lawyer, turns by clever use of that more directive figure, the simile, to a condemnation of a considerable sweep of creatures: courtiers, kings, asses, whores, kings again, and divines. The inviolability of clergy and the *arcana imperii* are rent away like flimsy veils to reveal an ugliness beneath. It would be difficult to exaggerate the daring and the subversive innuendo that the court of Elizabeth I would associate with the attribution of bastardy to king's titles. In other words, the force behind the lines is

---

[2] On the characteristics of Roman formal verse satire, see Mary Claire Randolph, "The Structural Design of Formal Verse Satire," *Philological Quarterly*, xxi (1942), 368–84, the most influential essay. See also Maynard Mack, "The Muse of Satire," *Yale Review*, xli (1951–52), 80–92; and Alvin Kernan, *The Cankered Muse* (New Haven, 1959), Yale Studies in English, vol. 142, who has a good deal to say about Donne.

enormous, and it generates in outrage and hatred. Surprisingly, the end of the passage, with its image of the sea in flood, does not bring the nausea that it might, but a lyricism manquée. Often Donne's satire deals not with things merely evils in themselves but perversions of good. Given the value that he attributed to love, or that it has to any normal person, he is able to expand upon a mere hatred of what is good:

> Why should'st thou that dost not onely approve,
> But in ranke itchie lust, desire, and love
> The nakednesse and barenesse to enjoy,
> Of thy plumpe muddy whore, or prostitute boy
> Hate vertue, though shee be naked, and bare.
> (*Satyre I*, 37–41)

The perversion of values and the universality of threat carry farther still, even entering into the private world of the speaker:

> At home in wholesome solitarinesse
> My precious soule began, the wretchednesse
> Of suiters at court to mourne, and a trance
> Like his, who dreamt he saw hell, did advance
> It selfe on mee.
> (*Satyre IV*, 155–59)

The prime refuge of lyric affirmation, the private self, is perverted into nightmare.

Donne's elegies moderate the evil but possess a strong element of satire. The tendency for detail to be lyrical and affirmative emerges more strongly in a properly positive than a perverted sense. There are at least alternatives to what is wrong—I may compare my mistress to thine in "The Comparison":

> Like Proserpines white beauty-keeping chest,
> Or Joves best fortunes urne, is her faire brest.
> Thine's like worme eaten trunkes, cloth'd in seals skin,

Or grave, that's dust without, and stinke within . . .
Are not your kisses then as filthy, 'and more,
As a worme sucking an invenom'd sore?
Doth not thy fearefull hand in feeling quake,
As one which gath'ring flowers, still feares a snake?
Is not your last act harsh, and violent,
As when a Plough a stony ground doth rent?

(23–26, 43–48)

The "comparison" is precisely between what may be lyrically
affirmed and what must be satirically denied. Donne goes
further throughout "The Anagram" and in a passage like
the following from *Loves Progress*:

Rich Nature hath in women wisely made
Two purses, and their mouths aversely laid:
They then, which to the lower tribute owe,
That way which that Exchequer looks, must go:
He which doth not, his error is as great,
As who by Clyster gave the Stomach meat.

(91–96)

That is of course a joke, but it is a coarse, cynical, and arro-
gant joke dehumanizing women by representing them by but
one part of the body and that in relation to far from appealing bodily incursions. Yet it is typical that such deliberately
outrageous talk should be put in unusually rhythmical lines.
All the elegies but one, "The Autumnall," show such antagonism to any romantic or ideal conception of love, and "The
Autumnall" is so far-fetched as to carry conviction only of its
own wit. Much must indeed be allowed to these elegies as
Roman or Ovidian wit directed against ordinary, accepted
standards. Sometimes, as in *To his Mistres Going to Bed*, the
antagonism is translated into a male erotic vision of considerable power:

166

License my roaving hands, and let them go,
Behind, before, above, between, below.
O my America, my new-found land . . .   (25–27)

That third line is so marvelous precisely because it renders
eroticism into art and antagonism into the lyric thrill of
discovery. There are other such lines, but it is an impatient
cynicism that emerges at the end:

To teach thee I am naked first; Why than
What needst thou have more covering than a man.
                                                    (47–48)

The very high spirits seem to allow the woman no independent value.

There is no need to assume that Donne is describing his
own amorous adventures in the elegies, since the one adven-
ture we do know of, with Anne More, was a wild romantic
gesture with an illiterate woman he loved so dearly that he
ruined his career for her out of genuine and lasting love:
"John Donne, Anne Donne, undone." Even accounting for
the differences in status of the two sexes, the elegies are
remarkably antagonistic toward women, and in this antagonism, expressed so many ways, lies their chief satiric force.
That force is directed to showing that conventional attitudes
in poetry are wrong, and that man need not be an abject
suitor. Woman is often ugly, is as biological as man, and is as
much man's possession to play with as he had been her
servant in Petrarchan poetry. The only possible way to come
to an acceptable human truth in the elegies is to regard them
as fictional and to see them in the context of the conventional poetry of the sixteenth century. Donne therefore
creates a different world, sometimes an adulterous world after
the fashion of the Ovidian elegy (*Jealosie*), or else simply the
world of adult sophistication and experience. As the Mistress
going to bed is told:

cast all, yea, this white lynnen hence,
There is no pennance due to innocence.

(45–46)

Obviously the cynicism derives from the assumption that "There is no pennance due to innocence." The world of the satires is one in which the most vigorous possible efforts are required to retain individual integrity in a world of corruption and threat. In the elegies, Donne turns from the public world to the private world of love or, at most, the social world of the family, and he finds the women in it no better than himself, or that it is he himself who bears the spoiler's hand. Both groups of poems presume, for their situations though not for biographical detail, a contact and experience of the world. The satires show the individual recoiling, partly in disgust and partly in fear. The elegies reveal a brazen wiping aside of idealism, a momentary acceptance followed by disdain, or a lyric gaiety hardened at times into grimace. In the elegies, the male speakers have acquired control of their world, in no small part by directing a satiric energy against it. The poet whose satire in some ways most resembles Donne's is Rochester, but it is remarkable that Rochester found it impossible to combine, as did Donne, a sense of real antagonism with real lyricism.

The *Songs and Sonnets* provide a much greater variety of tone, though downright coarseness or hatred is really impossible to find. We have moved a further step toward lyric affirmation, though something of the mockery of the elegies will be found in poems like "Communitie":

If then at first wise Nature had
Made women either good or bad,
    Then some wee might hate, and some chuse,
But since shee did them so create,
That we may neither love, nor hate,
Onely this rests, All, all may use.   (7–12)

But there is also a new willingness to argue with women, which suggests a closer approach to equality than that implied by the usual tone of the elegies. Sometimes, as in the deliberately mistitled "Womans constancy," Donne goes so far as to attribute to the woman a long chain of reasoning to justify her infidelity. That is the same sort of witty dialectic that the male speaker was advancing in the passage just quoted from "Communitie." Now he concludes for her:

> Or, your owne end to Justifie,
> For having purpos'd change, and falsehood; you
> Can have no way but falsehood to be true?
> Vaine lunatique, against these scapes I could
> Dispute, and conquer, if I would,
> Which I abstaine to doe,
> For by to morrow, I may thinke so too.   (11–17)

The wit is lighter, gayer. It is more elastic, more capable of sudden shifts and unexpected turns. It is a freer agent. And yet there is still some of the fear of experience of the satires and the evasion from it of the elegies—along with Donne's persistent compulsion to experience. The arena of contact has narrowed to a private and very intimate scene. What we see in this somewhat artificial progress from the satires to the elegies to the *Songs and Sonnets* (I am not implying any fixed chronology) is that command of one's world and affirmation of it are directly proportional to the intimacy of the situation and the distance from the world, and therefore inversely proportional to the presence of society and its institutions. To put it crudely, after the manner of Mandeville, Donne's thematic postulates are public vice, private benefits. Once he is able to restrict the area of contact, he is able not only to experience but often to enjoy human involvement.

Insofar as they have different themes, the satires can be said to fear experience because the arena of contact and the nature of what is to be contacted arouses fear; the elegies run boldly and contemptuously into experience, because although the area is manageable what is found there is usually no better than oneself; and the *Songs and Sonnets* accept and affirm experience because it is confined to an intimate world where what is found is really as good as oneself. A few examples will suggest the special tone of the *Songs and Sonnets*:

> And now good morrow to our waking soules,
> Which watch not one another out of feare.
>
> ("The good-morrow," 8–9)

> If yet I have not all thy love,
> Deare, I shall never have it all.
>
> ("Loves infinitenesse," 1–2)

> Sweetest love, I do not goe,
>   For wearinesse of thee,
> Nor in the hope the world can show
>   A fitter Love for mee.   ("Song," 1–4)

> Deare love, for nothing lesse then thee
> Would I have broke this happy dreame.
>
> ("The Dreame," 1–2)

In such passages the satiric bitterness and fear is gone, the brazen cheekiness of the elegies might never have been. They are lines that every reader of Donne recognizes with pleasure, and recognizes to be lyrical. And yet what is in some ways most remarkable—and what cannot be insisted on enough— is that by any usual definition of Metaphysical styles they are not Metaphysical at all. Here are none of the strong lines, ironic wit, conceits, and the related characteristics we have been taught to regard as Metaphysical. By the criteria used in this book, they are rather more Metaphysical in being private and dramatic; and although only the first quotation uses a technique at all approaching definition, the further movement is dialectical. What is implied by the disparity between the lyric element in Donne's poems and the usual conceptions of them is that those poems lacking in a residual or open satiric force are less Metaphysical, or at least less Metaphysical than others possessing it. (Or else that the usual criteria are irrelevant, or in need of addition.) I think it more temperate to say that the farther the lyric element in Donne's poems approaches affirmation and sweetness—and song—the closer it moves towards the mainstream of Renaissance lyricism; and similarly that the more satiric is the force directing the poetry, the farther it is removed from the main line.

Yet it is also true that in some poems or passages Donne combines, if not full song, then at least lyric affirmation, with such a basic Metaphysical feature as dialectic. To return to the first example given of his lyricism:

> And now good morrow to our waking soules,
> Which watch not one another out of feare;
> For love, all love of other sights controules,
> And makes one little roome, an every where.
> ("The good-morrow," 8–11)

Our souls are defined or distinguished from others; the reason for their lack of fear (a very revealing admission for many of Donne's other poems) is explained by defining the active power of true love.

The most extended example of affirmation without any prominent satiric current is *The Extasie*, in which antagonism is all but gone and which is yet a poem Metaphysical to everyone's mind. The complexity of its dialectic, its drama of speaker and dual audience, and the much disputed character of its second half, all show the poem to be one of the most involved and complex of Donne's poems, which is surely to say a good deal for a lyric poem. But the poem is also in a sense a simple lyric. Its uncomplicated structure may easily be represented.

Lines 1–4: when
    5–20: then
  21–24: if
  25–28: then
  29–48: our souls say
  49–76: let's to bodies

The lyricism of the poem is most obvious in its simple quatrain stanza, but it is best expressed in the degree of regularity of rhythm Donne has chosen for his complicated ideas. (His accomplished craftsmanship seldom gets the credit it deserves, because we always wish to talk about what he has done with his craft.)

The features of *The Extasie* that have been stressed are its basic lyricism, its affirmation, and its Metaphysical modes of definition, dialectic, private poetry, and drama. Since the lyric element in Donne's poetry needs as much stress as the satiric, it is worthwhile to see what Lord Herbert of Cherbury found worthy of imitation in *The Extasie*. His *Ode upon a Question moved, Whether Love should continue for ever?* is an "ode," a lyric adapting Donne's abab quatrain rhyme to abba. The structure is basically similar:

Lines 1–20: when
  21–36: then
  37–60: she says
 61–132: he says
133–40: they are "ravish'd"

The last four stanzas show how far the Metaphysical modes have been followed and how much Lord Herbert has seized upon the lyrical element in Donne's poem to define his own aims. The last two may, therefore, be quoted again:

This said, in her up-lifted face,
  Her eyes which did that beauty crown,

172

Were like two starrs, that having faln down
Look up again to find their place:

While such a moveless silent peace
    Did seize on their becalmed sense,
    One would have thought some Influence
Their ravish'd spirits did possess.   (133–40)

In calling his poem an ode, Lord Herbert no doubt had the
Horatian model in mind, whether Donne did or not. But at
all events, he has isolated and magnified the two basic features of Donne's lyricism: its greater sweetness of technique
and its affirmation.

Donne's divine poems give the lyricism its most frequent,
if not necessarily its fullest, expression. So far is the technique
lyrical that some of the poems were meant for musical set-
tings, and most of them take the form of a sonnet or hymn.
And the affirmation is to be found in the fact that there is
almost none of that antagonism of the secular poems against
his audience. It is true that he can group "the world" with its
traditional comrades in evil, "the flesh, and devill" (Holy
Sonnet: "This is my playes last scene"). But the reality of
that world has been reduced nearly to nil, and that of which
the speaker is now most conscious outside himself is of
course God:

The Sonne of glory came downe, and was slaine,
Us whom he'had made, and Satan stolne, to unbinde.
'Twas much, that man was made like God before,
But, that God should be made like man, much more.
        (Holy Sonnet 11, 1633, "Wilt thou love God," 11–14)

O strong Ramme, which hast batter'd heaven for mee,
Mild lambe, which with thy blood, hast mark'd the path;
Bright torch, which shin'st, that I the way may see,
Oh, with thy owne blood quench thy owne just wrath,

And if thy holy Spirit, my Muse did raise,
Deigne at my hands this crowne of prayer and praise.
(La Corona, no. 7, 9–14)

The *"prayer and praise"* of the divine poems is far removed
from the bitterness and fear of the satires, and the religious
poems therefore represent the final step in the thematic
progression that I have been following. (It should be said
again that I am not arguing for a dating of Donne's poems.)
What has been most obvious in the thematic shift is that it
depends upon a changing response to that lying outside the
perceiving subject, the speaker and, if carefully enough considered, outside Donne himself. The satires are strongest in
the emotion with which they recoil from a world that still
draws one in. The elegies yield somewhat, altering fear and
bitterness to a brazen contempt sometimes tempered by a
degree of affection. Lyrics like "The Indifferent" or "Womans
constancy" temper the antagonism yet further by admitting
the other, the woman, as a near equal. The most lyric poems
(e.g., "Sweetest love, I do not goe") and the most evidently
affirmative (e.g., "The good-morrow," *The Extasie*) show a
harmony between the speaker and his other concern, his
beloved. The religious poems of course show a stage in which
the other concern, God, has become superior to the subject,
the "I."

The shift in the norm of goodness or integrity from the
endangered private speaker of the satires to God is accompanied by a second shift in the religious poems. The second
admits a new version of the satiric by directing the attack
and criticism at a new object. Whereas in the satires, elegies,
and many lyrics the world was culpable, inferior, and often
wrong, in the religious poetry the culpability, inferiority, and
wrong center in the speaker himself. The drama remains, and
the speaker may even be possessed by a new grandeur of
vision, almost by the spirit of prophecy:

174

At the round earths imagin'd corners, blow
Your trumpets, Angells, and arise, arise
From death, you numberlesse infinities
Of soules, and to your scattred bodies goe . . .
(Holy Sonnet 4, 1633, 1–4)

And yet the speaker now turns upon himself, as it were, in a temper of self-criticism very different from anything in the secular poems:

But let them sleepe, Lord, and mee mourne a space,
For, if above all these, my sinnes abound,
'Tis late to aske abundance of thy grace,
When wee are there; here on this lowly ground,
Teach mee how to repent; for that's as good
As if thou'hadst seal'd my pardon, with thy blood.
(9–14)

We remember numerous turns or twists at the end of his secular poems—all proving the speaker right and his audience wrong. Now we witness a reversal, and sometimes the sense of the speaker's inadequacy provokes a violence even greater than in the satires:

But who am I, that dare dispute with thee?
O God, Oh! of thine onely worthy blood,
And my teares, make a heavenly Lethean flood,
And drowne in it my sinnes blacke memorie.
(Holy Sonnet 5, 1633, 9–12)

Spit in my face yee Jewes, and pierce my side,
Buffet, and scoffe, scourge, and crucifie mee . . .
(Holy Sonnet 7, 1633, 1–2)

Batter my heart, three person'd God; for, you
As yet but knocke, breathe, shine, and seeke to mend; . . .
Take mee to you, imprison mee, for I

Except you'enthrall mee, never shall be free,
Nor ever chast, except you ravish mee.
(Holy Sonnet 10, 1633, 1–2, 12–14)

But oh it [my world] must be burnt; alas the fire
Of lust and envie'have burnt it heretofore,
And made it fouler; Let their flames retire,
And burne me ô Lord, with a fiery zeale
Of thee'and thy house, which doth in eating heale.
(Holy Sonnet 2, 1635, 10–14)

Both the violence and its direction set the poems apart from Donne's secular verse.

What has happened, then, is that Donne has relocated both the wrong (from the world to himself) and the norm (from himself to an exterior being, God). In the first chapter, we saw that the satires were motivated in considerable measure by one of the most powerful of human passions, fear. " 'I shooke like a spyed Spie" (IV, 237). In the secular poems of this kind, the urge to attack the exterior world was in reality a defense measure. In the divine poems there is also a fear, but now of personal inadequacy before an omnipotent, just, and omniscient albeit gracious God:

Wilt thou forgive that sinne by which I wonne
Others to sinne? and, made my sinne their doore?
Wilt thou forgive that sinne which I did shunne
A yeare, or two: but wallowd in, a score?
When thou hast done, thou hast not done,
For I have more.

I have a sinne of feare, that when I have spunne
My last thred, I shall perish on the shore;
Sweare by thy selfe, that at my death thy Sunne
Shall shine as it shines now, and heretofore;
And, having done that, Thou hast done,
I have no more.
("A Hymne to God the Father," 7–18)

This very different fear of inadequacy is found in much of
Donne's religious poetry and, sometimes, as in this hymn, the
attitude comes close to that dispiriting, that despair of the
Redcrosse Knight, that mysterious sin against the Holy Ghost
which is usually explained as doubt of the possibility of one's
salvation. But just as in the secular verse, so here there is a
counter-tow. After all, the fear—if it is not excessive—is
wholly Christian. "Work out your own salvation in fear and
trembling," said the Apostle (Philippians 2:12). Donne believed that Solomon in his Proverbs (9:10; 15:33), like David
in his Psalm (121:10), identified wisdom with the fear of
the Lord. This was the lesson Milton's Adam was to learn
from the sorry spectacle of humankind presented in the last
two books of *Paradise Lost:*

> Henceforth I learn, that to obey is best,
> And love with fear the only God, to walk
> As in his presence, ever to observe
> His providence, and on him sole depend . . .

To which Michael responds: "This having learnt, thou hast
attain'd the sum / Of wisdom" (xii, 561–64, 575–76). In
other words, the wonderful energy given the secular poems
by what I have been calling satire continues in the religious
poems, but in a fashion directed to wholly orthodox ends.
Whatever the uses, it remains a critical energy still, as one
sees at once in Donne's greatest religious poem, *Goodfriday,
1613. Riding Westward:*

> O Saviour, as thou hang'st upon the tree;
> I turne my backe to thee, but to receive
> Corrections, till thy mercies bid thee leave.
> O thinke mee worth thine anger, punish mee,
> Burne off my rusts, and my deformity,
> Restore thine Image, so much, by thy grace,
> That thou may'st know mee, and I'll turne my face.
>
> (36–42)

177

It is difficult not to see from the spectrum of Donne's poems a thematic significance in the speaker's relation to the person he addresses. Donne's drama is not a morality play, but neither is it mere liveliness. His satiric theme implies suspicion, bitterness, and fear. In the secular poems, the theme implies a superiority of the speaker, the inferiority of everyone else. In the religious poems, the roles are reversed. The lyric theme implies either the equality of speaker-subject with the woman-object (as in the love poems) or the assured grace of the divine object to the speaker-subject (in the divine poems). What is common to the whole spectrum of Donne's poetry is the living commerce between subject and object, "I" and "thee" or "He." It is this conviction of experience, and the poetic illusion of it, that is so important in Donne. No one can be expected to consent to all details of the experience, but everyone must consent that it *is* experience and that the re-creation of it is valuable. The value is not simply as drama, good as Donne is at that, but for the far more fundamental human conviction, or theme, implied by the drama, that "I have lived and it was so." This theme is indeed one that private poetry excels in conveying, and one in particular that runs from Donne throughout the Metaphysical race as a heritage.

Donne's is not, however, a single theme but a gradation of themes unified by the central theme of the commitment to —and indeed fear of—experience; the gradation is adjusted by the central response of the subject to the object, of the speaker to his audience or the world. Having defined the thematic emphases of what I have characterized separately as satire and lyricism, I must now discuss the thematic significance of a fact observed at the outset, that the satiric antagonism and the lyric affirmation often combine. They do so because they are to some extent conditional upon each other, there being a reciprocal function between the speaker

or subject and the audience or the world as object. When
the object—the world and the court in the satires or the
woman in the elegies—is denigrated, the subject is the norm
of judgment. When, on the other hand, as in the divine
poems, the object, God, is the norm of value, then the
speaker is thought wrong. What happens is similar, though
it is differently directed. Although it is somewhat unnatural
to say so, at these extremes satire of the world changes to
self-satire. Self-criticism, guilt, and even self-loathing may be
discovered easily enough in the divine poems:

> As humorous is my contritione
> As my prophane Love, and as soone forgott:
> As ridlingly distemperd, cold and hott . . .
> So my devout fitts come and go away
> Like a fantastique Ague: save that here
> Those are my best dayes, and I shake with feare.
> (Westmoreland Holy Sonnet: "Oh, to vex me,"
> 5–7, 12–14)

There are, however, numerous poems that are not as extreme as the satires and the divine poems, poems that fuse
elements of satire and lyricism by other means than opposition between speaker and audience. The most common tactic
is to join the speaker and the audience as one side to oppose
to another, the "world": "['Twere] prophanation of our
joyes / To tell the layetie our love." That is one of Donne's
authentic notes, the division of the speaker and his beloved
from an inferior world. The analogy is sometimes, as in those
lines from "A Valediction forbidding mourning," between
the lovers as priests and the world as laity; at other times, as
in "The Canonization," the lovers are saints and the rest of
the world at best worshippers, and at worst foolish followers
of the culpable social routine. The theme is carried a good
deal farther, sometimes giving the lovers a magic:

179

> Wee dye and rise the same, and prove
> Mysterious by this love.
>> ("The Canonization," 26–27)

Or it may be that they alone are truly real:

> Princes doe but play us; compar'd to this,
> All honor's mimique; All wealth alchimie.
>> ("The Sunne Rising," 23–24)

And the same passage goes on to take the theme to its farthest and its most thrilling expression in Metaphysical poetry, the abolition of all but the lovers:

> She'is all States, and all Princes, I,
> Nothing else is.   (21–22)

The world so rejected is the social, public, customary world. The change from fear aroused by that world in the satires to assurance of command of it in some lyrics is shown by the bandying about of the sun:

> Must to thy motions lovers seasons run?
> Sawcy pedantique wretch, goe chide
> Late schoole boyes, and sowre prentices,
> Goe tell Court-huntsmen, that the King will ride,
> Call countrey ants to harvest offices.
>> ("The Sunne Rising," 4–8)

The superiority has an almost philosophical assurance:

> All other things, to their destruction draw,
> Only our love hath no decay.
>> ("The Anniversarie," 6–7)

Just as there is more than one audience in Donne's poetry, so is there more than one world. Set against the customary

world of men is another world, the universe, and therefore
a total reality which is set as an ideal shared by the lovers:

> Shine here to us, and thou art every where;
> This bed thy center is, these walls, thy sphere.
>
> ("The Sunne Rising," 29–30)

> Our bodies why doe wee forbeare?
> They'are ours, though they'are not wee, Wee are
> The'intelligences, they the spheares.
>
> (*The Extasie*, 50–52)

> I am a little world made cunningly
> Of Elements, and an Angelike spright.
>
> (Holy Sonnet 2, 1635, 1–2)

The correspondence between man's little world and the great
gives man considerable importance, dignity, and reality. This
world is as usually a font of value to Donne in his poetry as
the customary world of men is a force opposed to value.

There is finally, however, one further step in Donne, a
kind of thematic reversal, or thematic leakage, in which such
oppositions react upon each other. The simplest example is
that of the Holy Sonnets, in which imagery from the customary world is taken as imagery of normality or even of
value. There is, in "Batter my heart, three person'd God,"
for example, imagery of lord and subject, of betrothal, and of
imprisonment; or in "Father, part of his double interest,"
imagery of economics and law. It was observed in the first
chapter that the very private mode of the satires reveals a
degree of self-doubt and even self-loathing or guilt. In the
divine poems the counterpart of this is a certain harrying of
God, an unwillingness as it were to let Him alone, like a
teasing, inconsiderate child:

As thou
Art jealous, Lord, so I am jealous now.
Thou lov'st not, till from loving more, thou free
My soule: Who ever gives, takes libertie:
  O, if thou car'st not whom I love alas, thou lov'st not mee.
                    ("A Hymne to Christ," 19–23)

  When thou hast done, thou hast not done,
    For, I have more.
        ("A Hymne to God the Father," 5–6, 11–12)

There is a tendency to set God to His lesson ("Who ever
gives, takes libertie") and an inclination to tell God what to
do. It is precisely just this mingled attitude toward the self
and the person addressed, and indeed even toward the customary world, that accounts for the varieties of antagonism
and affirmation in Donne's poetry and for the exceedingly
complex mingling of tones in much of what he wrote.

The most extraordinary examples in his poetry of what I
have been calling satiric antagonism and lyric affirmation are
of course the *Anniversaries*. In them the speaker finds his
source of value in what the dead Elizabeth Drury represents,
and he finds in the world his source of what must be repro-
bated. The speaker himself is caught between the dead girl
and what she represents (she being no God, he can hardly
pray to her), and yet his awareness of her value prevents his
attachment to the world. (In this case, significantly, the
"world" is both the customary world and the physical universe.) In other words, Donne's object, the world, has fused
two worlds that usually have quite contrary value in his
poetry, and he has denied himself his usual audiences.
(*Anniversary II* has the speaker addressing his soul as his
audience, but the middle sections of *Anniversary I* have not
even so tenuous a dramatic audience.) For such reason, although structurally the most important sections of both

poems are the meditations and the eulogies of that "shee," Donne's satire is directed one scarcely knows where, and his affirmation is of a girl rendered sufficiently symbolic and yet real so that no one from Ben Jonson to the present has been altogether at ease with the *Anniversaries*. The tone of the two poems does differ very considerably. *Anniversary II* is a good deal more optimistic, its satire and lyricism combining after the manner of much of Donne's poetry, to make a complicated whole. The poems suggest, what is confirmed by later poets in Donne's train, that almost the only way to write a lengthy Metaphysical poem was to explore a satiric theme. Satire allowed for a long lecture on the world; the private lyric breath was short.

The mingling of satire and song in the *Anniversaries* can best be shown by comparison of two passages similar in alchemical imagery, in one of which the satiric element is uppermost, in the other the lyric:

> She, of whom th'Auncients seem'd to prophesie,
> When they call'd vertues by the name of shee;
> She in whom vertue was so much refin'd,
> That for Allay unto so pure a minde
> Shee tooke the weaker Sex, she that could drive
> The poysonous tincture, and the stayne of *Eve*,
> Out of her thoughts, and deeds; and purifie
> All, by a true religious Alchimy;
> Shee, shee is dead; shee's dead: when thou knowest this,
> Thou knowest how poore a trifling thing man is.
>
> *(Anniversary I, 175–84)*

The lyric affirmation is plain enough in the beginning of the passage and in the refrain-like iteration of "she," "shee," and similar syntactic forms. But the tone and movement of the passage drive the lyricism into an attack upon that which is so inferior to the ideal. "She" is contrasted with faulty Eve and with "trifling . . . man." How dominant the satiric tone is can be understood readily enough by comparing the passage with a similar one in Dryden's *Eleonora*, which he fashioned on his panegyric conception of the *Anniversaries*.[3] Dryden in fact echoes the very passage just quoted, making the same guilty Eve trope a means not of having panegyric serve satiric ends, but of satire serving panegyric:

> A wife as tender, and as true withall,
> As the first Woman was, before her fall:
> Made for the Man, of whom she was a part;
> Made, to attract his Eyes, and keep his Heart.
> A second *Eve*, but by no crime accurst;
> As beauteous, not as brittle as the first.
> Had she been first, still Paradise had bin,
> And Death had found no entrance by her sin.
> So she not only had preserv'd from ill
> Her Sex and ours, but liv'd their Pattern still.
>
> (*Eleonora*, 166–75)

The difference may be crudely set forth: Donne speaks of his woman only in every other line, Dryden in all but two.

Dryden compares Eve at her best with Eleonora and contrasts her at her worst. And he connects: Eleonora would have preserved us, as Eve nearly doomed us, and she remains a pattern for us. Donne contrasts, opposes, is conscious of the gulf between the ideal and the real; it is his agonized sense of antagonism between the two that gives a satiric current even to his more lyric *Anniversary II*, as another passage with alchemical imagery will show:

> Shee, of whose soule, if we may say, t'was Gold,
> Her body was th'Electrum, and did hold

---

[3] Dryden's use of Donne in *Eleonora* is treated in my *Dryden's Poetry* (Bloomington and London, 1967), ch. vi, and will be further discussed in our forthcoming third volume of *The Works of John Dryden*.

Many degrees of that; we understood
Her by her sight, her pure and eloquent blood
Spoke in her cheekes, and so distinckly wrought,
That one might almost say, her bodie thought,
Shee, shee, thus richly,'and largely hous'd, is gone:
And chides us slow-pac'd snailes, who crawle upon
Our prisons prison, earth, nor thinkes us well
Longer, then whil'st we beare our brittle shell.

(Anniversary II, 241–50)

The passage is far more affirmative and even panegyric than
that quoted from Anniversary I. In this it approaches
Dryden's concern with the object of praise rather than one's
own concerned meditation. But once again Donne's direction
comes from his antagonistic contrast between the "shee" and
us of "our brittle shell," which is the customary world,
though the physical world, "earth," is also wrong. The
alchemical images are the same; the tone is more affirmative;
but the element of satiric force is what determines the tone
and theme of the poems.

Louis L. Martz has shown that the Anniversaries are made
up of introduction and conclusion and, in the main section
between, of repeated sections alternating meditation and
eulogy (and sometimes other passages related to one or the
other of the main).[4] It can be seen from this that although
the satiric theme dominates in the Anniversaries, it does so
in a basic lyric structure. In effect Donne's technique (however indebted to meditational procedures) in the Anniversaries is to create a series of what might be called intellectual
stanzas, even down to a very refrain. Within each "stanza"
there is a tension between the satiric antagonism of the
meditation and the lyric affirmation of the eulogy. It is

<hr />

[4] Martz, The Poetry of Meditation (New Haven, 1954), pp. 222–23,
236–37.

difficult to think of a single Metaphysical poem of any length and quality that is not in stanzas, either so indicated, or divided as Donne's are in the *Anniversaries* by intellectual and tonal function. Crashaw's longest poem is stanzaic, and so is Marvell's, and they are the two important Metaphysical poets most often given to something other than stanzas. But Donne as much as Herbert is given to thinking in terms of stanzas in his private poetry. (His public is another matter on several counts.) We can see once again how a fundamental tension between satire and song, antagonism and affirmation, determines Donne's poetry, even when he sets out to write long panegyric. To some degree the *Anniversaries* brought Donne back to the satires with their near hysteria over the encroachments of evil. But what is of greatest importance is that throughout Donne's poetry there is a feverish engagement with experience: he and other people and the world are defined by intimate relationships. And throughout the poetry there is enough ambiguity in Donne's response to his world to create and to require contrarieties of tone and theme. All poets and all human beings share with Donne differing responses to experience. What is unusual with Donne is less the vivacity with which he creates experience, precious though that is, than the way in which contrary responses are made to depend upon each other for their fullest expression.

Crashaw is the least satiric of the major Metaphysical poets (and Traherne of the minor). So given is he to praise and affirmation that the satirical element, the personal antagonism, the tension of opposed elements—the things that give Donne's poetry much of its drive—are either absent or transformed in his best-known poetry. In "The Hymne" to Saint Teresa, for example, the Moors who will martyr her are not even stage villains:

> Since 'tis not to bee had at home,
> Sheel travell to a martyrdome.

186

No home for her confesses shee,
But where shee may a martyr bee.
Sheel to the Moores, And trade with them,
For this unvalued Diadem. (43–48)

With the Moors traders, the only problem is how to bargain
with them to kill her. Similarly, the only tension is normally
that between erotic imagery and religious ecstasy, but since
such imagery is common enough in mystical poetry and because Crashaw uses it for traditional sacred parody, his usual
treatment does not warrant the name of satire, even in an
extended sense.

One must look among his less-known poems for works with
some element of satiric antagonism. A brief example is "To
Pontius washing his blood-stained hands," and significantly
it is built up of a contrast between the satiric antagonist,
Pontius Pilate, and the lyric heroine, the weeping Mother of
Christ. A poem even more in Donne's line is Crashaw's
venture into the long work, *Sospetto d'Herode*. The intention was clearly to write a long biblical narrative, though only
the first book was done. (Crashaw's good friend Cowley had
only somewhat better fortune in his *Davideis*, but it is a sign
of the times that his poem is closer in technique to *Paradise
Lost* than to Crashaw or Donne's long poems.) The story
concerns Herod, the Innocents, and the flight into Egypt, but
he would be a desperate reader who studied the poem for its
plot. It is in fact rather an extended diffuse lyric almost as
much dramatic as narrative, and it is built precisely on
Donne's principle of repeated units embodying a contrasted
antagonism and affirmation, as the sixty-fifth stanza shows:

Why art thou troubled *Herod?* what vaine feare
Thy blood-revolving Brest to rage doth move?
Heavens King, who doffs himselfe weake flesh to weare,
Comes Not to rule in wrath, but serve in love.
Nor would he this thy fear'd Crown from [thee] Teare,

187

But give thee a better with himselfe above.
Poore jealousie! why should he wish to prey
Upon thy Crowne, who gives his owne away?

The dramatic address somewhat reminds us of Donne, and
Crashaw shares the technique with Herbert as well. Moreover, the opposition of Christ to Herod as a king is one that
might appear in the religious poems of any of the three. The
difference between him and Donne, in say the *Anniversaries,*
is that in Donne we sometimes have difficulty in taking the
affirmation seriously, whereas with Crashaw it is the antagonism that seems more perfunctory. Having chosen, with the
Council of Trent, to resolve all doubts in splendor, Crashaw
seems really to have found it difficult to bring back to poetry
a sufficient negative response to give his poetry a tension. His
theme is affirmation, and even Herod slaughtering the Innocents seems scarcely to pose a threat.

Herbert's poetry is distinguished by a comparable drama
and sweetness, but with much greater concentration of mind
and language. The lyric sweetness is indisputable, but, unlike
Crashaw, Herbert shows that he had to win it by considerable
struggle with himself. His particular combination of affirmation and antagonism is best represented by the title and a
few verses from a poem, "Bitter-sweet":

> I will complain, yet praise;
> I will bewail, approve:
> And all my sowre-sweet dayes
> I will lament, and love.   (5–8)

The verses are not very important for their poetry, but they
do show in Herbert the same contrast or opposition of dissimilar forces that we see so quickly in Donne. His longest,
The Church-porch, gives the "sowre" note of Herbert its
clearest expression, and although "satiric" in its usual sense
is not the best name for the tone, the motive in a kind of

disgruntled, didactic, and indeed querulous corner of Herbert's personality is very marked:

> He that is drunken, may his mother kill
> Bigge with his sister: he hath lost the reins,
> Is outlawd by himself: all kinde of ill
> Did with his liquour slide into his veins.
> The drunkard forfets Man, and doth devest
> All worldly right, save what he hath by beast.
>
> (36–36)

The 460 lines of the poem may well catechize us properly for entering the Church, but as this or any sample would show, they really lack the sweet to go with the "sowre." Once again we observe how the longer Metaphysical poem falls into satire, while yet keeping the lyric structure of repeated stanzas for rolling on. Unfortunately, the personality emerging from this dull poem is not the attractive one we find elsewhere in Herbert's poetry.

At his best, which is a standard maintained in many poems, Herbert is wonderfully successful in conceiving dramatic situations to embody an opposed antagonism and affirmation. Sometime the elements may seem to come in sequence, as in "The Collar":

> I Struck the board, and cry'd, No more.
> I will abroad.
> What? shall I ever sigh and pine?
> My lines and life are free; free as the rode,
> Loose as the winde, as large as store.   (1–5)

There is even an irony rare in Herbert:

> Forsake thy cage,
> Thy rope of sands,
> Which pettie thoughts have made, and made to thee

> Good cable, to enforce and draw
> And be thy law.   (21–25)

But of course, for all such "fierce and wilde" rebellion, only
God's voice is necessary for a change to acceptance and
affirmation:

> Me thoughts I heard one calling, *Child!*
> And I reply'd, *My Lord.*   (35–36)

One of Herbert's relatively longer poems, *The Sacrifice*,
has something of the querulousness of *The Church-porch*, a
basically undirected antagonism that has put off some
readers. But, for others of us, it does succeed in creating a
sustaining tension in the poem by opposing to the lament
and the dominant complaints of Christ a strong sense of
love. And since the situation is the Crucifixion, the tone may
well be heightened without our feeling as nervous as with
the condescending vicar's voice in *The Church-porch*. Yet
that negative tone is present—and indeed is essential to the
functioning of the poem, a satiric drive carrying the poem to
its greater than usual length through, as in other such Metaphysical poems, the lyric stanza measure:

> See, they lay hold on me, not with the hands
> Of faith, but furie: yet at their commands
> I suffer binding, who have loos'd their bands:
>   Was ever grief like mine?

> All my Disciples flie; fear puts a barre
> Betwixt my friends and me. They leave the starre,
> That brought the wise men of the East from farre.
>   Was ever grief like mine?

> Then from one ruler to another bound
> They leade me; urging, that it was not sound
> What I taught: Comments would the text confound.
>   Was ever grief like mine?

The Priest and rulers all false witnesse seek
'Gainst him, who seeks not life, but is the meek
And readie Paschal Lambe of this great week:
      Was ever grief like mine?   (45–60)

The poem does not have the concentration of Herbert's shorter poems, but it may be argued that no longish Metaphysical poem is entirely successful; and though it is uneven, it certainly is not dull, because cut across its satiric force and lyric roll is an often exciting though implicit narrative of Passion Week. Yet the real force is dramatic, since what happens over several days is concentrated in one monologue; and that voice of Christ is at once full of reprobation and loving sorrow, a combination for that character on that occasion which is absolutely appropriate.

Like Donne, Herbert gets much of his effect from the felt dramatic strength of his speaker and audience, but with Herbert the divisions are seldom those opposed at the same time within the speaker. If they are within the speaker, they usually appear in sequence, yielding to the lovely simplifications one sees at the end of "The Collar." What is less apparent than in Donne, though in its way equally important, is that the satiric antagonism is evoked both from within the speaker (as in "The Collar" and numerous other poems) and from a contrast of an inferior "world" to an ideal one. The ideal world is of course a religious ideal transforming this present time and place. The inferior world is one that emerges only upon occasion in the poetry, but then clearly enough to show that it was an important force in Herbert's thought. "The Pearl" affords one such occasion, and its second stanza illustrates (indeed the others do, too) the usual means employed by Herbert to create that world he is (or was) drawn to but rejects:

I know the wayes of Honour, what maintains
The quick returns of courtesie and wit:

In vies of favours whether partie gains,
When glorie swells the heart, and moldeth it
To all expressions both of hand and eye,
Which on the world a true-love-knot may tie,
And bear the bundle, wheresoe're it goes:
How many drammes of spirit there must be
To sell my life unto my friends or foes:

     Yet I love thee. (11–20)

Herbert looks back on his earlier aspirations for preferment, knowing their attractions full well. Perhaps he still suffers some hesitation of will. But the energy of the poem is directed to criticizing that world and even himself for feeling drawn by it. Such antagonism is set off against the simple affirmation: "Yet I love thee." A similar situation is developed in "The Quip," in which the world to which Metaphysical poets respond negatively emerges explicitly:

The merrie world did on a day
With his train-bands and mates agree
To meet together, where I lay,
And all in sport to geere at me. . . .

Then Money came, and chinking still,
What tune is this, poore man? said he:
I heard in Musick you had skill.
But thou shalt answer, Lord, for me.

Then came brave Glorie puffing by
In silks that whistled, who but he?
He scarce allow'd me half an eie.
But thou shalt answer, Lord, for me. . . .

Yet when the houre of thy designe
To answer these fine things shall come;
Speak not at large; say, I am thine:
And then they have their answer home.

     (1–4; 9–16; 21–24)

The "merrie world" and his friends strut and threat before the resolved and patient Christian. (Like many of the godly, Herbert, or his speaker, thinks the world jeers at him. Bunyan was to make the best prose fiction of the century out of such kinds of experience treated by Herbert.) If it were not for the chamber drama, and the knowledge that the claims of the world rouse some faint echo in him, we would have out-and-out satire here. As it is, we have the motive to satire, antagonism, as one of the two lively contrary forces such as Herbert himself told Ferrar he would find in his poems: "a picture of the many spiritual Conflicts that have past betwixt God and my Soul, before I could subject mine to the will of Jesus my Master, in whose service I have now found perfect freedom." [5] The rebelliousness, the antagonism now towards God and now towards the world, provide Herbert's poetry with much of its force, and the contrary lyricism much of its sweet beauty. The central theme of Herbert's poetry concerns the resolution of antagonisms—to the world, to God, and sometimes to himself—in such a way that will yield to peace in God. The poetry would perhaps be more perfectly religious if there were not that antagonism, if there were sheer lyric affirmation such as may be found in the nineteenth-century hymnodists. But there would be less poetry. As in Donne, so in Herbert, the vitality of the poetry, its complexity and its direction, depend upon what I have termed satire, even while for Herbert the final predication depends upon song.

Vaughan concerns us less in this discussion. It is not that he is less satiric, but that when he is the element is apt to come out too strongly and upset the balance of his poetry. His most famous poem, "The World," begins in a beautifully exalted fashion but, as with the other Metaphysical poets, turns "sowre" when "the world" is mentioned:

[5] *The Works of George Herbert*, ed. F. E. Hutchinson (Oxford, 1953), p. xxxvii.

193

I Saw Eternity the other night
Like a great *Ring* of pure and endless light,
  All calm, as it was bright,
And round beneath it, Time in hours, days, years
    Driv'n by the spheres
Like a vast shadow mov'd, In which the world
  And all her train were hurl'd;
The doting Lover in his queintest strain . . .   (1–8)

It is quite remarkable how the change comes upon mention of "the world," leading Vaughan on to "The doting Lover," the "darksome States-man," the "fearfull miser," and the "down-right Epicure," while "poor, despised truth sate Counting by / Their victory." To such "fools" the poet contrasts some few who fly up into the ring of eternity (the conclusion is in some ways even more moving than the breathtaking beginning). The structure of the poem (from affirmation to satire to a final mingling) works very well. There is a wide sweep of vision throughout, and there are many fine details like that of Truth sitting by ignored. I should not like to persuade anyone who feels otherwise that there is any serious defect. But I confess that for myself the change from that so beautiful opening to a series of stock villains comes as a falling-off. It is too simple, unlike the assured treatment of the world in Vaughan's unjustly ignored secular verse. In the quotation just given, he shows very clearly that "the world" is the villain arousing antagonism in Metaphysical poetry, and that the affirmation beyond it is deeply lyrical. But to my tastes, he was not able to take seriously enough, as Donne or Herbert could, the possibility that the world might claim *him* for its own, that there were disruptive forces *within*. The clearer the threat, the less complex Vaughan's response became—as in a dull poem like "Misery." His happiest solution to the poetic problem was to transform the bad world into an idea, to which he might contrast an affirmed childhood, or into an image, especially darkness, to which he might contrast the light. In such guise the rather too cut-and-dried opposition of the middle sections of "The World" could result in not only a number of very moving poems, but poems sustained far better: "Man," "Cock-crowing," or "They are all gone into the world of light," for example.

In Cowley's poems we find the opposed attitudes transformed by Cavalier wit into a merger rather than an opposition of the two qualities. This merger brings a new distance from the subject and situation, as can readily be seen from "Resolved to Love":

> These are but *Trifles*, I confess,
>   Which me, weak Mortal, move;
> Nor is your *busie Seriousness*
>   Less trifling than my Love.
> The wisest *King* who from his Sacred *Breast*
> Pronounc'd *all* V*an'ity*, chose it for the *best*.
>
> (25–30)

If the Metaphysical tone is not so clear in talk of Solomon, the Cavalier note is even more evident in "Loves Ingratitude":

> I little thought, thou fond *ingrateful Sin*,
>   When first I let thee in,
>   And gave thee but a Part
>   In my unwary *Heart*,
>   That thou wouldst e'er have grown,
> So *false* or *strong* to make it all thine own.
>
> (1–6)

By merging antagonism and affirmation, Cowley (like Suckling before him) stands farther off from his subject and his audience and grows more conscious of his reader. Such a tendency was common in mid-century, and it is only occasionally that in Cowley at least we find poems that seem at once more Metaphysical than Cavalier and yet manage to sustain the dual forces apart. One, or rather two, of these poems is his pair, "Against Hope" and "For Hope." In a sense the separation of satiric antagonism and lyric affirmation is complete, but the two poems are obviously paired versions of a single theme and require being read together to understand Cowley's full theme:

> *Brother* of *Fear,* more gaily clad!
> The *merr'ier Fool* o'th' two, yet quite as *Mad:*
> Sire of *Repentance, Child* of fond *Desire!*
> That blow'st the *Chymicks,* and the *Lovers Fire!*
> Leading them still insensibly 'on
> By the strange *Witchcraft* of Anon!
> By *Thee* the one does changing *Nature* through
> Her endless *Labyrinths* pursue,
> And th'other chases *Woman,* whilst She goes
> More Ways and Turns than *hunted Nature* knows.
> ("Against Hope," 31–40)

> *Brother* of *Faith,* 'twixt whom and Thee
> The Joys of *Heav'n* and *Earth* divided be!
> Though *Faith* be *Heir,* and have the *fix'd Estate,*
> Thy *Portion* yet in *Moveables* is great.
> *Happiness* it self's all one
> In *Thee,* or in *Possession!*
> Only the *Future's Thine,* the *Present His!*
> Thine's the more hard and noble Bliss;
> Best *Apprehender* of our Joys, which hast
> So long a *Reach,* and yet canst hold so *fast.*
> ("For Hope," 21–30)

As with Vaughan a moment ago, so now with Cowley, I am dealing too hastily with a fine poet. These two passages from two very good, if somewhat over-extended, poems are (it goes without saying) most important for their intrinsic merits. But they are also very valuable as illustrations for their being clearly Metaphysical—the Cavalier strains of the earlier poems quoted earlier have yielded to Metaphysical definition and dialectic. The paired poems also demonstrate the opposite strains in Metaphysical poetry with uncommon neatness, demonstrating, in addition, what might have been suspected, that the rhetorical training in writing on both sides of an issue and the rhetorical principle that satire and panegyric are but counterparts are matters affecting Metaphysical poetry. If we do not think of such matters while reading Donne, it is because he exercises too great a spell over us while we read. But it is also because the two contrary motives are intermingled in his personality and his writing in a way that Cowley usually could not manage in the more private Metaphysical mode, but only in the more social Cavalier.

Both as a Cavalier and as a Metaphysical poet, Cowley is a good introduction to Marvell, because what Cowley separated into different styles Marvell brought back together again, as it were, in a mixed style. Marvell's poetry has not indeed the passionate immediacy of Donne's (how many English poets do?), but he does possess a lightness of thought and a fineness of shading between thought and thought and between thought and feeling that is unrivalled in his sphere. In fact, it is precisely in matters of interest to this chapter that Marvell most excels, and sometimes most baffles, adjusting idea to idea or emotion to emotion in his complex personality in ways that are so delicately weighed that scarcely a feather of a thought can be moved without tumbling the whole. Historically the explanation for his fine minglings is no doubt that in retirement he joined the Metaphysical directness of commitment to the subject and situation with the Cavalier disengagement and well mannered hesitation. But:

if we would speak true,
Much to the man is due.

He found among subjects and genres familiar or new a corner
of English poetry previously, and since, uncultivated and
there made his garden, and there he sang:

My Soul into the boughs does glide:
There like a Bird it sits, and sings,
Then whets, and combs its silver Wings.

But what is Metaphysical is that the song must be cut by dis-
cord, and the surpassing green stanza of *The Garden* is followed by a coarser satiric irony:

Such was that happy Garden-state,
While Man there walk'd without a Mate:
After a Place so pure, and sweet,
What other Help could yet be meet!
But 'twas beyond a Mortal's share
To wander solitary there.   (57–62)

Just as in *The Garden* the pure lyric note yields to the
harsh rankling joke (how often Marvell seems to distrust
sex), so in *The last Instructions to a Painter* the satire yields
to lyric touches. The mordant satire is generally accepted to
be Marvell's, though the evidence is, strictly speaking, in-
conclusive.[6] Whose-ever it is, it shows the obverse or counter-

---

[6] In *Marvell's Poems and Letters* (Oxford, 1952), 1, 268, H. M.
Margoliouth comments in a fashion followed by many others: "Of all
the satires attributed to Marvell there is none of which we can feel less
doubt." The logic runs that, being the best of a group of satiric poems,
The last Instructions must be by Marvell. In a book appearing too late
for me to incorporate fully, *Destiny his Choice* (Cambridge, 1968),
John M. Wallace appears to employ the criterion of quality and of
moderation in attacking Charles II for ascribing the poem to Marvell;
see ch. iv. The truth is that the only objective evidence for authorship
is not altogether trustworthy contemporary ascription, which means
little for specific poems. In any event, Marvell wrote other poems that

part of a number of the lyrics we have been looking at. The
tone of the satire is very coarse, as in the passage that Margoliouth conceded to be based on untrue and "revolting
charges" against Anne Hyde, Duchess of York:

> Paint her with Oyster Lip, and breath of Fame,
> Wide Mouth that Sparagus may well proclaim:
> With Chanc'lor's Belly, and so large a Rump.
> There, not behind the Coach, her Pages jump.
>
> (61–64)

How far this seems from "a green Thought in a green Shade."
Encountering such satiric license in Donne or in Marvell (the
poems on Tom May and Richard Flecknoe are certainly
Marvell's), one wonders at the injustice of calling Dryden
coarse or Pope cruel. And yet the point is that, however we
judge such attitudes, they function alongside a delicacy and
fineness of lyric approbation. The handsomest piece of description by a Metaphysical poet (if it is by one) appears in a
passage referred to earlier in this chapter, that in *The last
Instructions* describing de Ruyter's invasion of English rivers:

> Ruyter the while, that had our Ocean curb'd,
> Sail'd now among our Rivers undisturb'd:
> Survey'd their Crystal Streams, and Banks so green,
> And Beauties e're this never naked seen.
> Through the vain sedge the bashful *Nymphs* he ey'd;
> Bosomes, and all which from themselves they hide.
> The Sun much brighter, and the Skies more clear,
> He finds the Air, and all things, sweeter here. . . .
> Among the Shrowds the Seamen sit and sing,

---

may be coarse satires or delicate lyrics, so that the qualities which I
isolate in *The Last Instructions* can be found, if not so starkly contrasted, elsewhere. See my article, "The 'Poetic Picture, Painted Poetry'
of *The Last Instructions to a Painter*," *Modern Philology*, LXIII (1966),
288–94.

And wanton Boys on every Rope do cling.
Old *Neptune* springs the Tydes, and Water lent:
(The Gods themselves do help the provident.)
And, where the deep Keel on the shallow cleaves,
With *Trident's* Leaver, and great Shoulder heaves.
Aeolus their sails inspires with *Eastern* Wind,
Puffs them along, and breathes upon them kind.
With Pearly shell the *Tritons* all the while
Sound the Sea-march, and guide to *Sheppy Isle*.

(523–30; 541–50)

There is nothing surprising about a few lyric notes in an eighteenth-century satire, as *The Rape of the Lock* shows at once. But so long, and so curiously genuine, a lyric passage in a seventeenth-century satire would seem very peculiar if by now we had not seen how much in their other verse the satiric and the lyric were conditions of the successful poetic existence of each other. The echo in the passage of the opening lines of Catullus, lxiv, confirms the mixture. Also in *The last Instructions* there is a passage of nearly fifty lines (649–96) of panegyric on the brave young Scot, Archibald Douglas, and the tone is without question completely laudatory. It is not as fine as the de Ruyter passage, perhaps because it does not raise such complex issues: just how could Marvell or any patriot of his time create an almost pastoral vision of alien men-of-war sailing up English rivers? The device seems to me to work wholly successfully, contributing beauty as well as a shame of violation to the poem, just as to me the eighth stanza of *The Garden* is unsuccessful because it does not really engage itself with the lyric affirmation of the rest of the poem.

What in any event is most marked in his best poetry is a tendency to think of that which would seem to be opposed to, or destructive of, what he is affirming. The opening of *The Garden* recalls the active life in order to praise the retired; the opening of the *Horatian Ode* on Cromwell recalls the retired in order to praise the active. The country ideal admits original sin ("The Mower against Gardens") or thoughts of the falls of princes ("The Mower to the Glo-Worms"). Even one of his most wholly Cavalier poems draws upon such opposition, though it is of course therefore less a division in his mind than an effort to persuade his coy mistress that *she* should make love because *he* fears time. Probably the best illustration of the tendency in his poetry to poise, to opposition, and to total balance is his most Metaphysical poem, "The Definition of Love," in which their love, "so truly *Paralel*, / Though infinite can never meet" (27–28). Examples are broadcast in his poetry. After my strictures upon the eighth stanza of *The Garden*, however, it is only fair to take as an example a passage similar in kind, wholly successful, and utterly Marvellian.

In *Upon Appleton House, to my Lord Fairfax*, the gardens are described as "the just Figure of a Fort" (286). The public, heroic life is used to describe the private and retired; war describes peace, man describes nature, politics cultivation, and so on. The lengthy passage (281–400) of course glances at the Civil Wars, and the reason for such combinations, as well as the reason for their success, is that like Fairfax, Marvell was himself deeply divided. His description resembles some minute but altogether living clockwork:

> When in the *East* the Morning Ray
> Hangs out the Colours of the Day,
> The Bee through these known Allies hums,
> Beating the *Dian* with its *Drumms*.
> Then Flow'rs their drowsie Eylids raise,
> Their Silken Ensigns each displays,
> And dries its Pan yet dank with Dew,
> And fills its Flask with Odours new.   (289–96)

This is pure Marvell, outside the touch of any other poet, perfectly suited in style and thought. As so often with Marvell's more extended style, many of the lines have two nouns; and in this case, where two such different modes of thought **are** involved, Marvell sometimes gives to one half of a couplet one (e.g., floral) significance, and to its rhyme-mate another (military) significance:

> When in the *East* the Morning Ray
> Hangs out the Colours of the Day.

Sometimes the concentration goes yet further by opposing the nouns in each line:

> And dries its Pan yet dank with Dew,
> And fills its Flask with Odours new.

The poise or opposition in style of course corresponds, and is part of, a similar tension of thought and attitude. Marvell is not, after all, creating a pretty metaphor or a quaint Metaphysical conceit. He is talking about both the gardens of Appleton House to which he in one sense, and the Parliamentary General Fairfax in another, have retired; and through the gardens he is talking about the state, England, and the military life:

> And yet there walks one on the Sod
> Who, had it pleased him and *God*,
> Might once have made our Gardens spring
> Fresh as his own and flourishing.
> But he preferr'd to the *Cinque Ports*
> These five imaginary Forts:
> And, in those half-dry Trenches, spann'd
> Pow'r which the Ocean might command.
>
> (345–52)

Here, as often in Marvell, the closer he comes to explicit statement of his theme the more subjective he tends to become: the nouns tend to drop yet farther away, as in some

Japanese poems yielding to the predication of verbs and adjectives. The style is clearer but the implications are less obvious. Just what is implied by the statement that England might have been made a thriving garden, "Fresh as his own and flourishing"? One reason for the difficulty is the lack of abstraction, another is the extremity of tact or hesitation that Marvell shows: England might be "flourishing"—"had it pleased him and God." The same almost eager acceptance of the inscrutability of Heaven that marks the *Horatian Ode* is here, and with it the same refusal, as if Marvell would not like to see what he expects to find if he looked into the mind of his hero.

Even beyond such stylistic and psychological balances and hesitations, there is from time to time a true enigmatic style of metaphor:

> Unhappy! shall we never more
> That sweet *Militia* restore,
> When Gardens only had their Towrs,
> And all the Garrisons were Flowrs,
> When Roses only Arms might bear,
> And Men did rosie Garlands wear?
> Tulips, in several Colours barr'd,
> Were then the *Switzers* of our *Guard*.
>
> (329–36)

Here again there are the paired nouns, and here, too, a poise of meanings scarcely to be resolved. The garden is an obvious figure, but for what? By analogy to the stanza quoted just before this one (though that follows this in the poem by an interval of one stanza), the "Gardens" should be England, and that which is sought is the ideal peace and land that existed like a Paradise before the Civil Wars. (The Paradise/Kingdom figure runs familiarly from Shakespeare to Pope.)

But the fall of man is also meant, as part of the intervening stanza shows:

> Oh Thou, that dear and happy Isle
> The Garden of the World ere while . . .
> What luckless Apple did we tast,
> To make us Mortal, and The Wast?
>
> (321–22; 327–28)

There are two questions. The easier is largely technical: how far does the garden trope convey the meanings of paradise and of kingdom? The answer is surely all the way, the garden being the intermediate vehicle for two quite different though traditional tenors (paradise, kingdom). The second question concerns Marvell's attitude toward what he says, and that is difficult. Putting aside (as one in conscience should not), the issues of his attitude, really, toward mere gardens and his political associations with Paradise, we are still left with the question whether he really thinks that England was an ideal state, a garden or paradise before the Civil Wars. The Parliamentary cause may indeed have been too good a cause to have been fought for, but surely he who was believed by his contemporaries to have so mordantly attacked the milder rule of Charles II must have regarded the harsher reign of Charles I in yet less sympathetic terms. Or is there simply the nostalgia of one who "Sings still of ancient Rights and better Times," as he put it in the poem on *Tom May's Death?* Marvell is one of the few writers for whom the simple answer to a question is unlikely to be the correct one. It is precisely because his loves and hates, his approvals and reprobations, his affirmations and attacks are either so finely mingled or so set off by contrast within and between poems that we scarcely know where we are. What has been represented throughout this chapter in terms of satire and song became in Marvell a strange harmony of implicitly discordant

204

notes. The *discordia concors*, which Dr. Johnson saw at the basis of Metaphysical wit, goes straight through Marvell's writing, from such elementary stylistic features as his frequent opposition in his characteristic two-noun lines to such balances and oppositions of thought as we can see in the themes of individual poems or between individual poems. To the extent that the *discordia concors* is essentially Metaphysical, Marvell is (for all his dominant Cavalier and Restoration tendencies) an essential Metaphysical poet.[7] Those who praise him for his purity probably have in mind what I consider his elegant fineness of thought, but pure, in the sense of being unmixed, Marvell is not.

The surprising thing is that Marvell should so often seem to wish to protect himself by provisionals in his statements and by withdrawals from his affirmations. In the poem "On Mr. Milton's Paradise Lost"—an occasion at the head of the book where pure praise was all but obligatory, and no poet was thought to be on oath—Marvell enters strange doubts, which he attributes to pious "surmise":

> the Argument
> Held me a while misdoubting his Intent
> That he would ruine (for I saw him strong)
> The sacred Truths to Fable and old Song,
> (So *Sampson* groap'd the Temples Posts in spight)
> That World o'rewhelming to revenge his Sight.
>
> (5–10)

---

[7] For the sake of clarity I should probably stress the difference between the Johnsonian meaning of *discordia concors* and the meaning of *concordia discors* as developed in the highly influential essay by Earl Wasserman treating Sir John Denham's *Cooper's Hill*. The latter discussion, contained in *The Subtler Language* (Baltimore, 1959), concerns a major *topos*, expressed in numerous tropes and graphic designs, of harmony proceeding from reconciliation of various discords and polarities. Dr. Johnson's differing conception is of a cognitive mode expressed in syntax and metaphor to the end of wit: "The most heterogeneous ideas are yoked by violence together."

He seems to have thought the fall of man too good a subject to have been written about. Marvell is surely the foremost misdoubter of the century, not suspicious, but uncannily able to see—and present—so many sides to a case that an essentially less passionate man would be purely evasive. In short his celebration of the greatest poem in the language is very odd panegyric. And his conclusion (45–54) is pure satire of rhyming poets. At the very end he returns to Milton, with a contrast between his poetry and that of the rhymers:

> Thy verse created like thy *Theme* sublime,
> In Number, Weight, and Measure, needs not *Rhime*.
>
> (53–54)

So much, some have said, for Marvell on Dryden. But what Marvell really *says* is that with so exalted a subject and style Milton does not *need* rhyme. If we say that Pope did not need lyric gifts to write as brilliantly as he does, does that mean that he is better off without them? It may be remarked that here and in his other English poetry Andrew Marvell uses rhyme.

Such compulsive dubiety is partially indebted to the enigmatic mode of a good deal of mid-seventeenth-century poetry, especially that by Royalists during the Civil War and the inter-regnum. Although this is a topic to which I shall return in the next chapter, it is necessary here to establish however briefly the nature of that tradition. By now one of the most familiar poems of the enigmatic line is Lovelace's "The Grasse-hopper," which has political meanings clear enough in principle but less easily discussed: [8]

[8] On the other hand, by staying with the tradition rather than with the poetry, D. C. Allen more easily discusses the thought than clarifies the experience in his essay, to which we are all indebted, "An Explication of Lovelace's 'The Grasse-Hopper,' " *Modern Language Quarterly,* XVIII (1957), 25–43.

Dropping *December* shall come weeping in,
   Bewayle th'usurping of his Raigne;
But when in show'rs of old Greeke we beginne,
   Shall crie, he hath his Crowne againe!   (29–32)

The glance at the problems of Charles I is (or seems) obvious, but the sorting of political ideas, especially in the
Cavalier, Anacreontic context of the poem, requires the utmost tact. Another of Lovelace's poems, "The Falcon," deals
very handsomely indeed with the doubly fatal aerial battle of
the Falcon and a Heron. And the poem maintains its
enigmatic mode to perfection:

   Bright Heir t' th' Bird Imperial,
From whose avenging penons fall
Thunder and Lightning twisted Spun;
Brave Cousin-german to the Sun,
That didst forsake thy Throne and Sphere,
To be an humble Pris'ner here;
And for a pirch of her soft hand,
Resign the Royal Woods command.   (7–14)

Those are among the most explicit lines in the poem as far
as suggestion of a darker meaning is concerned. What one
means in calling its mode enigmatic is that it seems as impossible to resist as to elucidate the political significance of such
lines. But with both of Lovelace's poems we have (whatever
the obscurity of what he is talking about) Cavalier clarity of
attitude and tone. The poems may be political, but they are
lyrics, they carry affirmation, just as quite different poems
may be political and satiric. The enigma rests in the casting
of the subject matter, not in the tone, and not indeed even
in the theme, which would be clear at once if we knew the
subject.

Marvell is given to rather similar oblique procedures—the

last quotation from Lovelace sounds uncannily like Marvell, even to the octosyllabic couplets. But his uncertainties grow from "misdoubting" attitudes, from hesitations in accepting the very themes he knows necessarily follow from his postulates. *An Horatian Ode upon Cromwel's Return from Ireland* is notoriously difficult to sort out. The premise essential to the whole poem is that it is a panegyric on Cromwell, even to the point of following the usual heads of praise in the rhetorical handbooks (his origins, divine favor, actions, etc.). That premise is never rejected or countered, but it is misdoubted by the entry of other considerations, the concern with reasons for not praising, and the use of contrast with Charles I. Such "misdoubting" gives strong reasons, as it were, for another and very different poem on the same subject without for a moment actually turning this into that poem. There are scarcely five lines together that can be taken as simple praise of Cromwell. The hesitations are obvious enough in the description of him (33–34) as a man, who:

> Could by industrious Valour climbe
> To ruine the great Work of Time.

We need go but one step further, or rather take a view from another side of Marvell's Roman forum, and we have Dryden's Shaftesbury or MacFlecknoe. What Marvell has written is not simple praise, but it is praise of Cromwell, and opposed to it is the assessment of Charles I which is of course not too simple in expression but is deliberately simplified in evaluation, as if of a favorite child:

> *He* nothing common did or mean
> Upon that memorable Scene:
>   But with his keener Eye
>   The Axes edge did try:

> Nor call'd the *Gods* with vulgar spight
> To vindicate his helpless Right,

> But bow'd his comely Head,
> Down as upon a Bed.   (57–64)

As so often with Marvell, when he is not pairing nouns, he is pursuing crucial adjectives and verbs to use their greater subjectivity as the means of thematic predication. Charles does nothing "common" or "mean"; his eye is very keen; his cause is "helpless"; and his head is "comely." He "tried" the edge of the executioner's axe; he did not "call"; he "bow'd." Every detail is favorable, at least in context, but every detail reduces the portrait from a Vandyke to a Hilliard. From the evidence of this poem, Marvell appears to wish that Charles had stayed king—but the wish very much seems to postdate the execution. Never did a general with divided feelings like Fairfax have a more congenial resident poet.

In addition to the favorable, but not wholly affirmative, picture of the king, Marvell reveals his own inclination to phrases of scrupulous neutrality. The execution of Charles I is a "memorable Scene." The word recurs:

> This was that memorable Hour
> Which first assur'd the forced Pow'r. (65–66)

That "memorable"—for an event that set all England by the ears for over a decade—is the right Marvellian tone. And his inclination to offer evaluation in purely descriptive terms emerges in the second line. To the other side of descriptive neutrality lies of course the praise of Cromwell:

> They can affirm his Praises best,
> And have, though overcome, confest
>   How good he is, how just,
>   And fit for highest Trust:
>
> Nor yet grown stiffer with Command,
> But still in the *Republick*'s hand.   (77–82)

The rhetorical topics are those of testimony even from enemies and humility before the *patria*. The adjectives are again crucial: "good," "just," "fit for highest Trust." But it is curious that this praise, which makes Cromwell seem better as a ruler than Charles I, does not come from the poet himself; it is not *poëta loquitur*. There is, remarkably, no such "ethical proof" at all in this poem. Such tribute is normally confirmative of the orator's own causes for praise. And as for the last two lines, that "yet" and that "still" are very "misdoubting" provisoes.

What above all the poem reveals in such hesitations and proposals is so fine a mingling of qualified satire and song that the tonal harmony prevents separation into constituent notes. Behind this scrupulosity is, I believe, not so much a desire as a compulsion to be exact. There is also a very strong fear of excess, a shrinking from the inherent motion or inertia of human tendencies, as if events perhaps admirable in themselves may run so far as to become irreversibly wrong. In the satires, that fear of things getting out of hand has become hysteria, or at least the pose of hysteria. And in many of the earlier poems the urge to deal with the small or the young or the simple seems precisely a desire to keep control. In his best poems, there is usually a following of the tendency to what can only be thought its teleological purpose. That is, Marvell himself was swept along at times by the tendency to fearsome extremity inherent in full commitment. In *The Garden*, once the speaker turns from the active to the retired life, he goes farther and farther inward toward reflection. Though that is there considered a good thing, in the *Horatian Ode*, once the speaker rejects the retired for the active life, the direction assumed by the poem is toward the active, indeed the military, life:

> But thou the Wars and Fortunes Son
> March indefatigably on:

And for the last effect
Still keep thy Sword erect;
Besides the force it has to fright
The Spirits of the shady Night,
The same *Arts* that did *gain*
A *Pow'r* must it *maintain*.   (113–20)

Such *"Arts"* of extremity are necessary merely to maintain the *status quo* of the Commonwealth. Marvell was of course brilliantly right, but we expect poets to be more obviously committed to the cause they serve. Marvell shows how "rude" such assumptions may be. There are those who think him, basically, a royalist with reservations, and there are others who believe him, again with suitable reservations, a practical Machiavellian concerned with Destiny and character. But his best poems show him to have been independent, and fearful not only of excess but also of those efforts which might be taken to correct excess, because they too become excessive. That is to me the basic significance of the famous remark on the Parliamentary cause and the Civil Wars: "upon considering all, I think the cause was too good to have been fought for. Men ought to have trusted God, they ought to have trusted the King with that whole matter." [9] His distrust of positive, or rather full, action is even better brought out by a less familiar remark: He affirmed the idea that "even Law is force, and the execution of that law a greater violence; and therefore with rational creatures not to be used but upon the utmost extremity." [10] It is evident enough that Marvell's poetry prefers thought to action, "a green Thought in a Green shade" to those *"Arts* that did *gain* / A *Pow'r"* in active life. Significantly, the satire in *The Garden* is di-

[9] *The Rehearsal Transpros'd,* in Alexander B. Grosart, ed., *The Complete Prose Works of Andrew Marvell, M. P.,* 4 vols. (London, 1872–75), III, 212.
[10] *The Rehearsal Transpros'd,* Grosart, ed., *Prose Works,* III, 176.

rected outwards toward the world, even toward women, and is not so finely mingled with the lyric affirmation as in the *Horatian Ode*.

The one poem by Marvell that urges action and yet achieves repose is his most popular, "To his Coy Mistress." Its balance comes in no small measure from the fact that Cavalier assumptions and themes are preferred with Metaphysical wit:

> then Worms shall try
> That long preserv'd Virginity:
> And your quaint Honour turn to dust;
> And into ashes all my Lust.
> The Grave's a fine and private place,
> But none I think do there embrace. (27–32)

This, the most Metaphysical passage of the poem, suitably comes to rest on a definition. But there is also that fear of time and death rising in the middle section of the poem and at the very end. Such fears are very Cavalier, part indeed of one of the most important of Cavalier themes—transience or time, *tempus edax rerum*. But the Metaphysical element in the poem—chiefly a dialectic—revolves that fear like a dark globe taking form upon pivots of bright wit. Marvell for once not only contemplates the possibilities, but in his Metaphysical half, takes amusement. The wit glances gaily about, the dialectical argument moves with great rigor to prove nothing to the woman. (The Cavalier argument proves too much to the arguing man.) In his fully Metaphysical poetry Marvell achieves such repose only by that tendency to paradox represented so well by "The Definition of Love" or by that transcendence shown at its finest in the stanza of *The Garden* on the mind.

What Marvell shows very clearly is that the Metaphysical withdrawal to private poetry, or to poetic treatment of private life, was sufficiently felt and deliberate to leave a consciousness amounting almost to yearning at times for the public or active life and its values. Marvell valued his independence and achieved it in privacy; but he was conscious of a public world in which what one shared with other men was of prime importance. The difference between him and Donne in this respect is that Donne is much more a part of what he sees; he is much more engaged, involved, even if against his will. Donne is ultimately so valuable as a poet because we find the experience he treats of significance even when he does not like it, when he suffers, or when it seems disagreeable to him and us. Marvell, on the other hand, perpetually hesitates, refuses to identify himself even with that which he likes, and questions what he admires. Both share fears that are reflected in the excesses of those satires with which Donne perhaps began, and Marvell probably ended, the main Metaphysical line. Both share as well affirmations of passion and thought that mark their more lyric works. Satire and song, or the attitudes associated with them, set the boundaries, and frequently provide the main constituents, of Metaphysical poetry throughout its development.

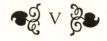

THREE POEMS

—by these hymnes, all shall approve.
— Donne

THE OTHER chapters of this book are primarily concerned
with delineation of the distinguishing features of Metaphysical poetry. Such delineation has at times occasioned attention
to the traditional contexts of the poems and has led at times
to more or less extended examination of them. But the major
emphasis has been upon definition and discrimination of
stylistic and other properties that distinguish Metaphysical
poets from other poets and the Metaphysical poets from each
other. The emphasis of this chapter falls less on Metaphysical poetry than on three poems by Metaphysical poets. If I
am successful, the earlier chapters will have set terms for
considering the literary ancestry as well as the individual lives
of these three significant poems, and this chapter will confirm, if but implicitly, the concerns of the preceding chapters.
The kinds of "ancestry" I have sought to emphasize differ
with each of the three poems discussed, but they combine
contemporary experience, biblical or classical tradition, and
analogous forms of artistic expression. Dealing with other
poems, one might have reason to consider other matters—
continental developments, science, philosophy, or the Cavalier poets. I have simply turned where the poems seemed to
direct me. To discuss the literary life of the poems, I have
tried to leave earlier chapters, and the other elements just
mentioned onstage, but to allow the three poems critically
considered to play the main role. The poems have been
chosen partly for exemplary reasons, as their authors and

titles show: Donne's elegy, *The Perfume*; Herbert's longer poem, *The Flower*; and Marvell's narrative, *The Nymph complaining for the death of her Faun*. But it would be disingenuous of me not to add that these are poems I find especially interesting and sufficiently free of previous extended discussion to allow me the chance of saying something new about them.

i. *The Perfume*

The effectiveness of *The Perfume* is due primarily to its immediacy. The language, the cadences, and the rapid movement draw us at once into the private lyric drama which makes up the world of the poem:

> Once, and but once found in thy company,
> All thy suppos'd escapes are laid on mee. (1–2)

Here is the authentic note of human speech, and behind it a male personality at once involved with and exasperated with his audience. It is unquestionably from the same poet who could write, "For Godsake hold your tongue, and let me love." It is this immediacy and also this tone of something between full attention to the woman and attack upon her that distinguish Donne's secular poems from other love poetry in English. Many reasons may be given, and have been, for this difference. One of the simplest is that behind the lines there is working an antagonism that forces passion into speech. The last couplet of *The Perfume* shows this very well:

> All my perfumes, I give most willingly
> To'embalme thy fathers corse; What? will he die?
>
> (71–72)

Donne's elegies stand between the satires and the *Songs and Sonnets*, thematically and indeed poetically, as the middle ground of his finest secular verse. It is true that their strong satiric undercurrent has not brought them the popularity of the more wholly lyric *Songs and Sonnets*. But anyone who is willing to accept a love poetry that denies numerous romantic assumptions will find that Donne's elegies carry their special conviction.

Unquestionably, however, it is the romantic traditions of love poetry that have proved most popular in English. Idealism, male service, and aspiration (rather than fulfillment) have been its objectives (until the severe modifications of this century). The basis for this poetry lies in contributions from numerous conventions—modified courtly love, Petrarchanism, Marinism, and other traditions that valued praise of feminine worth. But we recall that to Guillaume de Lorris' ideal first half of the *Roman de la Rose* Jean de Meung added a realistic or satirical second. And there were numerous palinodes. But it was far more important that a poet writing in Donne's day could have recourse to a complete alternative to romantic poetry, an alternative best called Roman or Ovidian, although "elegiac" is more exact if perhaps confusing. The Ovidian strain was known to Chaucer and was highly influential on Dryden. To Donne it was a crucial modification of the romantic. He was of course aware of the romantic ideal—as his frequent parodies show. *The Anagram* is a devastating version of the worshipful Elizabethan blazon of a woman's itemized beauty. The elegy beginning, "Natures lay Ideot" parodies the Petrarchan idea of love as education. Without such things as "tear floods" and "sigh tempests," without techniques like the blazon and conceit from Petrarchanism, and without the neo-Platonic conceptions of the over-riding importance of love, Donne's love poetry could not have been written. But of course no one else wrote as he did, because in part no one else drew as he did on these elements and, at the same time, in the same way on classical love poetry. Other major poets at the time—and we must remember that the time was the 1590's—usually turned to Ovid either for eroticism or for a sense of impermanence, mutability. Writing, as perhaps he was, in the interval between the publication of the two major parts of *The Faerie Queene*, Donne seems to have been the only major writer to conceive of love as an experience accommodating both the romantic and Ovidian versions. He took much of the technique of passionate address from the *Heroides* and yet more from the Roman love elegy, and primarily, I believe, from Ovid's *Amores*.

The Ovidian, or Roman, love elegy became popular in England almost at the same time as formal verse satire.[1] In his *Poemata* (1595), Campion laid claim to being the first British elegist:

> Et vatem celebrent Bruti de nomine primum
> Qui molles elegos et sua furta canat.

The claim holds for precedence in publication, but it is likely that Donne was composing most of his elegies at about the same time. And Donne wrote in English. Very few of Donne's poems can be dated with any certainty, but when Jonson said that Donne had written his best work before he was twenty-five, he had a date somewhere around 1597 in mind. Since none of the passages from Donne that he is reported to have memorized is from the *Songs and Sonnets* or divine poems, while one elegy (*The Bracelet*) did stay in his memory, and since it is as elegist that Jonson himself approaches Metaphysical poetry so closely that to this day the canon of the two men is uncertain—for these reasons, it

---

[1] This paragraph draws on the Introduction to the Elegies in Dame Helen Gardner's edition, *The Elegies and Songs and Sonnets*. N. J. C. Andreasen also has some very useful comments about Donne's use of Ovid in her *John Donne: Conservative Revolutionary* (Princeton, 1967), ch. ii.

seems most likely that Jonson at least thought that Donne's elegies dated from a period ending some few years before the close of the seventeenth century. (Of course *The Autumnall* is often supposed to be later for reasons presuming association with Lady Magdalene Herbert.) It is known from contemporary testimony that Donne's satires circulated as a book, a "Book of Satires." Dame Helen Gardner is no doubt right in her assumption, from such evidence as textual traditions among manuscripts, that there was also a "Book of Elegies." This is all the more likely because of certain analogies. Classical writers grouped their elegies into books, and, closer to hand, Campion had put his poems into a *Liber Elegiarum*. The fact that both Donne and Campion have a funeral elegy among their amorous elegies suggests that they had gone the whole distance in imitating Ovid, whose third book continues an elegy (ix) on the death of Tibullus. Finally, "books" of elegies were obviously circulating informally, since elegies not by Donne were added to his in manuscript compilations.

The last decade of the sixteenth century surely is the most remarkable ten years in English literary history. The stage was just rising to its height; Spenser was giving England its first really assured humanistic poetry; and certain "new" forms were beginning to circulate in manuscript—satire, elegy, and epigram. To speak of Donne's elegies alone: they clearly reflect a fashion, which they helped establish, and a sense of a distinct form. Of the fashion it can scarcely be said often enough that although Donne's poems, in this instance his elegies, are valuable because they convey conviction of experience, they are responsive as well to fashion and therefore are not to be taken as biographical fact. The confessional view of poetry dates only from the eighteenth century, and the truth of Donne's poems is one of a universal human relevance rather than of biographical fact.

The principle of the non-biographical relevance of Donne's elegies and *Songs and Sonnets* is widely acknowledged and widely ignored. The sense of distinct form in these works is not widely acknowledged. Such a sense of form is to a considerable sense a conception of genre, because the sixteenth and the seventeenth centuries attached great significance to the kinds of experience, the kinds of occasions, the social or moral significance, and the rhetorical decorum of different genres. (There was of course continual leakage of the generic current—Virgil himself notoriously incorporated the heroic and the satiric in his pastorals.) The harshness and crudeness of the satires of Donne, Hall, and Marston are as decorous as the sweet grace of Spenser's sonnets. Moreover, the related new movements in verse and prose are essentially neo-classical. The Roman elegists and satirists are called upon to bring norms of poetry and reality by which to judge not only the experience of the day but also a kind of poetry increasingly felt to misrepresent the experience of the day. Only those who think classicism, or neo-classicism, monolithic fail to see that the same habits of mind and even the familiarity with a shared body of classical writers could yield entirely different results if Sappho was preferred to Horace for lyricism, or if the epic ideal was forgot in favor of satire. In other words, there is great significance in the choice of a genre or of an author to be emulated, and there is almost a certainty that a given writer will do better in two or three of the genres than in others. It is further significant that for his poetic breakthrough in the last decade of the sixteenth century Donne chose satire and elegy. Fashion and choice must be weighed very carefully in this. But the inclusion of an unusually abstract topic, religion, among the satires, the recurrent outbursts of anger in the elegies, and the great uneasiness with the court—these and other symptoms give evidence of a felt truth behind fashion and the high spirits of the elegies.

Donne's fashioning of the private world of his poetry out of these elements has been discussed in an earlier chapter. All that need be added here can be presented in terms of the characteristics of the Roman love elegy.[2] These characteristics suggest what Campion, Donne, and Jonson could set before themselves as possibilities.

The three best-known Roman elegists—Ovid, Catullus, and Tibullus—differ in numerous respects; the Roman definition of an elegy was, after all, basically prosodic (see *Amores*, I, i). But from his apparent favorite, Ovid, much of Donne's most striking achievement can be seen in better light. The Roman elegy was of great utility in creating a new kind of love poetry. For one thing, the Romans treated the woman as an equal or an inferior, not as an unapproachable goddess. For another, they assumed sophistication rather than innocence. Ovid's Corinna (who may of course be purely fictional) is married, and it is usually such an adulterous or otherwise experienced woman whom the elegist pursues. To bring these two elements into a world whose poetic tribunes were the sonneteers was obviously subversive and well calculated to draw attention to oneself. But it is also true that these two features of the Roman love elegy gave Donne his America, his new found land of experience to explore; and he could hardly have been unaware of the implications of his

[2] Quite another characterization than mine of the Roman elegy and its relation to seventeenth-century poetry is needed; it would involve not only the practice of a number of poets of the time, in Latin as well as English, but also the discussions of elegies by Renaissance scholars. For two such discussions, see *Ivlii Caesaris Scaligeri Poetices Libri Septem*, 5th ed. (Heidelberg, 1617), I, 1; III, cxxiv; etc.; and Giovanni Pontano, *Reformata Poeseos Institvtio*, cap. xxxv and cap. xxxvi. I have read Pontano in Johann Buchler, *Sacrarum Profanarumque Phrasivm Poeticarvm Thesavrvs*, 13th ed. (London, 1642), pp. 384–88. Instead of sailing into these waters, I have tried to read Donne against the practice of the Roman elegists, assuming that, whatever his debt to Renaissance scholars, his turning to the Latin elegists was sufficiently radical to imply above all his personal study of the Roman elegy.

choice. What he allowed himself to explore was, in any event, sex and passion rather than wooing and service, and therefore psychology replaced morality as the obvious concern of the poet. The "Come, Madame, come" of *To his Mistris Going to Bed* is obviously an impatient address to a woman of the town; the almost last sally—"There is no pennance due to innocence" (46)—shows how far the excitement of sex has become a frank subject of interest. The pair in *The Perfume* include a young man, the speaker of the poem, and his experienced but attractive and unmarried girl friend. He recalls "those sweet nights." If those are not the casual nights of *Going to Bed* (and they are not), they are still worlds away from the love situations of Spenser, Watson, Drayton, or Sidney.

The Roman elegy also created a social world with a special ethos and considerable sense of time and place. It is the more or less wealthy class of the capital (e.g., Ovid, ii, vii, and viii), those who can afford travel (Ovid, ii, xi), who have servants (Ovid, i, xi, and xii) and slaves (Ovid, ii, vii and viii). Dramatic moments are often created, sometimes in the imagination of the speaker (Ovid, i, ii), and there will be details of dress, pets, food, waiting at doors, and much else that gives a strong sense of actuality. In this world, no one seems to have any work to do, unless it is the self-conscious poet who speaks of his art from time to time. In *The Perfume*, such a social ethos is wonderfully Londonized into the household of the aristocrat, the gentry, or a city family. There is that "grim eight-foot-high iron-bound serving-man," whose role is to "barre the first gate." The degree of wealth implied is increased, or confirmed, by reference to the mistress' expected fortune (11). The court society of the satires in a sense turns Renaissance panegyric topsy-turvy, and in the fear conveyed by most of the satires, there is something of a tragic tone as well. The elegies either go lower in the social scale or, what seems more likely, simply treat the private life of men and women similar to those at court in the much different social tone of comedy.

The Roman elegy provided, as well as the ethos, the best model for Donne's use of speaker and audience in terms of address. Ovid goes farthest in this respect, addressing even Aurora or a ring about to be sent off to his mistress. But the usual audience is either Corinna, her maid, or her slave. Some poems have no particular audience in the poem (II, xvii), but usually there is either a kind of immediate, "dramatic" situation (I, iv, *etc.*) or a recalled "narrative" situation in which address to the woman is included as one of several features (I, v, etc.). What was usual, drama, with the Roman elegists is consistent and heightened by Donne. In his elegies, the address is almost always to the woman (*The Comparison* is to a man) so creating that directness and that sense of immediate experience that makes the poems seem so dramatic:

> Once, and but once found in thy company,
> All thy suppos'd escapes are laid on mee... (1–2)

> Though thy immortall mother which doth lye
> Still buried in her bed, yet will not dye ... (13–14)

> Thy little brethren, which like Faiery Sprights
> Oft skipt into our chamber, those sweet nights ...
> (27–28)

In one final respect, the Roman elegy, especially Ovid's, must have had special appeal to Donne. Its combination of passion and wit (often to produce a certain naughtiness of tone) must have appealed to him as just the kind of poetry that might serve as a proper corrective to the usual cant about love. Donne's wit involved a greater parade of learning and allusion—and that element is couched in terms closer to Ovid in the elegies than it is in the *Songs and Sonnets*. In both the Roman elegists and Donne there is a novelty of conception and a verbal wit to match the intellectual. Like the Roman elegy, then, Donne's characteristic version of the elegy form is distinguished by: an equal or lower status for the woman; a postulate of sophistication; a wealthy urban and domestic society; a clearly defined audience and a clear situation functioning so that it expands into a little drama or narrative; and a combination of passion with wit. These same elements will be found in the *Songs and Sonnets*. They may be found directed to the excesses of an elegy like *The Anagram*, to the sweetness of the opening of *The Bracelet*, and in other tones suited to a new lyric purpose. It is quite true that Donne rejected Petrarchanism (it is also true that he kept a good deal in the rejection); but it should not be pretended that he wrote *ex nihilo*. He was more neo-classical, if not more conventional, in his debts than were the sonneteers. It was Roman silver that he, as Monarch of Wit, stamped with his own head into full poetic currency.

The Perfume[3] is a poem of moderate length, its seventy-two lines falling between the longest (114 ll.) and the shortest (20 ll.) of Donne's elegies. The situation softens the frequent Roman adultery to an affair with a girl under her family's noses (cf. Tibullus, I, ii). In spite of all the obstacles they have laid in his way, he has managed his affair with considerable success. Roughly the first half of the poem (1–38) conveys their triumph over her parents. Indeed it is striking that Donne so often found a passage of about forty lines as far as he chose to go, or could go, in a given direction, in a given strophe or section. The second half of the poem (39–72), like the second half of *The Extasie*, or like the turns of many of his poems, moves in reverse fashion, describing the man's self-betrayal by the perfume he wore. In this section, his precautions are as little successful as those of her

---

[3] The text of the poem is given in the Appendix, pp. 273 ff.

parents had been in the first. After a sort of neutral or transitional passage (39–52), the address suddenly changes from the girl to the perfume (53–70), shifting back to the girl only at the very end (71–72). Once again, we are faced with the problem of a shift in the direction and the plane of experience. It is one thing to have a young man address a young woman in terms mingling some affection with irritation, pride, anger, and self-regard. It is another thing to have him address the ball of perfume that betrayed him and to question himself.

The first half of the poem is in effect made up of three stanzas, in which first the father, then the mother, and at last the "serving-man" are spoken of as the obstacles to the secret love of the speaker and his girl friend. Each section ends with a "refrain" taking satisfaction that such opposition has been outwitted. However hard the "Hydroptique" father tried, "Yet close and secret, as our soules, we'have beene" (12). The mother may try all her arts to extract some sign or confession of guilt from her daughter:

> And kissing notes the colour of thy face,
> And fearing least thou'art swolne, doth thee embrace;
> To trie if thou long, doth name strange meates,
> And notes thy palenesse, blushing, sighs, and sweats;
> And politiquely will to thee confesse
> The sinnes of her owne youths ranke lustinesse.
>
> (19–24)

And yet, pat comes the refrain:

> Yet love these Sorceries did remove, and move
> Thee to gull thine owne mother for my love.   (25–26)

Nor can the "serving-man" discover anything:

> Though by thy father he were hir'd for this,
> Could never witnesse any touch or kisse.   (37–38)

These incidents are not incorporated into a sequence and so are not narrative. Each is a parallel drama recalled after the initial confession that he has been apprehended.

The attitude toward the girl's parents is one of hatred relieved only by mockery and disgust. The father dominates the poem as much as anyone other than the speaker, being the first hated in each half of the poem, and the object of the speaker's last exasperated comment: "What? will hee die?" (The expression, "what," is an older interjection of impatience, and the first question mark is obviously that of an older day which did double duty for the exclamation as well. The function of the second is less clear.) As for the mother, he only wishes she would die. His attitude toward the girl is much more complex. He does resent the fact that all her "suppos'd escapes are laid on" him (2)—that is, all her wrong-doings, especially sexual—but in doing so, he admits them to be "suppos'd." There is a value to him in the past, in "those sweet nights" they have shared, but it is not clear how much this implies of tenderness and how much of self-gratification. The crucial passage in the first half of the poem is that on the father's threat:

> Though hee hath oft sworne, that hee would remove
> Thy beauties beautie, and food of our love,
> Hope of his goods . . .   (9–11)

It is possible to read this as the father's criticism of this particular young man: "He would take away your inheritance, which (he says) is all I am after." [4] If that is the case, it is difficult to understand why the tenth line is there at all, and the most natural way of reading the lines is as presenting a double appositive: "He has sworn that he would take away what is the special character of your beauty, and that which sustains our love, namely, hope to inherit his money." His

[4] Dame Helen Gardner suggests that this "may be" all that is meant.

hopes for the death of her father and mother confirm this view almost to a certainty, but it should be noticed that he assumes that she has the same motivations: "food of *our* love" (my stress). What the speaker suggests is that it is likely that they might have been dissuaded from enduring in so difficult a suit if they had not had so powerful an economic incentive to sustain them. On balance, the first half of the poem is a success story of love against odds, Hero and Leander, Romeo and Juliet—but in the tone of the Roman elegy. The second half of the elegy has the same elements but recounts a failure:

> But Oh, too common ill, I brought with mee
> That, which betray'd mee to my enemie:
> A loud perfume, which at my entrance cryed
> Even at thy fathers nose, so were wee spied.
>
> (39–42)

The "loud perfume" [5] reminds us of the title and perhaps makes us wonder how the first half of the poem relates to this apparently major part of the poem. The chief logical connection has already been suggested: having succeeded in their love against the obstacles placed by the family, he now finds that the guardian family proves successful through his own self-betrayal. The betrayal is to his "enemie," her father, who dominates the poem as the antagonist. That dominance of the antagonist and the need to rely on shifts and one's wits is another feature unifying the poem, giving it its tone of fear, antagonism, and even of some sense of danger. In the use of such an antagonist and in the defensive posture of the speaker we have a more particularized or more dramatic version of the situation in most of Donne's satires.

[5] Donne's usage of *loud* for "Powerful; offensive" antedates by nearly half a century the earliest usage recorded in the *Oxford English Dictionary*, by Milton, in 1641. Donne of course plays upon its usual meaning.

So much is easy enough. The most difficult matter to decide upon is that of the role of the girl friend in the two halves of the poem. That is, she has a very obvious place in the first half—and no very obvious role at all in the second half, which seems almost entirely to concern her father and the traitorous perfume. For many years I suspected, and sometimes have argued, that there is a quasi-identification between the girl and the perfume. Two passages seem to suggest as much:

> I taught my silkes, their whistling to forbeare,
> Even my opprest shoes, dumbe and speechlesse were,
> Onely, thou bitter sweet, whom I had laid
> Next mee, mee traiterously hast betraid ...   (51–54)

> You'are loathsome all, being taken simply'alone,
> Shall wee love ill things joyn'd, and hate each one?
> If you were good, your good doth soone decay;
> And you are rare, that takes the good away.
> All my perfumes, I give most willingly
> To'embalme thy fathers corse; What? will hee die?
>   (67–72)

Previous to the former passage, the second-person pronoun had been used only for address to the girl; it is natural that we should go on in this passage on the same assumption, so that "thou bitter sweet," which has "laid / Next" him is the girl rather than a pomander ball or some other form of solid perfume such as was used at the time. The latter passage seems, on the contrary, to be speaking of perfumes with the traditional paradox that their single good odors are compounded of many things that stink; yet suddenly it turns out that he is addressing the girl ("thy fathers corse") for what seems the first time in about thirty-five lines. Nor does the shift from *you* in l. 70 to the more familiar *thy* in l. 72 necessarily denote a different audience, because in the perfume section we find *thou* (53), *thee,* (59) *thee* (61), *you* (63), *yee* (65), *you* (66), *you* (69), and again *you* (70). On this evidence, we have a deliberate ambiguity.

There are passages, however, in the second half of the poem that make a reading of the perfume as a metaphor for the girl very difficult. In the first place, there is the dramatic situation —it is his perfume, not hers. In the second, there is the following:

> Base excrement of earth, which dost confound
> Sense, from distinguishing the sicke from sound;
> By thee the seely Amorous sucks his death
> By drawing in a leprous harlots breath.   (57–60)

Nothing in the tone of the first half of the poem justifies our thinking that he regards the girl as a diseased harlot. He feels irritation obviously, but her "escapes," he concedes, are only supposed by her parents. This passage, finally, does not sort with his reflection on those "sweet nights" they have shared. We can only seek a temperate description which is, I believe, that Donne did not intend an identification of the perfume and the girl, but that he manipulated his initial and closing address to the perfume in such a way that he can glide from, and at last to, address restricted to the girl. His shifting of audiences is by no means new. The most similar of Roman elegies, Tibullus, i, ii, moves about even more. Catullus and Ovid address all manner of audience, and Donne, as we have seen, shifted audiences at will in "The Indifferent." But to say that a technique is not unusual does not necessarily imply that it is successful in a given instance, even if there are witty transitional passages.

The meaning and the success of the seeming shift in address from the girl to the perfume and back to the girl at the very end are founded on the poem's central irony. Having won what he sought against the strong odds of the family, the speaker has betrayed himself. The true role of the girl in all this depends upon an exact understanding of the situation of the poem. The dramatic moments of which the poem is built (three or four or more escapes and one detection) are subsumed or recalled in one later moment, that of the present address to the girl. To quote the opening yet again:

> Once, and but once found in thy company,
> All thy suppos'd escapes are laid on mee ... (1–2)

We see that, after all, the dramatic address to the girl and the perfume is a replacement of ordinary narrative with narrative of recollection within direct address. The lovers are right there together, perhaps in bed, and he is expatiating on what she already knows to have happened, but on what his exasperation, pique with her, fury with his perfume, and self-dismay all require. Having managed to get together alone yet another time, he is talking to her *after* their detection, and *after* he has had to suffer her father's accusation for all her imagined affairs. This puts a new light on those "suppos'd escapes"—they are only "suppos'd" in the sense that he trusts that her escapades have all been with him. Whether that trust can be accepted by us is difficult to decide. Obviously the young man is a dandy—in silks, perfumed ("By thee, the greatest staine to mans estate / Falls on us, to be call'd effeminate")—but he realizes all this. What is really especially nice is that, as the two lie or sit together, he should pull out his solid perfume and histrionically address it as he does, perhaps with a glance at the girl at the beginning and end of his address.

Like most of the speakers of Donne's poems, the young man here seems more concerned with himself than with his girl, in spite of the fact that he addresses her throughout the poem. Indeed, the address to the perfume (53–70) should be in a kind of double quotation marks, part of his report, of his confession to her as they sit or lie there. And yet, at the same

time, the address to the perfume permits him to shift from
what is certainly an oblique statement of his love for her in
the first half of the poem to a confession or self-criticism and
to expression of downright hatred for her father. In the end,
the girl remains his only supporter—he cannot even trust
himself not to betray himself. It is this above all that draws
a contrast between the perfume and her. The rhetorical
gestures of address may draw a kind of connection, but the
relation is one of contrast rather than resemblance. Out of
context a line like "You'are loathsome all, being taken
simply'alone" (67) sounds very like the argument in "Communitie" and certain other poems—that women are made to
be taken in the large, not singly. But in *The Perfume*, cynical
and angry though he may be, much as he hates all her family
except her little brothers, much even as it passes his mind that
he might give up the connection if it were not for hope of
her money—still, he pays her the compliment of being the
only trustworthy, decent thing in his world, even including
himself.

The procedure to such an end is perhaps somewhat less
signposted than need be, but it must be allowed that the
poem undertakes a difficult task in its seventy-two lines. It
undertakes to create a dramatic situation of address to the
girl, and of address to the perfume within the address to the
girl. It employs this address to recall the speaker's grounds
for hating the girl's father and mother, to prove her father
their worst enemy and a despicable person besides; to absorb
three or four dramatic scenes of escape in the first half of the
poem; to absorb a larger scene of self-betrayal in the second
half. Above all, what the poem does is establish a remarkably
convincing equilibrium of the young man's feelings of self-
gratification, shame, bravado, love for his girl, and hatred of
her father and mother. The young man and his girl hardly
emerge as do Romeo and Juliet, but they nonetheless emerge
valuable, real. What we have here is the truth of the Roman

elegy; what we have in Shakespeare's play is the truth of romance. In some ways this elegy is more convincing—at least the parents are more fully felt. This oppressive and inimical outer world is made, through furtiveness and stealth, to give some room for realized private passion and true human attachment. The young man is not spared in any particular; he has enough faults to outfit more than one young coxcomb. But through his exaggeration we see his point: a hostile world will simply not leave them alone. The fine and private place sought by lovers is just not to be had in such a world. The social world of a strict Elizabethan family is no country for young men.

The poem also possesses remarkable vivacity, and it comes very near to including the total range of effect and experience of Donne's private secular poetry. Its privacy, its brilliant (if somewhat obscure) manipulation of time and place, its use of wit, its blend of satire and lyric affirmation—these features show how completely Donne's career in secular verse had been realized in the elegy, and how far the major characteristics of his followers are adumbrated. This poem alone would show that Metaphysical poetry was fully creative and operating in the 1590's, that it responded to modern fashion by modelling itself on a classical genre, and that it went on to acquire an accent and significance all its own. The poem is that rare thing, a convincing characterization of a young man's real experience of love; it is also, though not a full picture, a shadowy outline of a young woman whose family and heart do not agree. To me, this is the finest of Donne's elegies and a presumptive proof that all of them deserve closer examination, and appreciation, than they have had.

ii. *The Flower*

Many of Herbert's finest poems resemble *The Flower* in treating the agonies and joys of spiritual life. Many of his best poems are those, like *The Flower*, which propose in their title or elsewhere an image or an emblem that is developed in the course of the poem. Herbert clearly knew what he was doing in both respects. As for the first, it will be recalled that he remarked to Ferrar that his poems gave "a picture of the many spiritual Conflicts that have past between God and my Soul, before I could subject mine to the will of Jesus my Master, in whose service I have now found perfect freedom." [6] The vicissitudes of the soul reflect approaches to, or deflections from, the will of God. As for emblems and emblematic images, Herbert has been recognized to be the most emblematic of the major Metaphysical poets, just as Francis Quarles unquestionably is of the lesser. The kinds of experience combined in the poem are, then, at once highly personal and felt to be of the utmost significance on the one hand, and highly traditional on the other. Ministerial psychiatry did not begin in the twentieth century; Herbert shows that he knew, both in himself and in others, what the seventeenth century called "the case of conscience," an inner turmoil and uncertainty. The varying spiritual estate was one that he and his contemporaries knew all too well—scarcely a major poet can be found who did not undergo a major religious upheaval and usually some change of religion. The integrity and candor with which Herbert treats his own spiritual situation is obvious to readers today. But integrity in poetry is gained by poetic means, and we can glance again at the emblematic title and remark that it provides the poem with an image sustained more openly and at greater length than any of Donne's conceits. Neither openness nor length necessarily assure success, but the fact is that we have literary techniques to talk about. It is these that will chiefly concern me, and I shall assume that my reader is also his and is willing to agree with me that Herbert's poetry shows an integrity of life and that its distinctive feature is a humility

[6] *The Works of George Herbert*, ed. F. E. Hutchinson, p. xxxvii.

dearly bought from pride and a simplicity akin to magnificence.

Much has justly been made of the "poetry of meditation" in the seventeenth century, and specifically of the way in which varieties of the formal religious meditation were drawn upon by writers—as diverse as Donne, Crashaw, Herbert, and Richard Baxter—to give their writings coherence and religious atmosphere. Herbert's poem, *The Flower*, is indebted to two other traditions of religious writing. One, the emblematic, has already been mentioned; the other, that of the soul's vicissitudes, has already been hinted at and will be discussed subsequently.

Herbert characteristically uses his emblems in a particular way, and it is that which we need to try to distinguish. The second quarter of the century was a time of popularity for what may be called the *sic vita* motif, in which various things were set forth in order that a comparison to human life might be drawn. Henry King's poem entitled "Sic Vita" may be taken as a representative work in this line:

> Like to the Falling of a Starr;
> Or as the Flights of Eagles are;
> Or like the fresh Spring's gawdy hew;
> Or Silver Dropps of Morning Dew;
> Or like a Wind that chafes the flood;
> Or Bubbles which on Water stood;
> Even such is Man, whose borrow'd Light
> Is streight Call'd in, and Pay'd to Night.
>
> The Wind blowes out, the Bubble Dyes;
> The Spring entomb'd in Autumne lyes:
> The Dew dryes up: The Starr is shott:
> The Flight is past: And Man Forgott.[7]

---

[7] In her edition of *The Poems of Henry King* (Oxford, 1965), Margaret Crum gives persuasive reasons for accepting the traditional ascription of authorship of this poem to King.

There are numerous similar poems of the time. Of course there is a tradition running back to classical writers and glosses on Scripture; there are even Buddhist analogies. But each age chooses what it feels it needs from the past, and it is thought that the poem which started the *sic vita* fashion in the seventeenth century was one that exists in a number of places or contexts, and which is added, with his name, by Quarles to the end of his narrative poem, *Argalus and Parthenia* (1629). The latter half of the poem is more like King's, the former closer to Herbert's:

> Like to the Damask Rose you see,
> Or like the blossome on the tree,
> Or like the dainty flower of May,
> Or like the morning to the day,
> Or like the Sunne, or like the shade,
> Or like the Guord which Jonas had,
> > Even such is man, whose thread is spunne,
> > Drawne out and cut, and so is done.
>
> The Rose withers, the blossome blasteth,
> The flower fades, the morning hasteth:
> The Sunne sets, the shadow flies,
> The Guord consumes, and man he dies.[8]

Such poems are not despicable, but they certainly reveal how much more full of life, hope, movement, and particular personality Herbert's poetry is. It is important that we recognize both the difference in quality and the resemblance in kind. A simple test of both is given by Herbert's shorter poem, "Life," which we have no trouble in placing at once in the emblematic *sic vita* tradition:

[8] The poem can be found in *The Complete Works in Prose and Verse of Francis Quarles*, ed. Alexander B. Grosart, 3 vols. (London, 1880–81), III, 285.

I made a posie, while the day ran by:
Here will I smell my remnant out, and tie
           My life within this band.
But Time did beckon to the flowers, and they
By noon most cunningly did steal away,
           And wither'd in my hand.

Sic vita flora. Like *The Flower*, "Life" affords some hope (in its third stanza).

Farewell deare flowers, sweetly your time ye spent,
Fit, while ye liv'd, for smell or ornament,
           And after death for cures.
I follow straight without complaints or grief,
Since if my sent be good, I care not if
           It be as short as yours.

Numerous specific flowers provided the emblem. Herrick's "To Daffodils" gives one of the most common.[9] But Herbert's favorite was the rose,[10] and if any flower must be chosen as that of *The Flower*, it must be this. It is a root plant (11); it comes forth in buds (36); and it grows in gardens (46). Herbert's flower is, then, probably a rose and is certainly an emblem for life. And he expanded on the *sic vita* tradition to allow his well-scented plant to provide a hopeful emblem of the good life as well as an emblem for transitoriness.

The movement in Herbert's poem comes of course from his more complex Metaphysical art, but that art itself follows another tradition at once more complex and more comprehensive. Indeed, the tradition of writing on the soul's vicissi-

[9] On the transience traditionally associated with the daffodil, see the entry in the *Oxford English Dictionary*.

[10] Hutchinson's notes on the poem compare "The Rose," 1. 18; "Priest to the Temple," 1. 34; and *Providence*, 1. 78. Because it was a royal flower, because the rose had numerous emblematic uses, and because it was used medicinally, it was commonly thought in England to be the essential flower.

tudes is much more extensive and continuous than that of the meditation, and it runs from Hebrew to Christian writings (especially in Christian glosses on the Old Testament). Since there is not, to my knowledge, any detailed examination of literary uses of this tradition, I can hardly hope to set it forth in detail in a third of a chapter. But certain features may be mentioned. Treatment of the soul's vicissitudes might involve either Testament or the Apocrypha, but three books of the Old Testament stand out above all other sources: Job, Psalms, and the Canticles. Each of them had a distinctive role in treating the soul's vicissitudes, the fluctuations of the spiritual life. Job was primarily a source for evidence of anguish and awe, the Canticles for joy. The variety of the Psalms made them useful for either spiritual extreme, although in practice those concerned with grief or suffering seem to have been more often used.

The most illuminating treatment of such a tradition by a contemporary of Herbert's is that of Quarles in his *Emblemes* (1635, etc.), "far the most popular book of verse of the century." [11] The first two books of the five deal chiefly with the vanity of earthly things and so do not concern us. But the last three deal with the vicissitudes of the soul in a way that may be uneven in poetic quality but that is very moving when understood as a progression. The general progress is from anguish to joy, although the sorrows are sometimes tempered and the joys are sometimes interrupted. Such development leads to the domination of Book III by Job and Psalms. Book v takes its character from the Canticles. Of the fifteen emblem sections of Book III, for example, only four come from other books; six are from the Psalms, and five from Job. In so much shorter a work as *The Flower*, Herbert was

[11] Helen Gardner, *The Metaphysical Poets*, Penguin ed., rev. (1966), p. 317; but Quarles was probably equalled in popularity by Wither and was approached by Herbert.

obviously in no position to set forth spiritual development on so large a scale.[12] But he could, with his unusual skill in fashioning stanzas and yet in moving significantly to an end, give a sense both of repeated experience and of going toward a greater hope. The stanzaic structure—movement in repetition—is obvious in the earlier half of Donne's elegy, *The Perfume*, not to mention his *Songs and Sonnets*; and in an earlier chapter it was shown how integral that formal principle is to any long Metaphysical poem. Herbert was, therefore, hardly eccentric in his commitment to meaningful use of stanzas, but there is no other Metaphysical poet so skilled or so persistent in using the resources of the stanza. If, on other grounds, Donne is the Shakespeare among Metaphysicals, Herbert is the Spenser.

The poem begins with the return of spiritual springtime to the speaker of the poem.[13] The next two stanzas recall the earlier "shrivel'd" state of his heart and attribute its recovery to God's power. The fourth, or central, stanza expresses a longing for a state beyond change in God's garden, paradise. The next two stanzas (v and vi) deal once again, and yet more strongly, with the soul's agony under God's just wrath and with the recovery from that state. The final stanza changes the "Lord of power" (15) of the first section of the poem to "Lord of love" (43) and realizes that hope of planting oneself in God's garden (if abundance and pride

---

[12] If this were the place, I would set forth my reasons—both from the poems in *The Temple* and from Herbert's remark to Ferrar—for thinking that it is the vicissitudes of the soul, rather than meditations on the Eucharist, that define the dominant character of the work. There is of course much that is eucharistic in *The Temple*, but the second Anglican sacrament, baptism, is also treated—specifically; and to the extent that the reader of *The Temple* is, as it were, in a church, it is worship generally rather than communicating particularly that is involved. With this view, *The Flower* becomes a microcosm of the whole, and the eucharistic last poem, "Love (iii)," a last climax.

[13] The text of the poem is given in the Appendix, pp. 275 ff.

do not betray) which had been raised in the middle stanza. The movement of Herbert's poem is, therefore, more cyclical and somewhat less clearly progressive than the movement of Books III–v of Quarles' *Emblemes*, but it is the same hopeful movement toward God.

The element of hope is implicit in *The Flower* from the first stanza with its return of the soul's spring. Behind that return lies an important passage from the Canticles (ii. 10–12):

My beloved spake, and said unto me, Rise up, my Love, my faire one, and come away. For loe, the winter is past,
the raine is over and gone.
The flowers appear on the earth . . .[14]

By developing the *sic vita* tradition along the line of this passage, Herbert was able to give hope to his picture of the soul's vicissitudes. And the "lines" of the passage are the traditional one of biblical interpretation. Gregory had glossed "The flowers appear on the earth" in terms of the soul's anticipations of eternal joys: "For then *flowers appear in the land*, when the soul begins to foretaste certain stirrings of a sweetness from the eternal beatific life." [15] The imagery of the passing of unfavorable weather with the coming of spiritual spring is of course basic to Herbert's poem. Gregory's comment on "the raine is over and gone" shows that the happiness is due to Christ: "*The storm is past*. In my rising from

---

[14] The Vulgate version: "En dilectus meus loquitur mihi: surge, propera amica mea, columba mea, formosa mea, & veni. Iam enim transiit hyems, imber abiit, & recessit. Flores apparuerunt in terra nostra . . ."

[15] "Tunc enim *apparent flores in terra*, quando de aeterna beatitudinis vita quaedam suavitatis primordia praegustare anima" (*Biblia Sacra Cum Glossa Ordinaria*, 6 vols. [Douai and Antwerp, 1617], III, col. 1836, hereafter, *Biblia Sacra*. I cite this splendid Bible as the readiest means of indicating traditional commentary and exegesis, not to suggest that Herbert had necessarily read Gregory in it.)

the dead I have stilled the tempest and restored calm." [16] Or to call on Gregory yet once more, the spiritual hope to be found in the floral symbol is derived from the Canticles. The gloss is on *flores:* "They are said to have appeared on the earth, because although holy souls leave their bodies, they are received in heaven. And because, even though it was winter in this life, they did not grow sluggish in good works, so as soon as they departed, they flowered gloriously in the land of the living." [17]

The same chapter of the Canticles provided another significant association with flowers, because although in the Authorized Version, ii.5, reads, "Stay me with flagons, and comfort me with apples, for I am sick with love," the Vulgate is different: "Fulcite me *floribus,* stipate me malis, quia amore langueo" (italics mine). It is the Vulgate that Quarles follows, like many Protestants, though he renders it into English (see V,ii). His fourth stanza shows how a poet of considerable gifts but of less individual poetic vitality might treat the significance of flowers for the soul's vicissitudes:

Virgins, tuck up your silken laps, and fill ye
  With the faire wealth of *Floras* Magazine;
The purple Vy'let, and the pale-fac'd Lilly;
  The Pauncy and the Organ Colombine;
The flowring Thyme, the gilt-boule Daffadilly;
  The lowly Pinck, the lofty Eglentine:
    The blushing Rose, the Queene of Flow'rs, and best
    Of *Floras* beauty; but, above the rest,
Let Iesses sov'raigne Flow'r perfume my qualming breast.

---

[16] "*Imber abiit.* Ego a mortuis resurgens, tempestate compressa tranquillitatem reddidi" (*Biblia Sacra,* III, 1837).

[17] "*Flores.* Apparuisse in terra dicuntur, quia sanctae animae cum a corporibus recedunt, in coelo recipiuntur. Et quia in hac vita, quamvis hyems fuerit, a bono opere non torpuerunt: mox ut recesserunt, in terra viventium gloriose floruerunt" (*Biblia Sacra,* III, 1837).

He shares with Herbert the poet's tendency to follow the floral figure farther than is necessary for the spiritual significance, but the last line shows what that significance was. Lest there be any doubt, Quarles cites Bernard on Canticles ii.5:

> *By flowers understand faith; by fruit, good works: As the flower or blossome is before the fruit, so is faith before good works: So neither is the fruit without the flower, nor good works without faith.*

By reading the Canticles as a representation of the ardent love between God, especially God the Son, and the devout soul, theologians and poets alike were able to adapt strong passions to religious ends. Some of the finest medieval religious lyrics are those with a Latin refrain taken from Canticles ii.5 (and v. 8), "Quia amore langueo," usually to the end of showing Christ faint with love, about to expire on the cross. Similarly, "the feilds of Grace," in Crashaw's phrase, included that garden in which the whole drama of the soul's salvation was enacted. As William Alabaster put it:

> My soul within the bed of heaven doth grow,
> Where Christ hath set it in his own dear wound,
> That with all grace above it might abound,
> And spread his loaden branches here below.
> Why should not then my love still overflow,
> And flourish on so good a ground? [18]

The second chapter of the Canticles provides the basis for Herbert's picture of spiritual vicissitude, both in imagery

[18] For some of the *Quia amore langueo* lyrics, see *One Hundred Middle English Lyrics*, ed. Robert D. Stevick (Indianapolis, 1964). Alabaster's lines will be found in *The Sonnets of William Alabaster*, ed. G. M. Story and Helen Gardner (Oxford, 1959), p. 7. They are quoted by Stanley Stewart in *The Enclosed Garden* (Madison, Milwaukee, and London, 1964), p. 95. Almost all of Stewart's fine book is relevant to *The Flower*, but see especially, pp. 37, 81, 88–89, and 93–95.

and in movement, since in this poem (as in most in *The Temple*) he moves toward hope and reconciliation with God. The second and fifth stanzas, however, give a picture of times which, though now past, were occasions of great spiritual anguish:

> Who would have thought my shrivel'd heart
> Could have recover'd greennesse? It was gone
>   Quite under ground; as flowers depart
> To see their mother-root, when they have blown;
>   Where they together
>   All the hard weather,
> Dead to the world, keep house unknown.
>   (st. ii, 8–14)

The return of the flower to the root is an old trope to which Herbert gives a very fresh treatment.[19] But he is describing a profound lowness of spirit, a going as it were to the grave ("under ground"), a death in winter, or the agonies of hell:

> These are thy wonders, Lord of power,
> Killing and quickning, bringing down to hell
>   And up to heaven in an houre.   (st. iii, 15–17)

What he desires is to rise above such depression and to go beyond change, to be a flower in "Paradise" (23) or God's "garden" (46).

The explanation of such plunges of spirit may not much suit modern tastes, but Herbert set forth God's just wrath as an explanation for the death-like hell of anguish:

> But while I grow in a straight line,
> Still upwards bent, as if heav'n were mine own,
>   Thy anger comes, and I decline.   (st. v, 29–31)

The plunge of the soul under the anger of God has of course no connection with the Canticles. For this aspect of the poem,

---

[19] Hutchinson compared Herbert's *Memoriae Matris Sacrum*, v, 13: "Cuncta ad radices redeant."

we must consider Job 14:13: "O that thou wouldst hide me in the grave, that thou wouldst keep me secret till thy wrath be past." [20] Although as it were employing the same symbols, the Vulgate is again closer than the Authorized Version to Herbert's poem: "Quis mihi hoc tribuat, ut in *inferno* protegas me, & abscondas me donec pertranseat furor tuus" (italics mine). Gregory's brief comment covers the whole ground of the passages just quoted from Herbert (8–14, 15–17, 29–31): "The wrath of the Lord, in respect to the souls of the elect, has passed over in our Redeemer's coming, because he has brought them back from the gates of hell to the joys of paradise." [21] What is implied is nothing less than the whole redemptive order, as may be inferred from Gregory or be seen explicitly in the commentary of Chrysostom: "So, before the coming of the Mediator of God and man, there is no doubt but that each man, though he was of proven life in the world, descended to the gates of hell—because man, who fell through himself, could not return to the quiet of paradise through himself, unless that One would come who would open for us the path of this same paradise by the mystery of His incarnation." [22] Or, in the more concise words of the *moraliter* gloss of "wrath": "That is, Thy indignation against the human race, which was reconciled with God by the death of Christ." [23]

[20] For a use of the passage similar to Herbert's, see Quarles, *Emblemes*, iii, xii.

[21] "Furor Domini quantum ad electorum animae in redemptoris nostri adventu pertransiit: quia eas ab inferni claustris ad paradisi gaudia reduxit" (*Biblia Sacra*, iii, 179).

[22] "Quia ante adventum mediatoris Dei & hominis, omnis homo, quamvis mundae probataeque vitae fuerit, ad inferni claustra descendit, dubium non est: quoniam homo, qui per se cecidit, per se ad paradisi requiem redire non potuit, nisi veniret ille, qui suae incarnationis mysterio eiusdem nobis paradisi iter aperiret" (*Biblia Sacra*, iii, 178).

[23] "*furor tuus.* id est indignatio tua contra genus humanum, quod in morte Christi fuit Deo reconciliatum" (*Biblia Sacra*, iii, 178–80).

The traditional significance of the grim passage from Job shows, then, that God's anger, which is just and which causes a desolation to fall upon the soul, is nonetheless an aspect of the divine plan of redemption.[24] Herbert is very aware of the seasons of spiritual suffering, but he is also conscious of the hope implicit even in the verse from Job and explicit in the glossings of the second chapter of the Canticles:

> How fresh, O Lord, how sweet and clean
> Are thy returns; ev'n as the flowers in spring.
>
> (st. i, 1–2)

What follows in the poem shows very clearly how necessary such "returns" are to the devout soul/flower, but the stress on hope and joy, the expectation of heaven, gives the poem its character. To describe the poem in terms of the biblical traditions we have been following: it deals with the soul's vicissitudes in the redemptive order of God; and they involve a recollection of the sufferings of Job under inscrutable divine providence and a faith in the rapturous vision of the Canticles.

There can be little doubt that Herbert was writing in a well-established tradition, and now my concern must be to try to say what is special about his poetry in that tradition. Quarles also follows a hopeful progression in his *Emblemes*, iii–v. He is also a Metaphysical poet, and at times a very

---

[24] It is this emphasis that makes the traditional reading of Job more apt for *The Flower* in my judgment than the spiritual sufferings depicted in certain Psalms. But two examples will show how appropriate they are to this note in Herbert's poetry. Psalm 30:10: "My life is spent with grief, my years with sighing." The emphasis of the commentators is on the grievous position of the human estate, "because human frailty has no good in itself" ("quia humana fragilitas nihil boni habet in se," *Biblia Sacra*, iii, 647). Ps. 142 (Ps. 141 in the Vulgate): "Bring my soul out of prison, that I may prayse thy name." The commentary treats the passage as the soul's longing that it be freed from the body (*Biblia Sacra*, III, 1539–40).

good one.[25] But his poetry differs from Herbert's. One of the differences reveals something highly significant about Herbert's art. Whereas Quarles tends to concatenate lyrics into a narrative progression of the soul's vicissitudes, often without any clear sign of time or place, Herbert tends to give his spiritual times in a series of concatenated dramatic lyrics, any one of which may sum up the whole of a spiritual life. Herbert also has the gift for concentrated poetry that characterizes the best Metaphysical achievement. There are in such of his finest poems as *The Flower* not just a remarkable lyric grace with a considerable pressure of ideas but also a hard won simplicity of spirit that led his contemporaries to venerate him almost as a saint:

> How fresh, O Lord, how sweet and clean
> Are thy returns! ev'n as the flowers in spring.

"Sweet" is unquestionably Herbert's favorite epithet, and it is here proved by "fresh" and "clean." One would not have guessed that this man had been Public Orator at Cambridge University. God's *returns* sounds very fresh in English, but it is a freshness without newfangledness that marks the diction and the whole poem. The central figure of the poem is introduced in the second stanza, but not in any simple *sic vita* floral simile. We had sensed in those first lines a greater weight than is at once measurable, and it comes through clearly at the opening of the second stanza with its almost supererogatory felicity in imagery:

> Who would have thought my shrivel'd heart
> Could have recover'd greennesse?   (st. ii, 8–9)

But the poem is also the great one it is by virtue of its resonance. Behind it lies the literature of the soul's vicissitudes

---

[25] For as close a comparison as seems possible, see Quarles, *Emblemes*, v, iii, 16: "My beloved is mine, and I am his; He feedeth among the lillies." It is a fine poem.

and, as we have seen, commentaries or tradition surrounding the Canticles and Job. These give a weight, a universality, that private poetry needs to acquire.

In short, Herbert packs the biblical tradition into the brevity of the *sic vita* of the emblematic tradition by making it seem that he is writing of his whole life, and our whole lives. He suggests a cyclical, or rather a changing, state of his soul, and he does so not by simple depiction, but by his floral conceit. There are in this numerous temporal suggestions ("May," "hard weather," "again," etc.), and the significant use of the stanza form assists him in his effects of change, of alteration in a regular rhythm. But across such strong suggestions of fluctuation are cut numerous complex movements suggesting order or a different pattern. The change is of course directed for the better, because the poem concerns divine providence and the redemptive scheme. The element of hope can be found in the sequence from "Lord" (1) to the rather overwhelming "Lord of power" (15) to the far more comfortable "Lord of love" (43). Similarly, the poem comes to open on a wider and wider perspective, from the returned spring of the first stanza, to the sense of a lifetime in the next five stanzas, and at last to a new garden and to eternity, with a glance backward to Eden:

> Thou hast a garden for us, where to bide,
>> Who would be more,
>> Swelling through store,
> Forfeit their Paradise by their pride.
>
> (st. viii, 46–49)

In all this, immediate place is transcended for metaphorical place or for a place in the divine garden; time is felt to be more real, but the fluctuating scenes, the address, and even the sense of climax coming from some remarkable imagery— all these contribute to make what ought to be a narrative, and what perhaps is narrative to some extent, a drama in its sense of immediate force. Someone, we feel, is there, talking, feeling at a given moment.

Herbert does these things in a way that is uncommonly natural, given images of green hearts, houses among the roots of plants, and a striking pun or two. There is not indeed the degree of immediacy possessed by Donne's poetry, but there is a greater purity, a chastened simplicity, of language and of thought. And in comparison with the other of the really superlative Metaphysicals, Marvell, Herbert does not take recourse to padding of lines, as Marvell sometimes does. Such naturalness is of course a supreme grace of art and is very hard-won, just as the simplicity of his life was earned in struggle from the much wider range of alternatives of which he was very much aware. The last word of the poem, "pride," is one that had a strong family and personal ring to it. The simplicity goes with magnificence, because the goodness of the man was accompanied by an equally pressed achievement of great poetry. The poetry has the significance it does because of its conviction of personal experience, a conviction nurtured by what centuries of men had joined to show was the nature of the spiritual life. Herbert's flower is grown from very old Christian and Jewish stock, and it is tended by hands at once "sweet and clean." The flower of the poem figures forth Herbert's whole spiritual life, his hopes of what is to come, and lasting verities of the soul.

iii. *The Nymph complaining for the death of her Faun*

By drawing upon the Latin love elegy, Donne had been able to make a radically fresh departure in English love poetry. By drawing upon Christian traditions of the vicissitudes of the soul, Herbert was able to invest his private experience and poetic expression with enduring truth. In the case of both Donne and Herbert, originality had enlivened what was inherited, and the inheritance had made the originality feasible and significant. It has proved possible for many critics to discuss both poets without emphasizing this interplay between their originality and their inheritance, but both are equally evident. The same is not true for Marvell's *Nymph complaining for the death of her Faun.* Original the poem certainly is, to the point of bafflement, but, as discussions of the poem have shown, the whole problem has been precisely one of knowing what tradition, genre, context, or matrix may be presumed relevant. I think it highly unlikely that anyone can produce evidence, of a high enough probability to constitute proof, that the poem precisely means so-and-so in any paraphrasable sense beyond a summary of its events. And yet, even as the poem baffles us, it invites scrutiny. It is in fact a rare challenge to the scrupulosity of one's critical and scholarly methods to say just what about the poem is certain, what is probable, what likely, what unlikely, and what wholly uncertain or out of the question.

The one important thing certain about the poem is, I believe, the source of the uncertainty, the wit. The poem displays Marvell's particular wit in even more extreme form than his *Horatian Ode;* in both poems, dialectic at its extreme functions in a fashion the reverse of Donne's. Instead of marshalling logic and rhetoric, ideas and feelings, definitions and arguments, abstractions and images to the end of irresistible proof, Marvell admits so much so hesitatingly, suggests so many things while withholding their force, that it is precisely what is "proved" that is least clear. In *Upon Appleton House,* more in the *Horatian Ode,* and most in *The Nymph complaining for the death of her Faun,* we discover that his wit provides for the maximum inclusiveness of experience in small compass and for the minimum pressure of the weight of any specifiable detail. His wit does not func-

tion so in all of his poems, but his wit functions in this way
in most of his best. His fear of excess was observed in the last
chapter, and that fear has, in the story of the Nymph, become
almost a distaste for commitment to the relevance of the
poem. In *The Garden,* all is absorbed into the consciousness
that we sense at once. In this poem, the consciousness has
become nearly complete transparency, and anything resembling self-committal has been rigorously barred. One is very
much reminded by this and certain other features of Marvell's poetry of that significant sentence in John Aubrey's
little memoir: "He had not a generall acquaintance." [26]

Such reserve, at least taken as far as Marvell took it, is as
rare in a major poet as is poetry in a Member of Parliament.
The question to be asked about the policy of diffidence is that
of just what kind the diffidence is. The poem is certainly
difficult by design, because Marvell could be clear enough
when he wished, when the occasion or the significance of a
given experience called for clarity. The more than four
hundred lines of *The First Anniversary of the Government
under O. C.* are as clear on the subject of Cromwell as the
Horatian Ode is hesitant:

> *Cromwell* alone with greater Vigour runs,
> (Sun-like) the Stages of succeeded Suns:
> And still the Day which he doth next restore,
> Is the just Wonder of the Day before.
> *Cromwell* alone doth with new Lustre spring,
> And shines the Jewel of the yearly Ring.   (7–12)

That is as clear as Cleveland on such subjects, and no better.
It is of course public poetry, but so is the *Horatian Ode.* The
same differences will be found in his Metaphysical verse.
On a Drop of Dew is a straightforward *sic vita* poem, very

---

[26] *Aubrey's Brief Lives,* ed. Oliver Lawson Dick (London, 1960),
p. 196.

clear and not a patch on *The Flower*. Generally speaking, Marvell wrote at his best when he employed his extraordinarily passive wit and undemonstrative dialectic.

We no longer think the Metaphysical poets uniquely difficult, but there are a few very difficult Metaphysical poems. One kind of difficulty is that of Herbert's "Jordan" poems, whose titles seem to suggest an area of intended meaning unapparent in the poems. The title of Marvell's poem is clear in its relation to the situation of the poem. Another kind of difficulty is one of tone, as in Donne's *Anniversaries:* can he be serious in saying such things about a girl he had never seen? This kind of difficulty is also not Marvell's. Everything seems entirely in place in his poem, and the poet, far from seeming to make extravagant claims for his Nymph, seems to plead the Muses' Fifth Amendment. There is another kind of difficulty, suggested in the last chapter. By bearing in mind *Upon Appleton House* and the *Horatian Ode,* we feel this to be most likely: the enigmatic mode as it was adapted in mid-century by writers like Lovelace. But to say so much is to come near drawing a logical circle, because to presume an enigmatic poem is to presume a political or historical implication to the poem, and that is something that requires rather than affords proof.

There are some matters of evident fact in *The Nymph complaining for the death of her Faun.*[27] The poem is a version of pastoral complaint. We have a Nymph and we have a swain, Sylvio, whose name is properly classical, even if he is a huntsman rather than a shepherd. The idealized world of the pastoral is developed in great physical and other detail. The Nymph becomes a sympathetic character. Into the pastoral, ideal world come the Troopers, who threaten to destroy it and who do break the heart of the Nymph by mortally wounding her Faun. Finally, there is some degree of amatory

---

[27] The text of the poem is given in the Appendix, pp. 277 ff.

relation between the Nymph and Sylvio, and this, too, suits with the pastoral.

That is not a great deal of certainty for so long a poem, but there are other matters that can be agreed upon. The plot, for example, seems not to have been discussed, because critics have not thought it worth their trouble. Since anything obvious in the poem is worth clinging to, we may spare the plot a few moments. The first consideration is the fact itself, that this is a narrative. The fact that this is the one truly important Metaphysical poem to be uncompromisingly narrative in nature is perhaps of some historical import. But to anyone seeking to understand the poem, the narrative mode is significant as a prime intrinsic concern. The first purpose of narrative is to tell of something that has happened, and the stress on the shooting of the Faun at the beginning and its death at the end echoes the title. Narrative is also significant in relating the sequence of events, and we observe of Marvell's story two things: that he does not follow the natural sequence in which the fictional events occurred; and that the effects are set forth in two sections of relatively great length (ll. 37–92, 93–122) whereas the causes are treated in two sections of relative brevity (ll. 1–24, 25–36). Here indeed is one of the basic causes of the poem's difficulty—the reasons for what has happened are what provide us with an understanding of events, but the reasons are quickly passed by; in fact, one of the crucial causal passages (ll. 25–36) is made very brief and placed in an unemphatic position. There are only four episodes to the poem, and Marvell's order of them is obvious enough not to be forgot; it will therefore prove, I think, to be revealing if we study the episodes in the order of their occurrence in the Nymph's life:

Episode 1: lines 25–36. The Nymph and her "Huntsman" Sylvio had been in love. While still not found to be "counterfeit," he gave her the Faun. His love did not last long, however, because "soon" he "beguil'd" her, leaving her with "his Faun," where before she had had his "Heart" (of course also playing on "hart").

Episode II: lines 37–92. The Nymph says that "Thenceforth I set my self to play / My solitary time away"— with the Faun. The long middle section of the poem succeeds the broken idyll of love with another idyll recounting her loving care of her pet, its beauty and good nature, and its purity.

Episode III: lines 1–24. Some "wanton Troopers" shoot the Faun, which lies bleeding to death before the Nymph as she questions the nature of such men and the heinousness of their act.

Episode IV: lines 93–122. The Faun languishes and dies. The Nymph resolves to have cut, as a memorial, a marble statue of her weeping self and, at its feet, an alabaster image of the Faun.

We observe that the first episode in the "real" chronology is that most suited to the pastoral convention, and that it is tucked away and given little space. We notice that the third episode has been made the first to be related in the order of the poem, thus beginning the poem near its climax, the death of the Faun, an event which is, however, delayed in the poem's sequence by narration of events anterior.

So far—it may not seem very far at all to anyone who has followed criticism of the poem—all is clear enough to pass for certainty. And all that has been said has significance, but the significance must be interpreted, a necessity that admits for a much lower degree of certainty. Still, we may begin with a question relevant to the plot, the relation (or relationships) between the characters: the Troopers, the Faun, Sylvio, and the Nymph. The Faun is contrasted both with Sylvio and the Troopers:

The Love was far more better then
The love of false and cruel men.   (53–54)

The application is obvious. Sylvio had been called "false" three lines before, and in the opening lines the Troopers are described as "wanton" (1) and "Ungentle" (3). We see why the Faun's love is better than Sylvio's—he "beguil'd" and left her as the Faun did not. But why is it better than that of "men" generally and of the Troopers particularly? Of course we may take the line as a kind of hypothesis of grief leading to categorical rejection of all men. But it is strange that the love of the Troopers (rather than their wanton cruelty) is what is the center of consideration. The question is not directly answered, but there is a kind of solution in the relation between Sylvio and the Troopers. Although the pastoral was flexible enough to allow many kinds of scene, Sylvio is not the usual pastoral figure, not the usual swain found with seventeenth-century English Nymphs. He is a self-styled "Huntsman" (31), and deer are of course the most important animal of the hunt in the century. The couplet therefore relates, thematically, the betrayal by Sylvio—his "counterfeit," "false" treatment of the Nymph—to the Troopers and their slaying of the Faun.

What such a relation implies and requires for logical consistency is another thematically conceived relation of characters: between the Nymph and the Faun. This is precisely the most extensively developed relation in the poem. The couplet last quoted is followed (in ll. 55–62) by a comparison of the Faun's beauties with those of the Nymph and even with those of "any Ladies of the Land" (62). In the next passage (63–70), the Faun's speed is compared to the lesser fleetness of the Nymph. After a lengthy comparison (71–92) of the Faun to the "flaxen Lillies" of the Nymph's garden, and after the death scene (93–110), the poem concludes with its description of the memorial statues. The last two lines imply a final comparison:

> For I would have thine Image be
> White as I can, though not as Thee.

The lines say that she cannot provide an alabaster as white as the Faun. But the accumulated superiorities of the Faun, the analogy with another passage (55–62), and the natural symbolism all lead to one conclusion: the Nymph is not as "white," not as pure as the Faun.

Not as white as the Faun, the Nymph is far whiter than Sylvio or the Troopers. We take her word for the first and her whole manner for evidence of the last two comparisons. But it requires the utmost care to describe just how "white" the Nymph herself is and to say on what evidence we are judging. I hope that I have shown that the wit and the structure of the poem do not allow us to *insist* upon anything so "Ungentle" as that the Nymph has lost her chastity; but, equally, we have a pastoral love plot and comparisons between the Nymph and her Faun. One may observe that it is the Faun that is said to have "pure virgin Limbs." It is clear enough that Sylvio is "Unconstant" (25), "counterfeit" (26), "wild" (34), and "false" (50, 54). The Nymph is not talking about his financial irresponsibility—nor is she confessing to immorality. Neither the description of the Faun nor the characterization of Sylvio, nor yet the strong force of the betrayed woman's complaint, makes it necessary for us to assume that the Nymph had yielded to Sylvio before he proved untrue: men may be untrue before as well as after love is consummated. More accurately, Marvell permits the suspicion but precludes any assurance whatsoever. What is implied by the parallel between the Troopers' slaying of the Faun and Sylvio's betrayal of the Nymph is the loss of innocence. Whereas the Faun had grown up knowing the Nymph, the Nymph herself grows up in another sense involving knowledge of Sylvio and the Troopers. She becomes the Faun's superior in experience and sophistication, both of them attributes inimical to innocence.

How far may we go in relating the loss of innocence to the love plot of the poem? The only answer is, in the event, a complication of the question. Toward the end of the poem, the Nymph speaks of making an offering of tears at *"Diana's* Shrine." In view of the recondite lore that one or two critics have brought to the poem,[28] I hesitate to come out with a remark so obvious as that Diana is goddess of the hunt and of chastity, although the pertinence of the fact might be thought sufficiently clear. The problem is: how is it pertinent? As goddess of the hunt, Diana is commonly pictured in statues and paintings as the Nymph finally imagines her marble and the Faun's alabaster statues to be grouped. It is also true that on at least one occasion Diana was upset to have a favorite stag killed.[29] But we cannot identify the Nymph with the goddess. Her world is very different from that of the Olympian deities and, what is yet more to the point, it is quite clear that she is the last person who would go to the hunt, who would destroy the beauty and innocence represented by the Faun. The manifest dissonance of this aspect of *"Diana's* Shrine" with its traditional trophies of the hunt very greatly qualifies any possible influence that the Nymph is any more a follower of Diana in chastity than in the hunt. What she offers the goddess is tears. She takes the "two crystal Tears" (102) shed by the Faun as it dies and, using them as a kind of essence, fills up the "golden Vial" (101) with her own tears. Under what conditions are such mingled tears an appropriate offering to Diana, goddess of chastity and the hunt? In my view, Marvell uses the detail

---

[28] For a survey of scholarship on the poem, see my article, "The Death of Innocence in Marvell's *Nymph Complaining for the death of her Faun*," *Modern Philology*, LXV (August 1967), 9–16. I wish that I had written, "The loss," to include the Nymph as well as the Faun, but I have been able in this chapter to correct, enlarge, and adduce new evidence.

[29] See Hyginus, *Fabulae*, xcviii; and Ovid, *Metaphorphoses*, XII, 24 ff.

to provide a partial appropriateness in both directions. Diana had grieved over the loss of her stag and sought revenge. The Nymph grieves, does not seek revenge, and does not hunt. Diana was very hard on those of her company who fell from the strict rule of chastity.[30] The Nymph's tears are suitable to a loss of innocence, but to insist upon chastity lost in a proper physical sense is more than Marvell permits us. The fact that Diana is goddess of the hunt qualifies our response to her being goddess of chastity quite as much as the reverse. We observe that it is the Faun that goes to a suitably classical Elysium to join "Swans and Turtles," "milk-white Lambs," and "Ermins pure." The whiteness symbolizes innocence, and if the Nymph is not as white as the Faun, she is nonetheless white and pure (55–62), at least very much more so than Sylvio and the Troopers. If that leaves a wide and uncertain margin, it is precisely the wideness and the uncertainty that must be admitted.

Having summarized what I think certain and what ambiguous in the poem, I shall now recollect what I think highly probable as well. There are two lines of plot, one dealing with the shooting and death of the Faun, and the other with a love story anterior to the shooting. The former is posterior in time but anterior in Marvell's relation, and the former is interrupted to include the latter, thereby in part assimilating it. The relationships and formal structural relations between the characters of the poem show, with the words of the Nymph, that the poem is a love complaint as well as a lament for the death of a pet. The parallelisms demonstrate further that the death of the Faun is relevant not just in itself as the death of an innocent but also as an analogy for the damaged innocence of the Nymph. The two sufferings or, to speak licentiously, the two deaths of the

---

[30] See *Metamorphoses*, ii, 441 ff., for the story of her merciless treatment of Callisto, who returned pregnant to the goddess's group.

Faun and the Nymph, establish the theme of the poem to be
the loss of innocence. The Faun literally dies from the sudden
intrusion of the "wanton Troopers" upon a pastoral world,
and the Nymph is damaged by her "counterfeit" and "false"
friend, the "Huntsman" Sylvio. In the one instance, the
action is decisive and the innocent dies, while Innocence remains as a principle. In the other instance, there is a betrayal
leading to experience and knowledge, the partial loss of innocence as a principle except in recollection. (I feel that I must
make it absolutely clear that I think there is no proof provided as to the loss, or retention, of physical chastity. The
question, not the answer, is raised because, I think, Marvell
wants to heighten the impact of the poem without limiting
the realm of innocence to a physical state.) The Nymph is
quite aware of her state and of her difference from the Faun,
and one major function of the animal is to provide her with
the psychological satisfaction of nursing an innocent when
she has grown experienced. This maternal, or rather this
feminine, prizing of a substitute for innocence lost is related
to the other surrogate role played by the Faun, the *surrogatus
amantis*, of which more presently. What, above all, the wit
of the poem suggests is that the loss of the Nymph's innocence is but partial. Her loss can be measured only by comparison with the absolutely pure Faun—ideal innocence—
but she still inhabits a pastoral world, which neither the
Troopers nor Sylvio in their wildness and cruelty have been
able wholly to destroy. But at the same time the wit also
demonstrates (because it is she who is the speaker, or narrator,
of the poem) that the Nymph's participating awareness is as
much involved as the actions of Sylvio.

So much, I think, can be said of the poem, with either
certainty or a high degree of probability. So conceived, the
poem is a meaningful one, and many readers may feel that
there is no need to have recourse to other conceptions of a

less probable kind. Yet most, perhaps all, of the critics of the poem have not been content to rest with the poem as I have outlined it—as if the pressure of significance is too strong to allow for so slender a line to be drawn about the whole. All of us should confess to our bafflement on a first (and perhaps a subsequent) reading of the poem, and our reason is no doubt the conviction that "there is more to it than that." The problem has been all along that one with which I introduced the poem: finding a proper context or tradition in which to set it.

One such context may be called psychological. It is obvious that the poem is comprised solely of the thoughts, reflections, and feelings of the Nymph—but where do these lead? One theory holds, in effect, that the Nymph's psychology represents Marvell's own. While it certainly is true that the Nymph's psychology represents Marvell's conception of it, that is merely a tautology for the obvious fact that he is the author, and I do not know of a shred of evidence to indicate that Marvell thought in the Nymph's simplified terms. Another interpretation holds that the Faun is a *surrogatus amoris* for the Nymph, and that the general situation is a traditional one for poems in the death of pets. The former part of this interpretation has been offered as a specialized version of the latter, although it is logically discrete. Of the latter, we may say with considerable certainty that of the many poems on the death of pets that have been adduced, only a few have the remotest resemblance to Marvell's, and only a few come from sources that one can presume he would probably have known. As for the Faun as surrogate, we can all sense from the Nymph's detailed account of the Faun, from her play with it, and from her love for it, that she has turned upon it the affection rebuffed by Sylvio. We must say more properly that if the Faun is a surrogate, it is a *surrogatus amantis* rather than a *surrogatus amoris*. The Nymph keeps her capacity for love—one of the most obvious facts of the poem—but she has had to change its object. It was, moreover, only after Sylvio had proved untrue that she turned for consolation to the Faun:

> Thenceforth [*sic*] I set my self to play
> My solitary time away,
> With this . . .   (37–39)

But beyond the obvious taking of consolation in the Faun and devoting to it the affection she had once given to Sylvio, what is there to be said of this interpretation? Either it is so obvious as not to take us two steps, or else it requires minute discriminations of the kind I tried to supply in the analysis of the plot. There is a danger, which is not confined to this poem or its author, that the simple may be rendered unduly complex, or that hints be taken as avowals and hesitations as refusals.

At all events, the psychological rendering, even when buttressed by quotations from the Fathers or from obscure poets, does not answer to our feeling that "there is more to it than that." It is natural, therefore, that many of us should turn to thematic interpretations. One such interpretation is religious and, like much of the reading of *The Flower* given above, it is based upon Canticles ii. The passage in Marvell does somewhat resemble the imagery of *The Flower* and of the biblical passage:

> I have a Garden of my own,
> But so with Roses over grown,
> And Lillies, that you would it guess
> To be a little Wilderness.
> And all the Spring time of the year
> It [the Faun] only loved to be there. . . .
>   (71–76)

It has been suggested on the basis of the resemblance that the main Christian use of the Canticles—the love of Christ for his Church—is involved in the poem's parallel of the Nymph's love for her Faun. I find it impossible to rule out completely the possibility that Marvell had the Song of Songs in mind when he wrote this passage. But what else did he have in mind? Those are questions that cannot be answered, although I think we can say what he did not have in mind. If we follow seventeenth-century habits of using biblical material, we must find some use for Sylvio and the Troopers. There is nothing *a priori* wrong with making Sylvio what the exegetes called the Synagogue (as opposed to the Church), Israel rather than Christianity; or with making the Troopers crucifying Romans. But this is all nonsense in the light of the poem. It is the Faun rather than the Nymph that dies. The Faun goes to a classical rather than a Christian afterlife. The Nymph is feminine, and nowhere that I know of in seventeenth-century writing will one find Christ represented by a female type. (I have had a fear that the "Roses" and "Lillies" would lead some critic to the Virgin Mary and her Son. Lest I prompt unwholesome thoughts, let me add that the Faun is referred to as "It" and apparently did not require parthenogenesis.) Apart from all this, there is only verbal resemblance in one passage to suggest that the poem is religious at all. What Marvell had in his mind with this recollection (if it is, as it seems, a recollection) of the Canticles must be taken as something we cannot ascertain. The furthest that I can go is to grant that in his garden passage (71–92) Marvell may have sought a glancing, witty but serious parody of the biblical passage, a parody revealing more about innocence lost by the Nymph and more about her solemnity concerning the Faun than about any patterning upon the love of Christ for his Church.

It has been more profitable, though in the end inconclu-

259

sive, to establish a thematic context for the poem in terms of sources and analogues. The most widely known of the proposed sources is William Browne's story of Fida's Hind in *Britannia's Pastorals*, i, iii–v. For its use of a version of pastoral and in its suggestion of wider significances in the death of a girl's pet, Browne's story deserves summary:

> i, iii. Remond and Fida sing their song of mutual love, overheard by Doridon, whose presence is betrayed when his dog chases Fida's pet hind. The hind had come to Fida weeping, "and with her head low laid / In Fida's lap, did humbly beg for aid" (327–28). On the animal's collar is written:
> "Maidens, since 'tis decreed a maid shall have me,
> Keep me till he shall kill me that must save me."
> Doridon apologizes, and all are reconciled.

> i, iv. Remond departs from Fida, and she rests in an arbor with her hind. Riot, in the figure of an old man, approaches and slays Fida's hind, but out of the animal's mangled body is born Aletheia (i.e., Truth).

> i, v. Riot reenters, is led to seek the good life, and (like Spenser's Redcrosse Knight) is taken to the house of Repentance. He is so changed in character and grown so fine a young swain that he is joined in love to Aletheia.

It may seem that this episode takes us into a sixteenth-century world of the Spenserians rather than provides us with a model for Marvell. Indeed, there is a good deal that is different. But to gain some sense of the *relative* likelihood of a connection between Browne's poem and Marvell's, we may examine another story of grief for a pet that has been claimed as a source for Marvell. It is the tale about Cyparissus in the *Metamorphoses*, x, 106–42:

> Apollo falls in love with the boy Cyparissus, who has a stag with great antlers. Cyparissus accidentally kills

his stag and is stricken with grief. He wishes to die and asks Apollo to let him grieve forever. The disturbed Apollo grants the request, turning the boy into a cypress.

By comparison, Fida's love for a hind (not a stag), her being loved normally (not homosexually, or by a god), and her being female (not male), make Browne's story much closer than Ovid's to *The Nymph complaining for the death of her Faun*. In addition, neither the Nymph nor Fida die, the two English poems share a pastoral setting, and in each there is a sudden, or "wanton" as Marvell puts it, slaying of the animal by a force from the outside. Browne and Marvell do differ (e.g., Truth born from the body of the hind; the reconciliation of Riot and Truth). On balance, Browne is far more likely than Ovid.

There is one further possible context that might have been more than a source. (I think it *is* a model and shall so argue, but it should be stressed that the evidence is not sufficient to constitute certain proof.) In the seventh *Aeneid* (475–509), there is a tragic interlude with the story of the death of Silvia's stag:

> While the Trojans have been campaigning against the Latins, the young Latin girl Silvia has been tending her deer with her own hands. The furious goddess Alecto, who has been trying to stir up the Latins against the Trojans, puts the hounds of the Trojan huntsman Iülus on the scent of the animal. Ascanius himself shoots the stag, and the action arouses the Latins to battle against the Trojans.

The episode is the third, and the only successful, attempt by Alecto to stir the Latins against the Trojans. The war is an obstacle to the founding of the new Troy, Rome, and the story of Silvia is a tragic idyll amid the larger workings of fate in the epic of a formation of a new nation. Again there are salient differences as well as resemblances. But what the

Virgilian passage possesses that is absent from other proposed sources is a theme such as Marvell dealt with in other poems.

In short, I wish to propose the hypothesis that the death of Marvell's Faun has a historical or political significance dependent upon allusion to the passage from the *Aeneid*. The connection in Marvell's poem is to be found with what first meets our eye there, the "wanton Troopers" of the opening line. The term "Troopers" was first applied to the Covenanting army of 1640. One of Marvell's best students speaks for several when he asks if it is "not likely [that in spite of earlier poems on the death of pets], however, that Marvell's untraditional particularisation of this traditional topic, the slaughter of a child's pet by foraging (and presumably Parliamentary) troopers was suggested to him by the sort of thing that was going on all around him, and had been going on all over England since the beginning of the Civil War . . . ?"[31] The question and the hesitation no doubt provide the right tone. In advocating a line of interpretation, I shall have to speak more dogmatically than the evidence allows.

The Virgilian parallel takes us to a qualification of the Nymph's view of what has happened, and obviously this qualification is as necessary here as in *What Maisie Knew*: simplicity is the narrator of complexity. The Nymph feels that she is wholly misused by Sylvio and that the death of her Faun is an unqualified tragedy. The attitude is right and natural. Virgil's narrative, however, treats such an episode as a highly pathetic and unfortunate occurrence in the desirable course of the establishment of a new and greater na-

---

[31] J. B. Leishman, *The Art of Marvell's Poetry* (London, 1966), p. 156. Leishman seems to have forgot the Virgilian episodes, and he makes the girl younger than she is in the poem; but the manuscript was not fully revised when death overtook this leading critic of Metaphysical poetry.

tion. What a parallel suggests is that Marvell's story is a similar although (in view of the narrative viewpoint and tone) a yet more regrettable episode in the shaping of England into a commonwealth. A parallel with Virgil implies that Marvell felt that the new order was as inevitable as that represented by Aeneas, *fato profugus*, but nonetheless tragic in its by-actions. If we regard Virgil as a source for theme and values and Browne as a source for some details, we see that both earlier stories of the death of pet deer carry a further significance like that which we imply to be present in Marvell's poem when we say that there is more to the tale of his Nymph than meets the eye. What is implied is a view of his poem as a vision of an older, more ideal world of pastoral sanctity invaded, and its prime representative destroyed by the invasion. Such a reading gives us, as in three concentric circles: the Nymph's fall from innocence to experience; the destruction of innocence in its most perfect embodiment, the Faun; and the loss of national innocence in the tragedy of a war overturning an ancestral order. This implies a fine Virgilian tone, and the requisite attitude of mind will be found sufficiently clearly in Marvell's pronouncements in *The Rehearsal Transpos'd* and his poems before the First Anniversary to allow for *a fortiori* acceptance of the possibility of the third concentric of meaning.

However, before seeking to strengthen presumption by taking stock of similar motifs in other writings by Marvell, we may pause to clarify the hypothesis, to say why the death of a Faun, the love of a Nymph, and a cruel "Huntsman" or Troopers might be thought capable of expressing three such seemingly diverse themes. The clarification is easy enough to provide, since deer furnished a number of literary tropes dealing with love, and since the hunt had an intimate connection with epic and love. To avoid abstruse examples, Shakespeare uses the trope of the stricken deer for one far gone in love, the tended deer as an erotic trope, the frightened deer as a trope for the woman violated, and the hunting of the deer as a trope for wooing a woman.[32] What these usages have in common is the deer as a figure for the lover or the beloved, and commonly for some degree of excess in passion. The origin of the trope is apparently a simile in the fourth *Aeneid*, 69, where Virgil compares the love-smitten Dido to an arrow-stricken deer: she is *qualis coniecta cerva sagitta*. Commentators have long since connected the arrow (or shaft) of this simile with those of Eros or Cupid.[33] It is not surprising that when in the Renaissance the epic was revived along romance lines, with more attention given to love, poets known to Marvell should have recovered the Virgilian image.[34]

There is every reason to think that Marvell was aware of the trope, and now it must be shown why Virgil himself is the likeliest predecessor. For one thing, Virgil developed the trope of *coniecta cerva sagitta* in Book IV into the idyll of Silvia in Book VII, thereby uniting it with the hunt. It is significant that Ascanius the huntsman is a link between Dido and Aeneas, as also later between peace and war, and youth

---

[32] For the stricken deer, see *The Winter's Tale*, I, ii, 115 ff. and *Titus Andronicus*, III, i, 88 ff.; for the tended deer, *Venus and Adonis*, 230–40; for the frightened deer, *The Rape of Lucrece*, 1149; and for the hunting of the deer, *The Passionate Pilgrim*, 299–300. See also Spenser's very interesting use in *Epithalamion*, 67 ff. Finally, since it is well known that Marvell often echoes Waller, the latter's "On a Girdle," 5–6, should be mentioned.

[33] See *Pvbli Vergili Maronis Aeneidos Liber Qvartvs*, ed. Arthur Stanley Pease, repr. ed. (Darmstadt, 1967), p. 147, s. v. 69. *sagitta*.

[34] Pease cites (p. 147) Petrarch, *Sonnets*, clv, 9–12; Boiardo, *Orlando Innamorata*, I, v, 14, 3–6; Ariosto, *Orlando Furioso*, xvi, iii, 5–8. It may be added that in his edition, *P. Vergili Maronis Aeneidos Liber Qvartvs* (Oxford, 1955), R. G. Austin glosses *Aeneid*, IV, 69 ff. by comparing, *inter alia*, Marvell's poem. Wyatt's sonnet, "Who so list to hount," may be added as a connection between Virgil and Petrarch and the English poets, although I doubt that Marvell had read the poem.

and manhood. This is no place to discourse upon the *Aeneid*, but the figure of Ascanius as huntsman is important, and it can be seen that Virgil introduces it at three very significant points of his epic: just before the storm that sends Dido and Aeneas to the cave (see IV, 156–157), at the outbreak (and indeed as immediate cause of the outbreak) of war with the Latins, when he slays Silvia's deer (VII, 477 ff.), and when he himself turns from the boyish pleasures of the hunt to participate as a man in war (IX, 590–92).

Such information strengthens the intelligibility of the hypothesis more than its proof. Perhaps it does add two or three featherweights of proof, and for Marvell's poem such additional weight is, it must be said, neither despicable nor decisive. What we have seen is that Shakespeare used the deer as an erotic trope on a number of occasions, and Marvell could claim a good deal more than a "small *Latine*," as people as far away as the court of the Tsar came to know. Virgil and Shakespeare show that there is nothing at all bizarre in Marvell's choice of subject or in his combination of a stricken Faun and a Nymph whose love has been "beguil'd." Indeed, the figure of Dido, *qualis coniecta cerva sagitta*, presents a fascinating comparison, striking in resemblance and difference, with the dual figures of the Nymph and her Faun. The Virgilian treatment of the Ascanius-huntsman figure shows that the deer (and love) may be part of a larger epic movement involving the destiny of a nation. Virgil provides a much fuller treatment of this than I have found desirable to recount here, and there is no need to dwell upon the way in which such elements are treated by Boiardo, Ariosto, Spenser, Shakespeare, or other writers. If further illustration is needed, I refer the reader to the charming painting by Claude Lorrain of Ascanius slaying the stag of Silvia, which hangs in the Ashmolean Museum at Oxford. I think the hypothesis is intelligible enough, and even interesting. But the problem remains: what actual evidence is there to show that Marvell had the larger national theme in mind with his Nymph and Faun, Huntsman and Troopers? There is some element of proof in the resemblances included in the hypothesis itself, but it is still a hypothesis of a kind incapable of fully proving itself. All one can do further is raise presumption toward proof by considering Marvell's practice in other poems.

Upon Appleton House makes a more explicit and demonstrable allusion to military and political matters in the description of Fairfax's garden as a fort, and England as a garden-paradise (sts. xxxvi–xlvi). What is remarkable about the resemblance of that story with *The Nymph complaining for the death of her Faun* is that the garden passage of *Upon Appleton House* immediately follows a curious love episode (sts. xi–xxxv) in which the elder Fairfax dispossesses a nunnery of "the blooming Virgin *Thwates*" (90). Whatever may be taken as the exact thematic combination of the longer poem, it shows that there is no reason why Marvell could not have sought in his pastoral narrative a combination of love, innocence, experience, pastoral, and war. The resemblance of the other subjects of the two poems makes it yet more likely that those "wanton Troopers" are Parliamentary forces.

An Horatian Ode upon Cromwel's Return from Ireland is an ode rather than a pastoral; it has no love plot and is not cast as a complaint. But it does weigh such elements as the "antient Rights" of "the Kingdome old" which Cromwell, with his "forced Pow'r," was establishing "Into another Mold" (38, 35, 66, 36). There is also something like a damaged innocent in the figure of Charles I, "the *Royal Actor*" on "The *Tragick Scaffold*" (53, 54). An idealized order must yield to larger forces from the outside. Of course in the *Horatian Ode*, the balance is favorable to Cromwell and "the forced Pow'r" rather than to the old order. As in

Virgil's episode of Silvia, so in the cases of the "Virgin *Thwates*," Charles I, and the Nymph with her Faun, we have characters of some degree of innocence acted upon by some degree of violence. As in the tragic idyll of Silvia and her deer shot by Ascanius, the innocent military pastoral of Fairfax's garden, the tragic drama of Charles I, and the violated pastoralism of the Nymph and her Faun involve a situation in which a more or less settled and good regime yields to superior strength and a new order. The poems (or passages) share many resemblances, and many differences; all are masterpieces of tonal adjustment.

The interpretation I propose involves, then, three themes: one (a pastoral theme) concerning the loss of innocence in the betrayal of the Nymph by Silvio; a second (a theme harmonizing pastoral and epic) the loss of innocence in the slaying of her Faun by the Troopers; and a third (an epic theme) the loss of innocence with the destruction of the old order. Along with these themes there is the birth of experience in the Nymph's increased understanding of herself and Sylvio, as also in her awareness that the Faun is purer than herself. Her pastoral tragedy suggests a national epic seen through the eyes of a pastoral figure, an epic in which a pastoral "garden" world with "antient Rights" is destroyed by the incursion of those "wanton Troopers" who, while reminding the Nymph of her faithless Sylvio, also remind Marvell of Ascanius and the birth of a new nation.

Just as the larger meaning I have suggested must be taken as one growing from the more immediate and simpler story of the Nymph's complaint, so must the larger meaning be relatable back, as it were, to the simpler, more apparent plot of the poem. In other words, if we are to accept that the Nymph's problems suggest a historical reading, that reading must in turn have implications illuminating, or at least not conflicting with, the immediately perceivable plot. The historical reading implies an older simplicity damaged and at least partially lost before a new, more complex order, which is at once more sophisticated and more violent. If this larger significance is accepted, it must relate to the Nymph's understanding. This I do think it does, and in two respects. The first respect concerns the change in her. The knowledge she gains through a partial loss of innocence is *ipso facto* partial, limited. If she were as little innocent as Sylvio and the Troopers, she would know as much, be as sophisticated as they. But her loss of innocence is deliberately restricted to a partial loss, whose degree can be understood by a comparison of her with the Faun on the one hand and with Sylvio and the Troopers on the other. Like the old order, she suffers at the hands of the new, but its values and her values reside precisely in their not becoming so altered by outside forces that they come to resemble that which is opposed to them. If the poem were a narrative of a loss of physical chastity and of a gain in understanding of the full violence, complexity, and reality of the world, we would have a very different poem, and instead of the Nymph bewailing the death of her Faun, we would need to mourn the corruption of innocence.

Such a restriction in the Nymph's loss of innocence and in her gain in knowledge leads us to the second respect in which the larger reading relates to her understanding. Throughout the poem, we have a narrator of limited understanding of a world more complex than her field of vision permits her to see. In other words our narrator, the Nymph, is still immured in a partial and damaged innocence—in a residual limitation of her understanding. This consideration tells us a good deal, I believe, about the tone of the poem and accounts for some part of its baffling nature. It implies an ironic discrepancy between the Nymph's relation and her realization of its significance, or between her understanding and that of her author and his readers. This must be emphasized. The irony is not a form of narrative devoted to a gradual unfolding of understanding, but an irony that reveals the discrepancy between kinds of experience in which the poet and the reader share what the Nymph does not. The poem is, therefore, less comparable to a Dickensian *Great Expectations* than to a Jamesian *What Maisie Knew*. The Nymph's innocence, like the older English order, is (I am arguing) partially lost but not destroyed. Her fall from perfect innocence to partial knowledge is, as it were, prior to the poem, and what the poem enacts by way of larger awareness is the growth of revelation, of the poet's disclosure and of the reader's understanding.

I have tried to be candid and clear as to what in this reading I think is certain, what probable, and what incapable of full proof. Other readers may well wish to advance in different directions from the certain and the probable, but I do think it clear that the poem arouses a response tantamount to conviction that "there is more to it than that," and my effort has been to suggest what I think that more may most likely be. Donne's use of the Roman elegy is patent, and Herbert's use in *The Flower* of the tradition of the soul's vicissitudes is clear once it is observed. Marvell's poem on the Nymph is very different in not drawing upon any of several traditions or contexts to the exclusion of others. In fact, it welcomes the pastoral, the epic, the amorous, the psychological, the religious, the classical, the political—but it refuses to sort them out. The refusal to sort out in certain ways implies that Marvell wished that we too would be unable to do so in those ways. He leaves us with an element of certainty rising chiefly from the plot and with a doubt as to the poetic sufficiency of what is certain; and he seems to me to use other, less certainly applicable or sortable, elements drawn from some earlier works. Where the dialectic, the wit, of Donne and Herbert had led both immediately and subtly to conclusiveness, the dialectic and wit of Marvell leads (in this and some others of his best poems) to a modicum of certainty and to a considerable reserve of inconclusiveness. That such procedure produced a very special, and to some degree baffling, poetry cannot be doubted. But I do not think it affectation or an irresponsible playing with the reader. Quite the contrary, Marvell's air of difficulty, once all is considered, implies a central truth of our mature experience: maturity demands that all be considered and, once it is, great difficulty attends the attempt to grasp (much more to express) how that all combines its constituent parts. Some of Marvell's poems show that he did not always essay so difficult a task. But when he did, he seems to have weighed possibilities—whether of idea, feeling, or his inheritance—like colors and to have enjoyed the necessity of balancing what became in his handling so light that we are ourselves baffled in our attempt to weigh. His mind did, at times, withdraw "into its happiness" to contemplate features of his world:

> Yet it creates, transcending these,
> Far other Worlds, and other Seas.

And there in that garden of the mind:

> There like a Bird it sits, and sings,
> Then whets, and combs its silver Wings;
> And, till prepar'd for longer flight,
> Waves in its Plumes the various Light.
> (The Garden, 45-46, 53-56)

Marvell has other ways of understanding the world, but this is his best. Such an understanding requires in us the greatest efforts to understand both the poetic scene immediately before us and the larger background of significant tradition— while yet not allowing ourselves to claim for human certitude more than a certain minimum that is, in its very suggestiveness, at once attractive and obscure.

Donne, Herbert, and Marvell are the three greatest and the three most original of the Metaphysical poets. The three poems discussed in this chapter explore possibilities of the private mode, and they seek to support in "lyric" affirmation what is most true to intimate experience and to deny with "satiric" denial what threatens the individual, whether that threat comes from without as with Donne, from within as with Herbert, or from a complicated entwining of both as in Marvell. All three poems are remarkable for a wit at once free in claiming its own special prerogatives and bound to the uses of the individual poetic whole. All three admit to lyric structures of time and place that adapt "dramatic" or "narrative" possibilities. Donne's elegy, *The Perfume*, is a recollection that might well have been couched as narrative but that in fact absorbs such possibilities in a dramatic confrontation. Herbert's poem, *The Flower*, admits narrative elements more fully, while yet preserving the sense of the drama of the soul's vicissitudes. Marvell's *Nymph complaining for the death of her Faun* develops a narrative of the loss of innocence within the but slightly felt dramatic address of complaint. Herbert's poem is arguably his greatest. The same claim should not be made for the other two poems, but they are, all three of them, excellent works bearing the stamps of their authors' particular kinds of genius. Moreover, much of the variety, and much of the historical development of Metaphysical poetry, can be understood in terms of these three poems. Each poem is, finally, at once original and relatable to important poetic and other traditions that the sixteenth and seventeenth centuries thought mattered to poetry and experience. In their response to literary traditions, as well as in their individual kinds of originality, we may see how the poets that we call Metaphysical might differ without yet forfeiting their race.

271

APPENDIX

POEMS DISCUSSED IN
CHAPTER V

i. John Donne, *The Perfume*

Once, and but once found in thy company,
All thy suppos'd escapes are laid on mee;
And as a thiefe at barre, is question'd there
By all the men, that have beene rob'd that yeare,
So am I, (by this traiterous meanes surpriz'd)   5
By thy Hydroptique father catechiz'd.
Though he had wont to search with glazed eyes,
As though he came to kill a Cockatrice,
Though hee hath oft sworne, that hee would remove
Thy beauties beautie, and food of our love,   10
Hope of his goods, if I with thee were seene,
Yet close and secret, as our soules, we'have beene.
Though thy immortall mother which doth lye
Still buried in her bed, yet will not dye,
Takes this advantage to sleepe out day-light,   15
And watch thy entries, and returnes all night,
And, when she takes thy hand, and would seeme kind,
Doth search what rings, and armelets she can finde,
And kissing notes the colour of thy face,
And fearing least thou'art swolne, doth thee embrace;   20
To trie if thou long, doth name strange meates,
And notes thy palenesse, blushing, sighs, and sweats;
And politiquely will to thee confesse
The sinnes of her owne youths ranke lustinesse;
Yet love these Sorceries did remove, and move   25
Thee to gull thine owne mother for my love.
Thy little brethren, which like Faiery Sprights

Oft skipt into our chamber, those sweet nights,
And kist, and ingled on thy fathers knee,
Were brib'd next day, to tell what they did see.　　　30
The grim eight-foot-high iron-bound serving-man,
That oft names God in oathes, and onely than,
He that to barre the first gate, doth as wide
As the great Rhodian Colossus stride,
Which, if in hell no other paines there were,　　　35
Makes mee feare hell, because he must be there:
Though by thy father he were hir'd to this,
Could never witnesse any touch or kisse;
But Oh, too common ill, I brought with mee
That, which betray'd mee to my enemie:　　　40
A loud perfume, which at my entrance cryed
Even at thy fathers nose, so were wee spied.
When, like a tyran King, that in his bed
Smelt gunpowder, the pale wretch shivered;
Had it beene some bad smell, he would have thought　　　45
That his owne feet, or breath, that smell had wrought.
But as wee in our Ile emprisoned,
Where cattell onely,'and diverse dogs are bred,
The pretious Unicornes, strange monsters, call,
So thought he good, strange, that had none at all.　　　50
I taught my silkes, their whistling to forbeare,
Even my opprest shoes, dumbe and speechlesse were,
Onely, thou bitter sweet, whom I had laid
Next mee, mee traiterously hast betraid,
And unsuspected hast invisibly　　　55
At once fled unto him, and staid with mee.
Base excrement of earth, which dost confound
Sense, from distinguishing the sicke from sound;
By thee the seely Amorous sucks his death
By drawing in a leprous harlots breath;　　　60
By thee, the greatest staine to mans estate

Falls on us, to be call'd effeminate;
Though you be much lov'd in the Princes hall,
There, things that seeme, exceed substantiall.
Gods, when yee fum'd on altars, were pleas'd well,   65
Because you'were burnt, not that they lik'd your smell;
You'are loathsome all, being taken simply'alone,
Shall wee love ill things joyn'd, and hate each one?
If you were good, your good doth soone decay;
And you are rare, that takes the good away.   70
All my perfumes, I give most willingly
To'embalme thy fathers corse; What? will hee die?

ii. George Herbert, *The Flower*

How fresh, O Lord, how sweet and clean
    Are thy returns! ev'n as the flowers in spring;
  To which, besides their own demean,
The late-past frosts tributes of pleasure bring.
        Grief melts away   5
        Like snow in May,
  As if there were no such cold thing.

  Who would have thought my shrivel'd heart
Could have recover'd greennesse? It was gone
    Quite under ground; as flowers depart   10
To see their mother-root, when they have blown;
        Where they together
        All the hard weather,
  Dead to the world, keep house unknown.

  These are thy wonders, Lord of power,   15
Killing and quickning, bringing down to hell
    And up to heaven in an houre;
Making a chiming of a passing-bell.

We say amisse,
This or that is: 20
Thy word is all, if we could spell.

O that I once past changing were,
Fast in thy Paradise, where no flower can wither!
Many a spring I shoot up fair,
Offring at heav'n, growing and groning thither: 25
Nor doth my flower
Want a spring-showre,
My sinnes and I joining together.

But while I grow in a straight line,
Still upwards bent, as if heav'n were mine own,   30
Thy anger comes, and I decline:
What frost to that? what pole is not the zone,
Where all things burn,
When thou dost turn,
And the least frown of thine is shown?   35

And now in age I bud again,
After so many deaths I live and write;
I once more smell the dew and rain,
And relish versing: O my onely light,
It cannot be   40
That I am he
On whom thy tempests fell all night.

These are thy wonders, Lord of love,
To make us see we are but flowers that glide:
Which when we once can finde and prove,   45
Thou hast a garden for us, where to bide.
Who would be more,
Swelling through store,
Forfeit their Paradise by their pride.

iii. Andrew Marvell, *The Nymph complaining for the death of her Faun*

The wanton Troopers riding by
Have shot my Faun and it will dye.
Ungentle men! They cannot thrive
To kill thee. Thou neer didst alive
Them any harm: alas nor cou'd   5
Thy death yet do them any good.
I'me sure I never wisht them ill;
Nor do I for all this; nor will:
But, if my simple Pray'rs may yet
Prevail with Heaven to forget   10
Thy murder, I will Joyn my Tears
Rather then fail. But, O my fears!
It cannot dye so. Heavens King
Keeps register of every thing:
And nothing may we use in vain.   15
Ev'n Beasts must be with justice slain;
Else Men are made their *Deodands*.
Though they should wash their guilty hands
In this warm life blood, which doth part
From thine, and wound me to the Heart,   20
Yet could they not be clean: their Stain
Is dy'd in such a Purple Grain.
There is not such another in
The World, to offer for their Sin.
Unconstant *Sylvio*, when yet   25
I had not found him counterfeit,
One morning (I remember well)
Ty'd in this silver Chain and Bell,
Gave it to me: nay and I know

What he said then; I'me sure I do.   30
Said He, look how your Huntsman here
Hath taught a Faun to hunt his *Dear*.
But *Sylvio* soon had me beguil'd.
This waxed tame; while he grew wild,
And quite regardless of my Smart,   35
Left me his Faun, but took his Heart.
   Thenceforth I set my self to play
My solitary time away,
With this: and very well content,
Could so mine idle Life have spent.   40
For it was full of sport; and light
Of foot, and heart; and did invite,
Me to its game: it seem'd to bless
Its self in me. How could I less
Than love it? O I cannot be   45
Unkind, t' a Beast that loveth me.
   Had it liv'd long, I do not know
Whether it too might have done so
As *Sylvio* did: his Gifts might be
Perhaps as false or more than he.   50
But I am sure, for ought that I
Could in so short a time espie,
Thy Love was far more better then
The love of false and cruel men.
   With sweetest milk, and sugar, first   55
I it at mine own fingers nurst.
And as it grew, so every day
It wax'd more white and sweet than they.
It had so sweet a Breath! And oft
I blusht to see its foot more soft,   60
And white, (shall I say then my hand?)
NAY any Ladies of the Land.
   It is a wond'rous thing, how fleet

'Twas on those little silver feet.
With what a pretty skipping grace,   65
It oft would challenge me the Race:
And when 'thad left me far away,
'Twould stay, and run again, and stay.
For it was nimbler much than Hindes;
And trod, as on the four Winds.   70
    I have a Garden of my own,
But so with Roses over grown,
And Lillies, that you would it guess
To be a little Wilderness.
And all the Spring time of the year   75
It onely loved to be there.
Among the beds of Lillyes, I
Have sought it oft, where it should lye;
Yet could not, till it self would rise,
Find it, although before mine Eyes.   80
For, in the flaxen Lillies shade,
It like a bank of Lillies laid.
Upon the Roses it would feed,
Until its Lips ev'n seem'd to bleed:
And then to me 'twould boldly trip,   85
And print those Roses on my Lip.
But all its chief delight was still
On Roses thus its self to fill:
And its pure virgin Limbs to fold
In whitest sheets of Lillies cold.   90
Had it liv'd long, it would have been
Lillies without, Roses within.
    O help! O help! I see it faint:
And dye as calmely as a Saint.
See how it weeps. The Tears do come   95
Sad, slowly dropping like a Gumme.
So weeps the wounded Balsome: so

The holy Frankincense doth flow.
The brotherless *Heliades*
Melt in such Amber Tears as these.   100
   I in a golden Vial will
Keep these two crystal Tears; and fill
It till it do o'reflow with mine;
Then place it in *Diana's* Shrine.
   Now my sweet Faun is vanish'd to   105
Whether the Swans and Turtles go:
In fair *Elizium* to endure,
With milk-white Lambs, and Ermins pure.
O do not run too fast: for I
Will but bespeak [thy] Grave, and dye.   110
   First my unhappy Statue shall
Be cut in Marble; and withal,
Let it be weeping too: but there
Th'Engraver sure his Art may spare;
For I so truly thee bemoane,   115
That I shall weep though I be Stone:
Until my Tears, still dropping, wear
My breast, themselves engraving there.
There at my feet shalt thou be laid,
Of purest Alabaster made: 120
For I would have thine Image be
White as I can, though not as Thee.

MAJOR EDITIONS USED
AND CONSULTED

(Asterisks distinguish the texts used for quotations,
determination of canon, etc.)

ANTHOLOGIES

Metaphysical Lyrics & Poems of the Seventeenth Century.
Ed H. J. C. Grierson. Oxford, 1921, and reprinted.
The Metaphysical Poets. Ed. Helen Gardner, Penguin Books,
rev. ed. Harmondsworth, Mddx., 1966.

JOHN DONNE

Donne's Poetical Works. 2 vols. Ed. H. J. C. Grierson. Oxford, 1912, and reprinted.
*John Donne . . . Complete Poetry and Selected Prose. Ed.
John Hayward. "Nonesuch ed." London and New York,
1929, and reprinted. For the prose quotations.
*John Donne: The Divine Poems. Ed. Helen Gardner. Oxford, 1952, and reprinted.
John Donne: The Anniversaries. Ed. Frank Manley. Baltimore, 1963.
John Donne: The Elegies and the Songs and Sonnets. Ed.
Helen Gardner. Oxford, 1965.
*The Complete Poetry of John Donne. Ed. John T. Shawcross. Garden City, New York, 1967.

JOSEPH HALL

The Poems of Joseph Hall . . . Ed. Arnold Davenport. Liverpool, 1949.

LORD HERBERT OF CHERBURY

**Edward, Lord Herbert of Cherbury. *The Poems* . . . Ed.
G. C. Moore Smith. Oxford, 1923.

Henry King

Poems. Ed. John Sparrow. London, 1912, and reprinted.
Poems. Ed. Lawrence Mason. New Haven, 1914.
*The Poems of Henry King. Ed. Margaret C. Crum. Oxford, 1965.

Francis Quarles

*The Complete Works in Prose and Verse. 3 vols. Ed. Alexander B. Grosart. London, 1880–1881.
*Emblemes. London, 1635.

Thomas Carew

The Poems of Thomas Carew. Ed. Rhodes Dunlap. Oxford, 1949, and reprinted.

Richard Crashaw

Poems by Richard Crashaw. Ed. A. R. Waller. Cambridge, 1904.
*The Poems . . . Ed. L. C. Martin. Oxford, 1957.

John Cleveland

The Poems of John Cleveland. Ed. Brian Morris and Eleanor Withington. Oxford, 1967.

Abraham Cowley

The English Works. Ed. A. R. Waller. *Poems,* Cambridge, 1905. *Essays, Plays and Sundry Verses,* Cambridge, 1906.
The Mistress with Other Select Poems. Ed. John Sparrow.
*The Works. 3 vols. "10th ed." London, 1707–1708.

Richard Lovelace

*The Poems of Richard Lovelace. Ed. C. H. Wilkinson. Oxford, 1930, and reprinted.

MAJOR EDITIONS USED

ANDREW MARVELL

The Poems & Letters of Andrew Marvell. 2 vols. Ed. H. M. Margoliouth. Oxford, 1927, and reprinted. (Text for *The last Instructions to a Painter*)

*The Poems of Andrew Marvell. Ed. Hugh Macdonald. London, 2nd ed., 1956, and reprinted.

GEORGE HERBERT

*The Works of George Herbert. Ed. F. E. Hutchinson. Oxford, 1941, and reprinted.

HENRY VAUGHAN

*The Works of Henry Vaughan. Ed. L. C. Martin. Oxford, 2nd ed., 1957, and reprinted.

The Complete Poetry of Henry Vaughan. Ed. French Fogle. New York, 1964.

THOMAS TRAHERNE

Thomas Traherne. Centuries, Poems, and Thanksgivings. Ed. H. M. Margoliouth. Oxford, 1958.

*Thomas Traherne. Poems, Centuries and Three Thanksgivings. Ed. Anne Ridler. Oxford, 1966. Corrects some textual errors in the preceding.

INDEX

The entries include names, topics, and the titles (under their authors' names) of works by Metaphysical poets when the works are quoted and discussed. The word "discussed" designates extended discussion of a poem.

Alabaster, William, 240
Allen, Don Cameron, 206n
analogy as logical procedure, 123
Andreasen, N. J. C., 121n, 217n
Aquinas, St. Thomas, 133, 147, 151
"argument" in Metaphysical poetry, 110–17
Ariosto, Lodovico, 265
Aristotle, 48–49, 119, 147, 151
astronomy in 17th-century views, 48–52
Aubrey, John, 248
Austin, R. G., 264n

Bacon, Sir Francis, 108n
Baker, Herschel, 51n
Baker, John Tull, 48
Baxter, Richard, 233
Bedford, Lucy, Countess of, 56
Bernard, St., 240
Bible, glosses on, 96, 236–43
Boiardo, Matteo Maria, 264n, 265
Brahe, Tycho, 49
Browning, Robert, 29
Brooks, Douglas, 108n
Browne, William, 260–61
Buchler, Johann, 220n
Burke, Kenneth, 120
Burton, Robert, 49n
Butler, Samuel, 45, 108n

Campion, Thomas, 217, 218, 220
Carew, Thomas, 43, 118
Catullus, 200, 220, 228

Cavalier poetry, 111, 114; sense of time in, 92
Charles I, 204, 208, 209, 210, 266
Charles II, 62, 66, 204
Chaucer, Geoffrey, 9, 152n, 156
Chrysostom, St. John, 242
Cicero, 119
Cleveland, John, 13, 26, 43, 44, 46, 140n, 149, 157, 248
"Copernican" universe, 49–52, 63
Cotton, Charles, the younger, 101
Cowley, Abraham, 3, 13, 26, 43, 44, 46, 100, 101, 140n, 149, 158, 163; "argument" in the poetry of, 110–117; Cavalier features of, 195; poetic mingling of qualities of, 195–97; "Against Hope," 196–97; "All over Love," 115; "For Hope," 196–97; "Inconstancy," 114; "The Innocent Ill," 111–12; "Love's Ingratitude," 195; "Resolved to Love," 195; "The Welcome," 116
Crashaw, Richard, 41, 44, 46, 48, 50, 55, 93, 110, 116, 118, 140, 141, 162, 163, 233, 240; tendency to affirmation of, 186–88; *Answer for Hope,* 99; "The Hymne" to St. Teresa, 186–87; "In the Holy Nativity of Our Lord God," 138; "A Letter . . . to the Countess of Denbigh," 97–98; *Sospetto d'Herode,* 187–88; *To the Name . . . of Jesus,* 98; "Vexilla Regis," 24; "The Weeper," 127

285

This book has been composed and printed by
The Maple Press Company
Designed by Jan Lilly
Edited by R. Miriam Brokaw
Typography: Electra and Bodoni
Paper: Warren's Olde Style
Binding by The Maple Press Company